STUCK

ALSO BY ANNELI RUFUS

Party of One: The Loners' Manifesto

The Farewell Chronicles: How We Really Respond to Death

*Magnificent Corpses: Searching Through Europe for St. Peter's Head,
St. Chiara's Heart, St. Stephen's Hand, and Other Saints' Relics*

The World Holiday Book: Celebrations for Every Day of the Year

*California Babylon: A Guide to Sites of Scandal, Mayhem, and Celluloid
in the Golden State* (coauthored with Kristan Lawson)

Weird Europe: A Guide to Bizarre, Macabre, and Just Plain Weird Sights
(coauthored with Kristan Lawson)

America Off the Wall: The West Coast: A Guide to Unusual Sights
(coauthored with Kristan Lawson)

Europe Off the Wall: A Guide to Unusual Sights
(coauthored with Kristan Lawson)

STUCK

Why We Can't

(Or Won't)

Move On

ANNELI RUFUS

JEREMY P. TARCHER/PENGUIN
a member of
Penguin Group (USA) Inc.
New York

JEREMY P. TARCHER/PENGUIN
Published by the Penguin Group
Penguin Group (USA) Inc., 375 Hudson Street, New York, New York 10014, USA •
Penguin Group (Canada), 90 Eglinton Avenue East, Suite 700, Toronto, Ontario
M4P 2Y3, Canada (a division of Pearson Penguin Canada Inc.) • Penguin Books Ltd,
80 Strand, London WC2R 0RL, England • Penguin Ireland, 25 St Stephen's Green, Dublin 2,
Ireland (a division of Penguin Books Ltd) • Penguin Group (Australia), 250 Camberwell Road,
Camberwell, Victoria 3124, Australia (a division of Pearson Australia Group
Pty Ltd) • Penguin Books India Pvt Ltd, 11 Community Centre, Panchsheel Park,
New Delhi–110 017, India • Penguin Group (NZ), 67 Apollo Drive, Rosedale, North
Shore 0632, New Zealand (a division of Pearson New Zealand Ltd) • Penguin Books
(South Africa) (Pty) Ltd, 24 Sturdee Avenue, Rosebank, Johannesburg 2196, South Africa

Penguin Books Ltd, Registered Offices:
80 Strand, London WC2R 0RL, England

First trade paperback edition 2009
Copyright © 2008 by Anneli Rufus

Most Tarcher/Penguin books are available at special quantity discounts for bulk
purchase for sales promotions, premiums, fund-raising, and educational needs.
Special books or book excerpts also can be created to fit specific needs.
For details, write Penguin Group (USA) Inc. Special Markets,
375 Hudson Street, New York, NY 10014.

The Library of Congress catalogued the hardcover edition as follows:

Rufus, Anneli S.
Stuck: why we can't (or won't) move on / Anneli Rufus.
p.   cm.
Includes bibliographical references.
ISBN 978-1-58542-667-6
1. United States—Social conditions—21st century.   2. American Dream.
3. Popular culture—United States.   4. Self-defeating behavior—United States.
5. Change (Psychology).   I. Title.
HN59.2.R838   2008   2008039066
158.10973—dc22

ISBN 978-1-58542-776-5 (paperback edition)

Printed in the United States of America
1 3 5 7 9 10 8 6 4 2

BOOK DESIGN BY MEIGHAN CAVANAUGH

While the author has made every effort to provide accurate telephone numbers
and Internet addresses at the time of publication, neither the publisher nor the
author assumes any responsibility for errors, or for changes that occur after
publication. Further, the publisher does not have any control over and does not
assume any responsibility for author or third-party websites or their content.

CONTENTS

Thanks a million times to:

S.L.

K.L.

S.H.

N.B.

INTRODUCTION

We're going nowhere fast.

I'm stuck.

We say it in despair. In desperation. In denial. It becomes a punch line, an excuse. Well, hey: I'm stuck.

We say it when we can't move on. Or won't. Or simply don't. We say it while immobilized, body and mind. We say it, too, when we are moving very fast indeed: in circles or running in place.

We say it about our jobs and relationships, our families and our habits and our homes. We say it when we cannot drive certain regrets out of our heads, certain desires, people, places, things, ideas, choices made that we cannot unmake. Or believe we cannot.

We call our stuckness by a thousand words, exquisite metaphors. *I'm frozen. Paralyzed. Marooned. Trapped. Enchanted. Enslaved.* We say: The world's passing me by. We say: Oops, I did it again.

Or: I can't get started.

I'm missing out.

I'm faking it.

I'm sick.

In lands of plenty, in the lap of luxury, in the fast lane, we're stuck doing—over and over—things we do not want to do. Stuck in places we do not want to be. Stuck with people we do not want to see. Stuck with stuff. Stuck without enough. What irony. You and I will almost surely never be sold into slavery. Those days are gone. We will not become indentured servants, will not be shanghaied and dragged off to sea, locked in the hold, hands chained to oars. We were not betrothed at age ten. *That's* stuck.

In all of history, no population anywhere has ever been so free as we.

And yet—somehow we all *feel* stuck.

We say so sadly. Angrily. Resentfully. Regretfully. In shame. It's so embarrassing to be exactly where you were before. To have to say so when folks ask: So are you still . . . ?

We fling it at others, a taunt, an accusation, saying: Know what you are? Stuck!

I am. Our lands of plenty yield as many ways to be stuck as there are of us, but here is mine:

I'm immature. I am a child inside. Oh, go ahead and say I'm not. Note that I am a forty-plus wife and homeowner with two university degrees and a career. All true, yet inside I feel seriously, absolutely, twelve. I am fearful, simple, and watchful, living in my frosted-cupcake world within a world. I mimic adults my actual age, aping their tones and smiles as if I understood what they mean when they speak, but I do not.

My real childhood blazed with bright sunlight, a gleaming sea.

Bright picture books and striped beach towels and costumed carnivals at school. And how was I to know in seventh grade that, long hair flying, lapels flapping, I would more or less stop growing then? For no reason I have ever discerned? That every day henceforth would require playing dress-up, playing keep-away, playing tea party and house and pretend, for real? My life depends on this. Passing for normal.

Faking it.

I'm stuck.

Could I grow up? A bit, perhaps. Through some hardship, say civil war or drifting on a raft after a shipwreck, spearing seagulls with a straightened hanger.

See?

More on this later.

But I have learned to adapt as a survival tactic. As have you, perhaps.

Who else is stuck?

My friend who spends six hours a day at eBay.

My other friend who is sleeping with a married man.

My friend who keeps moving from town to town, endlessly starting over.

My relative who always arrives late.

My other relative who spends too much.

Sam, who can no longer fit into the driver's seat of his candy-wrapper-strewn Honda.

Jake, who procrastinates.

Paul, who still feels the shock wave from the grenade every time he closes his eyes.

Caroline, who has been in grad school, off and on, for thirty years.

Kathy, with track marks down her arm.

Alex, who hands out conspiracy-theory flyers on the street corner.

Teresa, who makes plans and always cancels them.

Dale, with his drawerful of maxed-out credit cards.

Morgan, who looks sheepish and lights another cigarette.

If in these pages I appear ungentle, forgive me. I am my own worst critic—hard on myself, hard on you. *For our own good*.

I see stuck people.

Like all living things, Homo sapiens are creatures of habit. The more we think or do anything, the easier it becomes with time. After a while, it's second nature and we operate on autopilot. Which is not, for much of our our daily routine, in principle, so bad: we would waste time and energy having to assess every task anew. Practice makes perfect. Then it tips us into ruts.

Yet at what point does comfort become a drug?

We get stuck of our own volition. We do it to ourselves, though we are unwilling to admit this. Others do it to us, too. They snare us, stultify us, sneakily spread superglue under our shoes. Some do it out of love. Yet strangers do it, too. Powerful forces out there—commercial, social, political—want us extremely stuck indeed. The more immobilized we are, running in circles with one foot roped to a post, the more they stand to gain. The more immobilized we are, the more predictable we are, the more controlled. Easy to trick. Easy to trap. They have invested fortunes in researching how to get us stuck and keep us stuck on their products, their policies, and their philosophies.

Bet you can't eat just one.

No two stucknesses are quite alike, and yet . . .

The reasons we stay stuck are quite the same.

Three reasons, mainly, which will surface time and again in these pages. Pick a stuckness, almost any stuckness, and its reason will be one or more of these:

We stay stuck because we are lazy.

And/or because we are scared.

And/or because we have no idea who we are and do not want to know. When push comes to shove, we are stuck on ourselves.

If that sounds harsh, it should. But you can flip it if that makes you feel better:

Getting unstuck, becoming free, requires vitality. Bravery. And enough honesty with yourself, about yourself, to change.

There.

By lazy, I mean our temptation to take it easy, let it slide, pull the covers over our heads. Denial is a kind of laziness. Avoidance is another. Change—coming unstuck—is strenuous. Altering attitudes, routines, beliefs, goals is like training for a sport, toning "muscles" you might never have flexed before, meeting strangers and learning skills and saying yes or no and meaning it. Here in the lap of luxury we are accustomed to the easy, the instant, the automatic. Thus effort itself is now anathema to us. It seems wrong in principle. We have forgotten how to sweat.

Coming unstuck is terrifying, too. I know this fear. Coming unstuck means risk. Exposure. Trading the familiar for potential failure.

Coming unstuck requires facing who you are. The facts: whatever led you here and why. Facing your limitations and your
breadth, apart from what the world says. Hewing values out of
stone with your bare hands.

To stay stuck or to not stay stuck? That is the question.

Inertia is in the eye of the beholder. What looks to you like paralysis looks perhaps to another like passion. What looks to you like
a rut, others might say is commitment, true absorption in a topic,
a relationship, a career, a pursuit, a place. What looks to you like
boredom, others call commitment. And even contentment.

This is a book about not going anywhere and what to do about
it. You might call our community the United Stucks. Its borders are
marked by those barriers we know so well: Denial. Fear. Obsession.
Confusion. Delusion. Even love. The landscape here is rife with
echo chambers, quicksand, mires, morasses, ruts. Whirlwinds devil
our plains, maelstroms our coasts. How the heck did you get here?

You might not realize it yet, but you are free to go.

1.

ONCE UPON A TIME

Stuck in the Past

You see, this is my life! It always will be! . . . All right,
Mr. DeMille, I'm ready for my close-up.

—NORMA DESMOND, in the film *Sunset Boulevard*

In Tennessee Williams's play *The Glass Menagerie*, frustrated poet Tom Wingfield and his shy, disabled sister, Laura, share a shabby St. Louis flat with their ex–Southern belle mother, Amanda. The siblings' father—Amanda's husband—left them long ago.

Tom and Laura are realists, well aware of their unpromising futures and slim chances of success. By contrast, their mother flounces and struts around the dreary flat, forever dwelling on her lush but vanished past.

"One Sunday afternoon in Blue Mountain," Amanda trills, "your mother received—*seventeen!*—gentlemen callers! Why, sometimes there weren't chairs enough to accommodate them all."

Tom and Laura exchange here-we-go-again signals.

Modeling an age-ravaged gown—Williams calls it a "girlish frock"—that she has fished from a trunk, Amanda announces: "This is the dress in which I led the cotillion. Won the cakewalk twice at Sunset Hill, wore one Spring to the Governor's Ball in

Jackson! See how I sashayed around the ballroom, Laura? I wore it on Sundays for my gentlemen callers!"

Although her children appear unmoved as she swishes in the yellowed gown, Amanda narrates ardently:

"Evenings, dances! Afternoons, long, long rides! Picnics—lovely! So lovely, that country in May—all lacy with dogwood, literally flooded with jonquils."

Displaying an artifact from those long-ago days, Amanda flaunts a small dried bunch of the miniature daffodils.

"That was the spring I had the craze for jonquils. . . . Mother said, 'Honey, there's no more room for jonquils.' And still I kept on bringing in more jonquils. Whenever, wherever I saw them, I'd say, 'Stop! Stop! I see jonquils!' I made the young men help me gather the jonquils! It was a joke, Amanda and her jonquils. Finally there were no more vases to hold them, every available space was filled with jonquils."

In his stage directions, Williams instructs that this passage must be spoken "feverishly."

"The legend of her youth," the playwright tells us, "is nearly revived."

Maybe we stop short of still wearing our prom dresses, but we are all a little like Amanda. The past beckons—a panoramic land of *was*, of what-ifs, starring us . . . but airbrushed versions of ourselves. Good times, good times: the pretty past sucks us in and sometimes we cannot, will not, come out. But the bad past beckons, too. It's like watching an accident: our own.

The past is where we come from. It is only natural to want to stay. The past is home.

In the equation that is life on Earth, your future grows shorter each year and your past elongates, fills, swells. A refuge from present-day fears, even a bad past can feel safer than the present because at least past horrors are *known*—it shimmers in a warm if slightly unreal glow.

We can't airbrush the present. This ache right now, that whimpering child, this bill are all too real. Nor can the future be made to stop dwindling. Add to this the fair certainty that age brings illness and loss, that we are almost certain to feel worse henceforth than we do now, and the past becomes more magnetic. Time is our worst enemy, and only in our visions of the past can we control time. Only in our visions of the past does time stand still. This is how we get stuck.

Ambient sounds you hardly noticed at age two or ten or twelve or twenty-five, school bells and those Top 40 songs you mocked from hot backseats, are siren songs.

Nostalgia is a foregone conclusion.

And since we are only ever getting older, sicker, and closer to death, nostalgia is virtually genetically encoded. Awareness of who we are now hinges inextricably on who we were.

A lucky few are fully alive in the present, respecting the lessons of the past, yes, but forever facing forward. The rest of us envy their realism. Wind chafing their cheeks, these forward marchers scale the prow. They plan. They hope. Come what may, they keep saying: *Someday*.

They inhabit the *now*, the moment, savoring the sweet salt on their tongues, the whoosh of air, the snap of flags.

But some of us, try as we might, keep finding ourselves all turned around, spines against the horizon, staring back whence we came.

Transfixed.

Sometimes what pulls us back is tragedy, our old nightmares set on repeat. The past as prison. Others, the Amanda Wingfields, go back seeking glory. For them, the past is a pageant. If you had just seen me then, they say. If you had known me then.

Explained this way, being stuck in the past makes perfect sense. What could be wrong with staying stuck in happiness? Pinioned by pleasure? Mired in fun?

Nothing, in principle. Except that living in the past means . . . not fully inhabiting the present. Not to mention the future. I mean this literally: *not to mention* the future. And as regards our debt to society, contemplating the future and/or appreciating the present might be considered a moral obligation. That is, if you consider life a gift. Because every moment you live now is another new page in the story. To live in the past is to dismiss and devalue the present, thus to ignore everyone in the present, everyone and everything around you now. Ignore. Insult. Reject. Negate. Erase. We are forever forming future pasts. So living *in* the past means forming no new different ones. Which is a bit like being dead.

A Buddhist in a swimming pool once told me: *The only thing that never changes is the fact that nothing stays the same.*

Except the past.

In 1927, the British astronomer Arthur Eddington coined the term "arrow of time" to capture the concept that everything in the natural world hurtles irreversibly forward. The past is known. Only the future remains random. Thus, Eddington wrote, "The introduction of randomness is the only thing which cannot be undone."

Which, to most of us, is terrifying.

We try to get used to this idea. "The Moving Finger writes," Omar Khayyám warned in his *Rubaiyat* nearly nine hundred years ago, "and having writ, moves on: nor all thy piety nor wit shall lure it back to cancel half a line, nor all thy tears wash out a word of it."

Ouch.

When I was ten, I won a birthday-party game. My prize was a poster on which a girl gazed through a rain-streaked window. Printed on the poster was the message *Sometimes only memories seem real*. I swapped it for a rainbow Super Ball because I had no idea what those words on the poster meant.

Yet.

About a year later, my friend Nicki made a proclamation about me, herself, and our friend Rhonda. "I dwell in the past," Nicki said. "Rhonda dwells in the present. You dwell in the future." She'd nailed it. Nicki was romantic, always dreaming of good times gone, of meadows paved over as developers devoured our town, of boats and pinnacles once glimpsed on family trips and never seen again. By contrast, Rhonda was spontaneous, dynamic, every day brand new. Then there was me: perpetually, jaw-clenchingly terrified of saying something stupid, making my team lose, or making someone mad.

Flash forward: fifteen years later, after a lifetime spent mostly apologizing, I was startled to find love. Its effect was perverse. The more I should have thought about my future—*our* future—the more fixated I was on my past. The person I was now versus the person I was then. The more wonderful my new boyfriend (and eventual husband), Tuffy, was, his ringlets the color of new pennies shining in the sun, the more my childhood anguish seemed a tragic waste.

"If I'd known then what I know now," I kept repeating like the Ancient Mariner.

"Well, you didn't," he said. "Who ever does? Who cares?"

He wanted to go places, do things. Yet wherever we went, I kept up a running narrative of bygone misery. Not bona fide crises but slow suburban sorrows. Tuffy listened patiently to tales of saws and Etch A Sketches, swing sets and electric toothbrushes.

Our second summer together, we went to Europe. One evening in Germany, we swam in a mineral pool. Steam rose, smelling of sulfur, making us look half real and half dreamed. We floated at the shallow end.

"Wow," Tuffy said, curls plastered to his scalp. "The ancient Romans swam in these same springs."

I glanced around. "Uh-huh."

"And that up there"—he jerked his head toward trees outlined against a cobalt sky—"is the Black Forest, home of Rumpelstiltskin."

"Yeah." I chewed my fingernail. "Can you believe my dad called me a pig and dumped out my desk drawers onto my bedroom floor?"

"In nineteen sixty-eight," Tuffy said.

"Nineteen sixty-nine. And . . ."

That was what we talked about that night: the drawers, the floor, my pencils rolling toward the door. The next day on the train to Austria, past emerald hills dotted with ski chalets and crossroads crucifixes, we talked about how I accidentally spilled a bag of peanuts in the car one night and my dad pulled into a parking lot and hurled handfuls of nuts at me as strangers stared.

Tuffy nodded and clucked, watching vistas fly past behind my head: ten thousand tiled roofs, sunflowers, sunstruck lakes, and spires that we would never talk about.

We talked instead of me, of strangers he would never know, all long ago and far away.

I was cheating on Tuffy—not in the sexual sense but in choosing the past instead of him right then. I called it research. I called it recovery. I called it necessary, but now I will never get that summer back. I fed the present into the ravenous maw of the past and turned that present into yet another past whose wastage, if I am not very very careful, I will mourn by wasting future presents, too.

How long must one stare at the broken chains, marveling at their strength and heft, the clanking noise they made, before one just gets up and walks away?

Accepting the future enough to let go of the past requires courage, hope, and the kind of imagination that tends toward pots of gold and rainbows, not charred corpses. If you can speak in the future tense and smile, I think you are as brave as any soldier.

I fear the future the way most people fear disease. Just saying *tomorrow* makes me feel like a liar. Or a fool, ripe to be proven wrong. *And what an irony it will be if tomorrow never comes.*

The past is refuge, pageant, prison. But if, as most religions hold, all life is precious, we must learn to parcel out our reverence for the life we live now and the life we lived before and the life we have yet to live, allotting fond memories their due alongside awareness and anticipation. Treasuring the past is not a *bad* thing when it's part of an overall package. The trouble begins when we act as if we could outfox physics, outrace thermodynamics. We forget that running ever backward equals going nowhere. As time marches on every day, we must forever run backward one day farther to stay in that same moment of nostalgia. Imagine that you're on a wagon train in 1849, heading west from Delaware to California to join the gold rush. You share a wagon, one of eight in the train, with your wife and child. Two days into your westward migration, your beloved aunt Grace—who was traveling in the wagon behind yours—dies of a fever. Gathered around a freshly dug hillside grave under a majestic oak, the travelers say prayers and farewells, climb back onto their wagons and move on—you among them. Yet every day, as the wheels roll ever westward, first over Ohio and then Indiana, your devotion to the late Grace impels you to disembark, straggle back eastward alone, and visit the grave. Of course, the distance is farther and the journey more difficult every time. Then, after reaching the grave and experiencing the euphoria of an imagined reconnaissance with your beloved aunt, who was so kind to you when you were a child, you remember your family and your mission, then leap up and rush back toward the wagon train—only to turn around as soon as you reach it and head graveward again.

In a very short time, this becomes quixotic and absurd.

Yet it's what we do when we're stuck in the past: the endless running back and forth, missing the scenery, ditching responsibility, attached to what no longer exists. That we can do this without moving a muscle makes it more surreptitious but no less baroque.

Living in the past is life on hold.

You know that feeling, like a kind of drunkenness, when nothing new seems real. Circling that space after good-bye, before hello.

Thinking: I. Am. Not. Really. Here.

Those for whom the past is a prison often think they must serve life stentences.

Seventy years ago, on some Baltimore playground, a plump little girl named Jean flinched as, day after day, the catcalls came.

Tub.

Fatso.

Four-by-four.

After school and on weekends, because they both worked, Jean's parents put her in charge of her baby sister. Whatever went wrong, whatever the baby broke, Jean got blamed.

Your fault.

She gained weight as she grew up, hiding from cameras on holidays and family trips. Her slender little sister joined the catcallers:

Jean the giant.

My BIG big sis.

Some kids react to such treatment by growing angry, growing stronger, or growing resilient. Perhaps because no one—not her parents, certainly—was there to soothe her, Jean took the catcallers at their word. At twenty-five, she was her own worst enemy. She married and had kids in a glazed state of self-loathing and disbelief: not really there. The kids were still toddlers when, during a bout with irritable bowel syndrome, Jean shrank to a size eight and stayed there. She still loathed herself, hissing into the mirror. *Fatso.* Her kids grew up watching Jean punch herself in the face. She would not listen to their pleas to stop. When her sister got a divorce, Jean blamed herself, although she lived six states away and had nothing to do with it. *She's my responsibility*, Jean said. When her parents died—of stroke and pneumonia, at ripe old ages—she blamed herself.

Today Jean goes to church and senior clubs. She owns a comfortable home and drives an SUV. Widowed, she chats with neighbors at the supermarket. On the surface she looks like lots of well-off ladies her age. What no one knows is that she still starts every morning hissing at the mirror, pummeling her head. Her children see it when they visit: parents themselves now, they mourn and seethe, knowing she spent her life and half of theirs stuck in a past that has nothing to do with them. You live in luxury these days, her children say. You have been slim since 1970. Now, as then, Jean gazes, glazed, past them when they speak. She will not leave the playground.

Stuck-in-the-past characters populate film and fiction, funny and sad because they're so familiar:

In *Sunset Boulevard*, demented ex–silent movie star Norma Desmond dreams madly of making a comeback. In *Hush . . . Hush, Sweet Charlotte*, a crazed spinster refuses to relinquish to the wrecking crew the crumbling Southern mansion that was the scene of her girlhood joys and sorrows. In *Great Expectations*, old Miss Havisham has stopped all her clocks at the exact moment when, long ago, she was jilted. In *The Tin Drum*, three-year-old Oskar vows to never grow up—and while his mind matures, his body does not. In *Napoleon Dynamite*, middle-aged Uncle Rico drones on and on about his youthful football exploits: "Back in 'eighty-two I could throw a pigskin a quarter mile." Unsurprisingly, Rico buys a fake mail-order time machine. A recurring character in the British comedy series *The League of Gentlemen* is hospital aide Les McQueen, still stuck in the '70s, when he played guitar in a one-hit-wonder band called Creme Brulee that almost got a major record deal. McQueen wears huge outdated aviator glasses. He stays up late playing Creme Brulee records.

"Everyone knew me round here," Les remembers wistfully. "I'd walk in a urinal and heads would turn."

Now a prolific writer of true-crime books, Carol Anne Davis says her parents were "stuck in a time warp." In the Scotland of her youth, "they refused to use any product or service that *their* parents hadn't used. This meant, for example, that they refused to buy a refrigerator. In the summer, the butter would melt into an oily pool, the milk would curdle, and the cheese would sweat. Only my mother would eat them, though sometimes even she would renege and put the cheese out on the window ledge for the sparrows. I'm convinced that the decline in Britain's bird population dates back to this time." Davis laughs bitterly.

They also refused to install a telephone. This created continual communication breakdowns in that pre–cell phone era. Davis remembers one night when, as a teenager, she went out clubbing. Having told her parents what time she'd return, she planned to take a cab in order to make it home by then—only to find none available when she wanted to leave. A manager told the worried girl that if she waited until closing time, she and her friend could ride on the staff bus.

"But I had no way to warn my parents that I'd be two hours later than I'd promised," Davis tells me, "and by the time I got home my father had gone to a telephone kiosk and reported me missing to the police."

Their refusal to modernize stemmed from their own upbringing during harsher times. We often see that kind of stuckness in older Americans who grew up during the Great Depression. Still marked by the traumas of fear, deprivation, forced mobility, and watching their parents panic, they can be frugal and cautious to a fault.

Davis and her younger brother started working as soon as they could in order to buy their own modern conveniences. When she was seventeen and he was fifteen, they paid for a phone to be installed and split the bills.

"Bathing was yet another bone of contention," Davis tells me. "My parents only had a bath every Sunday night as children, so we were restricted to the same frequency and, even more unreasonably, the same time slot. When I started menstruating, I was desperate to bathe daily but my mother was adamant that we couldn't afford any additional hot water. So, when I started work, I arranged to pay her a certain amount per extra bath. She agreed to this, but I could feel her disapproval. She and my father were incredibly rigid people who held on tightly to their childhood rituals."

Yet despite her desperation to escape that lifestyle, *their* childhood rituals had become *her* childhood rituals and thus reflexive. She was still performing some of them even after she moved into her own apartment.

When "a boyfriend called around whilst I was making chips," she remembers, he was horrified to find that she owned no paper towels and drained the greasy fries on cheaper toilet paper and other scraps. Her mother had always told her that paper towels were too costly.

"He bought me some paper towels," Davis says now with embarrassment, "and I could immediately see that they were five times as absorbent."

She bought a fridge. She sampled foreign cuisines for the first time. She began bathing twice daily. But because her parents had always insisted that "education and work didn't matter for girls, that they were just things to be endured until a girl got married and had a family," Davis says, she "didn't feel equipped for a career."

Later in life than most, she enrolled in college and earned two degrees.

You know those times when life's been going fine, full speed ahead, but then you say: I just can't face another day? And then—you don't?

What provokes a blowback? Boredom. Heartbreak. Catastrophic illness. Workplace woe. It's insidious. It starts with a quick leaf through the yearbook, pages yellowed, binding creaky with disuse. It starts with Googling names long unsaid.

And this is done in secret, furtively, because the people in your present life would never understand your longing to escape them— to be anywhere but here, anywhere but this cold wet spot that feels like failure.

Sometimes only memories seem real.

Checking her e-mail one night, Donna saw a name that sent a lightning bolt down her spine. Tucked among the familiar senders and obvious spam, this one seemed to grow and glow before her eyes and pulsate, raising goose bumps.

She hadn't seen that name since she was fifteen. It belonged to a boy from her old neighborhood. She and Eric had gone to different schools—hers public, his Catholic—but for a few months, more than twenty years before, the pair had talked a lot, walking their dogs. Nothing physical had happened between them. Throughout those months, it forever seemed about to—always, almost—but, each time, she or he or both of them backed off.

So shy.

They both loved kung fu movies and magnolia trees. He was small for his age back then, which made him shyer still.

And then it ended. Donna started dating a boy who went to her school. Eric got his driver's license and acquired a secondhand car. When he drove past Donna, neither met the other's eyes.

And now, seeing his name—she realized she had never seen it typed before—made Donna throb. She pictured him, ordered herself to age-enhance the image, but as her flesh tingled it was the teenage Eric she saw. That prickly feeling on her nape: that swoony surge that, for a long time now, she had forgotten she could feel.

So I'm excited about a fifteen-year-old boy.

Who is the same age as my son.

Donna was married: happily, she'd always thought. Her home and work lives had seemed serene. That a simple e-mail—electronic, anodyne—could jolt her like this was frightening. And she hadn't even opened it yet.

She opened it.

Eric explained that he'd read a magazine article about the non-profit Donna had founded. She still used her maiden name, which he recognized.

"I got to thinking," Eric wrote. "I just thought: What the hey."

He was a real-estate agent, living two towns away. He, too, was married with kids. "It would be fun to catch up," Eric wrote.

She sent her phone number, telling herself that not to send it would be rude.

He called.

At first they were both blustery, falling into their old expressions. Then they talked of old acquaintances—whatever happened to . . . ?—the neighborhood, their favorite songs. And then, after a pause, he said: "We should have been together."

"I know," Donna said.

"I liked you."

"I liked *you*."

It hung there, both of them holding their phones, holding their breath. The conversation ended awkwardly. They hung up, rushed to call each other back.

"Sorry."

"Hmm. Well."

That night, Donna thought she would tell her husband about being contacted by an old friend. She always told him everything. And yet . . .

She didn't tell him this. Nor did she tell him Eric called the next day, nor the next, nor that she called Eric as well.

She thought: *Is this a midlife crisis?*

No, she told herself. *It feels too real.*

In those two weeks after hearing from Eric, Donna watched her serenity fall apart. At work, at home, she'd find herself hearkening back. She loved her husband: *But,* she told herself, *I made a wrong turn long ago. Now I want that chance back.* She would find herself walking down the street, chanting "I would, I would, I would" in rhythm with her feet. The past was sucking her in, fast.

She and Eric talked every day: hot stolen chats wrought with wishes, regrets.

"We have to stop this," Donna said.

"Or," Eric said, "we have to meet."

They set a date and place. He called it off. They made another. Donna got cold feet. They made another.

I would, I would, I . . .

At the last minute, she didn't go. Did he? She never knew. The day came and it went. They never spoke or wrote again. *Dodged a bullet*, she tells herself.

She Googles him sometimes.

_____

For some, the past is less a place than a principle. Some version of it, real or imaginary, is central to an ideology for groups such as Salafist Muslims or Hasidic Jews or the Amish, who reject the present as most of us know it. Of course, members of such groups experience *their own present*, each minute unfolding in real time for them, too. Theirs is a present in a past, shorn of the technology and trends that they would call surface trappings, or sin, but the rest of us would call signs of the times.

Their stuckness in the past and absence from the present is a chorused cri de coeur. A creed. The direction and speed at which the mainstream hurtles futureward offends them, disgusts them, shocks them, outrages them collectively. They want to stop time. Not just for themselves but in some cases for you, me, and everyone.

They don't consider themselves stuck. They consider themselves correct.

Belonging to an established religion de facto attaches one to the past. A religion's liturgy and lore are set in the time and place, usually long ago and far away, in which its founders and first followers lived. That sense of linkage lends authenticity to modern practice. Rooting spirituality in history makes it, for many, feel more real. We enthrall ourselves envisioning unbroken chains of fellow believers uttering the same prayers and performing the same rituals, back through time, wearing the garb and experiencing the travails of different eras. We feel embraced by those countless like-minded strangers, especially during dark nights of the soul. The heritage of a faith itself infuses the heritage of the faithful. Pilgrimages are journeys into the past.

Some devout groups take that sense of linkage even further.

They elect to manifest it not just in their hearts but in the way they dress, eat, speak. They leave the modern world and live as they imagine their fellow believers lived in that hopeful and holy era when their liturgy was new. They inhabit this ersatz past, stay stuck, as proof of faith. As contrasts grow between their lifestyles and the modern world, their identities are defined largely by the glaring fact of their rejection of the present in an artificial stopped-clock otherworld. Many such groups become objects of scrutiny or curiosity, laughter or fear. Their neighborhoods become tourist attractions. A scholarly eye observing them would note historical inaccuracies, impossibilities, the imposition of wishes over actual fact.

Islamic fundamentalism, charges Harvard University researcher Emran Qureshi, is "the intellectually enfeebled idea of returning to a pristine imaginary past." Fundamentalists—also known as Wahhabists or Salafists, from the Arabic term *salaf al-salih,* meaning "pious ancestors" or "pious early generations"—cling fiercely to the belief that Islam was perfect during Mohammed's lifetime and during the two subsequent generations, and thus should continue to be practiced now exactly as it was in the seventh century. They justify this with a hadith, a quote attributed to Mohammed, in which he is alleged to have decreed: "The people of my generation are the best, then those who follow them, and then whose who follow the latter."

Promoting eye-for-an-eye sharia law—unbearably harsh by Western standards—and wishing to impose it on the world at large, Salafists follow a strict network of religiously based rules affecting virtually every daily activity, from the number of fingers that must be used for eating (three), to the hand used to convey water to the mouth (right) in how many stages (three), to dress codes and restrictive behavioral and sexual codes for both women and men, all based on this perception of a pure and perfect past. Drawing inspiration from the eighteenth-century revivalist theologian Muhammad ibn 'Abd al-Wahhab—which is why they are also often called Wahhabists—Salafists reject Western ideologies, Western economies, Western social institutions, Western politics, and Western educational methods as manifestations of a modernism they abhor. In fact, they reject modernism not just in Westerners but in moderate and apostate Muslims. The punishment for escaping that rigid version of the past is often death.

Typically depicted piloting horse-drawn carriages down Pennsylvania roads, the Amish are separatist Christians who choose to live without electricity, telephones, and cars. Working their fields and driving those boxy wagons down country lanes, they look like actors in a period film, wearing capes, vests, straw hats, and long dresses whose modesty and plainness demonstrate the Amish dislike of pride—or *hochmut*, as it is called in Pennsylvania Dutch, the obscure archaic form of German that the Amish speak among themselves, though they speak English with the outside world. No group in America better embodies stuckness in the past than the Amish—except perhaps Hasidic Jews, whose large-hatted, long-bearded men and bewigged, long-skirted women evoke the eighteenth century, when the sect was founded in Eastern Europe. As in times of yore, the devout Hasidim keep to a strict prayer schedule. Most Hasidic marriages are arranged, married women do not show their hair in public, and many Hasidim, even young ones, speak among themselves in Yiddish, thus keeping very much alive a so-called dead language.

Morally and to varying extents technologically, the Amish and Hasidim are stuck in the past. But the big question is: So what? They barely interact with, much less harm, anyone outside their own circles. Amish ladies do not prowl neighborhoods ringing door-bells, distributing pamphlets, and lecturing passersby about God, as some other Christian groups do. And proselytizing is strictly for-bidden, not just among Hasidim but all Jews. Unlike Salafists, these groups do not wish to impose their rules on outsiders. They are true stuck-in-the-past separatists, inhabiting a separate world but enter-taining no agenda to pull you or me into it.

Belonging to a separatist religious group, like belonging to any club, affords a sense of solidarity. Spiritual underpinnings add to this a sense of superiority. Although living under strict archaic codes can be difficult, this harshness is counterpoised in such groups by the comfort of conformity and of putatively divine protocol. One never has to make individual decisions if one believes that every detail—including the mandate that one must live in the past—has been long ago worked out by the highest authority of all, a divine authority. Compared to modern secular life, in which the present and the prospect of the future demand incessant navigation and negotiation—so many questions demanding answers—the conform-ism and comfort of collective stuckness in the past are seductive and self-perpetuating. Dorothy Allred Solomon, the twenty-eighth of forty-eight children born to a polygamist Mormon father, describes in her memoir, *Predators, Prey, and Other Kinfolk*, the separatist Utah compound of her childhood: "For the most part, we were shy, gentle creatures who kept to ourselves, ruminants chewing on our private theology, who dealt with aggression by freezing or running."

Seductive, self-perpetuating—and solace for those who wish to stay stuck in the past: But what happens to those who don't? What happens to those who, after years of devotion, experience a change of heart or who, born into this milieu, reject a choice their parents made for them in which they had no part? As a young adult, Solomon broke ranks by choosing monogamy. As punishment, many close relatives disowned her.

Some Amish communities practice *Meidung,* or shunning—the deliberate ostracism of individuals who have left the faith. This is justified by such scriptural injunctions as "Now I beseech you, brethren, mark them which cause divisions and offences contrary to the doctrine which ye have learned; and avoid them" (Romans 16:17, KJV). *Meidung* is meant to usher strays back into the fold and save their souls, according to the National Committee for Amish Religious Freedom: "Belonging is important and shunning is meant to be redemptive. It is not an attempt to harm or ruin the individual and in most cases it does bring that member back into the fellowship again." Few punishments can feel harsher to those raised in a subculture that prizes togetherness. Among other, often severe, forms of avoidance, the relatives of shunned persons refuse to share dining tables with them.

But no one mutilates them or threatens them with death.

My classmates' moms were attending feminist consciousness-raising meetings and my seventh-grade gym class was grooving to Barry White as, halfway around the world, Ayaan Hirsi Ali—the five-year-old daughter of devout Somali Muslims—was circumcised with a rough pair of scissors: "My grandmother was living in the Iron Age," Hirsi Ali writes in her memoir, *Infidel,* recounting how the matriarch held her in position as an itinerant blacksmith did the cutting: "I heard it, like a butcher snipping the fat off a piece of meat." When she reached marriageable age, her father promised Hirsi Ali to a man who had approached him in a mosque two hours earlier: a distant cousin whom she had never met. Shortly after the marriage, while en route to join her groom in Canada,

Hirsi Ali fled to a Dutch refugee center. After defying demands from her husband and family to relent, she received a letter from her father, cutting off all further contact: "This is the last message you will receive from me," it read. "Go to hell! . . . MAY ALLAH PUNISH YOU." She later became a Dutch parliamentarian, was driven into hiding by death threats after making the 2004 film *Submission* (whose premise is that the Quran authorizes abuse against women) with later-murdered director Theo van Gogh, and moved to the United States.

Our children are our hostages in whatever era we inhabit.

At the turn of the nineteenth century, the Industrial Revolution was transforming the Western world, outfitting its newly urbanized populace with a parade of labor-saving inventions and with factories making new products in new ways. Yet not everyone was pleased with this progress, this leaving behind of the past. Among the disgruntled were old-school British knitters and other textile artisans who, mourning the loss of their livelihood, became saboteurs. Organizing into cells, their faces blackened by way of disguise, they staged attacks on wool and cotton mills, smashing the stocking frames and other futuristic machinery that symbolized the death of the old ways. These terrorists were called Luddites after the possibly mythical activist-hero Ned Ludd. The early nineteenth-century folk anthem "General Ludd's Triumph" hails this "Hero of Nottinghamshire" who "was to measures of violence unused":

Till his sufferings became so severe
That at last to defend his own Interest he rous'd
And for the great work did prepare. . . .

His wrath is entirely confined to wide frames
And to those that old prices abate
These Engines of mischief were sentenced to die . . .
And Ludd who can all opposition defy
Was the grand Executioner made.

Between 1811 and 1812, some thousand machines were smashed in Britain. In April 1812 alone, Luddites torched the West Houghton mill in Lancashire and mounted an assault on William Cartwright's mill in Yorkshire. Charlotte Brontë described the latter attack in her novel *Shirley*:

"A crash—smash— . . . the mill-yard, the mill itself, was full of battle movement: there was scarcely any cessation now of the discharge of firearms; and there was struggling, rushing, trampling, and shouting . . . from the counting-house front, when the mass of rioters rushed up . . ."

The attacks persisted even after industrial sabotage was made a capital crime in England and many Luddites were hanged—three in York in January 1813, over a dozen more within the next month. Others were deported.

The Luddites weren't exerting such effort and risk just to make symbolic gestures or demonstrate a point. They believed that their movement had a chance. They wanted to stop time, to freeze it for everyone, to halt with their hatchets and flames and crowbars the momentum of a shift we now see, with hindsight, as inevitable, inexorable, a force of progress like few that human civilization has ever known.

The Luddites have modern counterparts who call themselves neo-Luddites, and who decry technology as a destructive, dehumanizing force that kills natural social interaction and community life. Another such group are anarcho-primitivists, who, as their name implies, reject agriculture, modern science, and domestication. Their vision of a perfect world entails small, autonomous, nomadic hunter-gatherer tribes. The almost certain impossibility of this vision ever coming true does not stop anarcho-primitivists from forming organizations around the world, writing books, and even creating a flag to rally around: a rectangle diagonally split, half black to denote anarchism and the other half green, of course. Neo-tribalists are yet another group that rejects the forward flow of modern civilization, preferring the "noble savage" utopia envisioned by Jean-Jacques Rousseau, whose eighteenth-century writings promoted the idea that humankind was corrupted by society.

The Luddites were stuck in the past but it was their own past, an authentic if obsolescent past that they saw retreating before their eyes. Today's neo-Luddites, anarcho-primitivists, and neo-tribalists are stuck in a past that they not only never knew but that historians would argue never existed, a putative pure, primitive past whose inconvenient truths—such as the fact that, given free rein, aggressive tribes would annihilate placid ones, launching bloodbaths—mess up the fantasy.

Some of us look grown up but aren't.

We walk around with suits and briefcases and car keys, worrying about our mortgages. But inside, we are five. Or ten. Twelve. Sixteen.

We sit in boardrooms, fly airplanes, raise kids. But we are kids ourselves, still playing dress-up, playing house.

We are the ones who have been told *Grow up* so many times we tune it out. We are the ones that you call weepy, whiny, scatterbrained, impatient, irresponsible, illogical, flighty, commitmentphobic.

Here's another word for it: we're immature.

We are stuck in the past, not usually by choice but because, like dud popcorn kernels or bonsai trees, we failed to grow. The ones who were supposed to show us how did not. They did not know or were not there. Portals inscribed with mystical initiation signs gleamed in the moonlight through which we were meant to walk, but no: We wandered back the other way or balked. Or something happened way back when and bang. The end. Like Oskar in *The Tin Drum* in reverse, our bodies matured but our minds did not. Or something failed to happen, that initiation rite we somehow skipped.

Now—playing catch-up, playing spy—we feel left out of the adult world, certain that our would-be peers are whispering behind our backs or speaking in a code we do not know. See? What a childish fear, right there. *They're all talking in code!*

We, the immature, feel like freaks. We think back to a time before we felt like this, when our flesh and minds matched.

That was long ago. Getting longer.

Here's a fancy insult: arrested development.

In middle school, my best friend Rhonda started acting . . . different. Step by platform-sandaled step, she was altering right before my eyes. That slow, sly, sleepy smirk when boys walked by. The way she twirled her hair. The careless way she said *whatever*, like flicking ash from a cigarette. With other girls she exchanged glances, smiles like secret code.

We had been close for years but now, alone with me, she had a new tic: She tapped her heel *tiktik* like a woman waiting for a bus, eager to leave.

I knew something was wrong but not what: only that it was because of *me*.

Around that same time, a boy I liked told me: "I've passed you by." For months, we had talked nightly on the phone, been to the movies twice. But now—

I said, "Passed me by? How?"

He sighed. I could picture him shrugging six streets away, in his house, his thin shoulders in a SURF MAKAHA T-shirt. "Dunno. I just . . . passed you by."

Rhonda was growing up. So was he. So was everyone. Not me.

Rhonda was already thinking like a teen, like the ladies we used to dress up our Barbies as. She could do all sorts of adult things with her mind. She reasoned. Analyzed. Debated. Sparred.

I thought in simple sentences, in black and white.

I didn't realize it then.

Not that I could have, anyway.

That was just the beginning of my being left behind. Since then, they have moved on in droves, whole universes of friends and potential friends and would-be peers. At first, going on looks and numerals alone, they think we are alike. A moment always comes, *always*, when knowledge dawns in their eyes: They realize something is odd about me, though perhaps not what. As if reproaching me for tricking them, their eyes go from perplexed to vexed.

And they depart. I cannot blame them. I cannot behave like an adult.

Just as we all reach different heights, so too our hearts and minds reach certain levels of development, then stop. The inside normally matches the outside. Not always. Not mine.

My inside stopped around age twelve. Why? We could speculate. Did my self-loathing make me childish, or the other way around? Certainly growing up is hard if not impossible when around every bend you meet yourself coming the other way, scowling and calling you a creep.

I'm stunted.

Stuck.

Can this be fixed? Perhaps. If I circled the world alone, perhaps, or were an army nurse. Life being what it is, someday a tragedy will almost certainly befall me and I will be tested. Then we'll see. *Should* it be fixed? For now, for me, immaturity is a luxury. A bittersweet epiphany about not having any more epiphanies.

And yet—

Certain good things about childhood I want to keep. Transcendent things that were fun, true, and beautiful, so why relinquish them? Why feel ashamed, just because my flesh is a certain age, to want them?

A day at the beach!

My favorite song!

Which is to say that we, the unspoiled and innocent immature, are so easy to please.

These qualities will not help usher us through med school, law school, parenthood, or acts of God. But under certain circumstances, childish skills can be a kind of currency. That childish knack for red-balloon simplicity, peek-a-boo spontaneity, bow-wow-wow mimicry. Wide-open eyes.

These are commodities.

Which is to say that we, the childish, need not fail.

The downsides loom. My fears: Picture being afraid of monsters in your closet, afraid of the dark and being mocked and making people mad. Imagine knowing that you would lose nearly any argument with nearly any adults, that harsh words make you break out in tears. Imagine wanting to hide under beds. Imagine wanting to flee down the street in sneakers, to the swing set, to the sand— while juggling house payments and wearing bifocals *and being forty-eight years old*.

It's hard.

Those knowing glances grown-ups share. Those nods. I try to winkle-pick their meanings, but end up only pretending. I think they can tell. My peers, they peer. Were this a physical condition, I could carry a white cane, raise a prosthetic arm. But this? How do I relay the way in which I am stuck? Should I carry my favorite wind-up toy? It is a fake-fur bear in a red metal chair. Turn a key and it eats, bringing a minuscule spoon back and forth from its face to a bowl of cherries in its navy-trousered lap. I love this toy so much that I can barely look at it, much less actually wind it.

Even trying to explain all this to you right now feels like telling my babysitter: "Cynthia, I saw a circus clown!"

The title character in the 2002 film *Mr. Deeds* is a simple country bumpkin who inherits a fortune. Addressing a crowd of grown-up New Yorkers faced with a brutal business decision, he argues that adults have lost touch with their childhood dreams.

"Our eleven-year-old selves would wanna kick us in the ass all over the place," wails Longfellow Deeds. He is portrayed by

Adam Sandler, who has built a successful career on man-boy characters who retain their youthful integrity while revealing the adult world's hypocrisy. A man in the crowd Deeds is addressing confesses that, at age eleven, he dreamed of becoming a veterinarian but now runs a chain of slaughterhouses. Another, who dreamed at eleven of of becoming a magician, now operates a pornographic website.

"We've all compromised," Deeds says, then urges them to repent.

For the classic Sandler character, growing up doesn't mean selling out. Critics tend to dismiss Sandler's films as slapstick and jejune. Yet these films are hugely popular with audiences because they show stuckness in the past as a form of authenticity.

A popular country-rock singer in the '70s, Kinky Friedman then became a successful thriller writer, forming friendships with two very different presidents: Bill Clinton and George W. Bush. In 2004, Friedman ran for Texas governor, endorsed by a wide range of celebrities. During his colorful campaign, Friedman told a *New Yorker* reporter, "I'm still a child, very immature." He related how, when his music career stalled in the mid-'80s, he moved back in with his parents—who ran a summer camp for kids—and never moved out: "Never really grew up, never really did a conventional job." He offered the reporter a motto that he had learned from his father and still cherished: "Treat adults like children and children like adults."

We the immature do not recognize each other on the street. We do not recognize each other in cars or at work because we are faking so hard. We have to fake because adults say they love subcultures, but ours is one for which they display little empathy.

But we know how to have a great day at the beach.

And we know better than you how to love our favorite songs.

Politics is a never-ending struggle to wrest control of the present by making promises about the future based on the past—weighing one against the other with calibrated promises and threats. Even the least cynical observer can see this in action. It's how we make our own nonpolitical personal plans, after all, scanning our experiences for lessons that we can use as guidelines. *Hey, I know what happens when you buy the cheapest hose.*

The past upon which politics can draw is a vast and ever-growing omnibus of source material. With varying degrees of distortion, its figures and phases and events can be shaped into countless tableaux: Golden Ages that may or may not have ever really existed and to which we yearn to return, or historical nightmares for which harsh retribution is due. Atop actual history, politics can superimpose rosebuds or barbed wire, dissonant or mellow tunes, harking back again and again as a means to an end to scare, sicken, or galvanize a crowd.

Political ideologies spring from the particular social circumstances that inflect a certain place and time. Born of necessity, an ideology can look like salvation. It can proffer *the answer*—in its moment, to the masses, it makes sense. To exploited and vulnerable laborers in nineteenth-century Europe, Marxism made sense. To Germans panicking amid economic chaos after their country's humiliating loss of World War I, Hitler's National Socialism made sense. To once-stable Americans rendered destitute by 1929's Great Depression, Franklin D. Roosevelt's New Deal—federal relief programs now seen as the dawn of modern-day liberalism—made sense. To Chinese peasants whose horizons were confined by a rigid class system and wracked by a brutal Japanese invasion, Maoism made sense.

If politics were like food, then ideologies would be discarded when they "spoiled": that is, when the social circumstances that spawned them in the first place evolved so as to render them irrelevant, then obsolete. But, albeit with some exceptions—who remembers the Know-Nothing Party, or Distributism?—ideologies tend to persist, cherished and trumpeted long past their expiration dates.

Because most of us become politically aware in young adulthood, just as we savor our first spasms of real-world power, political beliefs have a way of fusing with our identities. So we retain them as we age. Nearly all of us maintain the same party affiliations throughout our lives. If a certain worldview was our salvation once, why keep searching?

But most political affiliations are versions of being stuck in various pasts. And part of politics is wishing that everyone agreed with you. And that means wanting everyone to inhabit your version of the past.

Derived from the Greek word for "ancient," the prefix "paleo" evokes Stone Age hominids hunting bison on steppes with flint-tipped spears. And "conservative" implies withholding, preserving, staying lodged in place: a double stuckness in the past. Yet the word "paleoconservative," though it sounds like an insult, was almost certainly created by paleoconservatives themselves. During the '80s, the term first began appearing in far-right publications such as *Chronicles: A Magazine of American Culture*. Today, many right-wingers eagerly embrace it.

"Yes, I am a paleocon. I am proud to admit it and I should be," writes one blogger in the Pacific Northwest. "After all, it was the paleocons . . . who first sounded the clarion call of immigration reform. We were right." Another blogger calls himself "The Paleo Pundit." Another dubs his blog "Paleocon Strikes!" An Amazon .com user beamingly titles his Listmania selection "Paleoconservative Essentials on History." The list includes volumes criticizing war and presidents and advocating states' rights and secession.

Those early articles in *Chronicles* outlined an isolationist worldview that adhered to an idealized past: America between the two world wars. Railing against post-'60s secularism and self-indulgence, distancing themselves even from mainstream Republicans and other more expansion-minded conservatives, paleos defined themselves as pro-Christian, anti-immigration, anti–central government, anticommunist, antimulticulturalist, and antiglobalist.

"Paleoconservativism is the expression of rootedness: a sense of place and of history, a sense of self derived from forebears, kin, and culture," according to *Chronicles* senior editor Chilton Williamson Jr. "Be true to your forebears," Williamson instructs, "and to the culture they created and—for nearly four centuries—sustained. Wear a coat and necktie in polite society, even on an airplane."

In polite society.

Is there a polite society? Was there ever, really—or just on *The Andy Griffith Show*, a Norman Rockwell dream where kids say, "Thank you, ma'am," and passing neighbors tip their hats? Polite to whom? And even if there ever was, where is it now? Nowhere I know of. Surely not on planes.

Yet in some ways, those who call themselves progressives are the ultimate irony—because despite the forward motion of the word "progressive," they glamorize what is in many ways an expired ideology repackaged to look fresh. Attracted by this new wrapper, eager generations march into the past and get stuck there without even realizing it. Unsurprisingly, "anachronistic" is the last thing progressives want to be called. They would say that is for conservatives, who relish it.

Yet with contemporary politics of every stripe being so inextricably tied to history, no affiliation is immune.

"Most people who were liberals in 1968 still are. Liberals. In 1968," jokes economist and Internet entrepreneur—and ex-liberal— Arnold Kling. He urges us to "contrast the way the world might have appeared to a reasonable liberal in 1968 with the way events have unfolded since then." In other words, how did those lofty ideals, so bold back then, work out?

"In 1968," Kling muses, "liberals thought that Communism could work reasonably well." In fact, "Many liberal intellectuals considered Communism a viable option for achieving development in the Third World." To counter this, he cites post-'68 mass exoduses from Cuba and Vietnam and recent revelations about life in the USSR. It's worth noting the decade's other massive casualties, often conveniently ignored: drugs' tragic death toll, the failures of urban renewal, the countless kids neglected (or worse) by parents immersed in their own ersatz enlightenment, flying eight miles high or doin' it in the road.

"If liberals had paid attention since 1968 rather than remaining in an ideological deep freeze," Kling scolds, "they would have seen the evidence." Taking that evidence to heart, he adds, "I am no longer a liberal (in the contemporary sense of the term), because my calendar did not get stuck on 1968." Today he's a libertarian.

Kling notes that we tend to maintain the utopian—albeit fact-challenged—ideals and loyalties that won our hearts when we were young. He calls the result "moral free riding": that is, holding an ideological stance that, while ostensibly extreme, poses no actual personal risk. It's relatively harmless to be radical in the postmodern West, where dissenters are not jailed for being dissenters.

The 1960s are like crazy-daisy Day-Glo pink patchouli-scented flypaper that tastes like Space Food Sticks and gets you high. Arguably, more people have been—and are—stuck in the '60s than in any other decade, ever. You don't even have to have actually lived through them to be jam-up-and-jelly-tight stuck on them. Many who were young then—or any age, just conscious—and experienced it firsthand frankly refuse to leave it behind. Stranger still, many who were not born until after it ended, even decades after it ended, cling just as fiercely to its fashions or renderings of its fashions, its music or their versions of its music, its ideologies or latter-day, game-of-telephone voicings of its ideologies. As a moment of epochal change in which nearly everything felt new and revolutionary, and in most cases was, that decade hovers in its ever-receding factual past, blaring out buzzwords that still enchant. As recent history goes, the '60s is like the popular kid in class. It's exciting, a little scary, not boring like those other kids sitting on either side, so everyone wants to say: "Hey! I'm with him!" The '60s is recent enough to be almost within reach, to be captured almost recognizably on record and film. So it's easier to imitate—to get stuck in—than, say, the 1410s.

The ambient sentiment during the '60s, a collective delusion of grandeur that was then free for the taking, was that one was making history. One could feel this, back then, even (as I know firsthand) when one was eight years old and playing Candyland, drinking strawberry Quik. Something was simply in the air.

And millions have been gasping that air ever since.

It's like one huge you-should've-been-there joke.

But psssst: It's over. Done. Just like the Punic Wars.

(You should've been there, though. Those Space Food Sticks were great.)

Many social battles waged back then were won. Doors flung open. Landmark laws passed. Shackles exploded. This is history.

When must the victory celebrations end?

Righteous, sexy '60s rebels are tenured professors now, earning substantial salaries. In one regard, they have become "the man." Yet they want it both ways. Their status as '60s celebrities keeps their classes full and their schools desirable and their names in the paper. And their popularity keeps academic rhetoric and university life stuck in that part of the past. The very nineteen- and twenty-year-olds who should be at their most rebellious and most forward-thinking, who should be all about the new, proudly wear Che Guevara T-shirts and Mao buttons hailing dead icons, safely recycling the same radicalism, with the exact same figureheads, that their parents and even grandparents flaunted years before.

A leader of the radical Weather Underground group that virtually declared war on the United States government and was linked with several bombings, Bernardine Dohrn was wanted on domestic terrorism charges and spent ten years as a fugitive before surrendering to authorities in 1980. Today she is a law professor at Northwestern University. During her keynote speech at a 2007 justice reform conference I attended at Berkeley—whose enthusiastic audience comprised mostly grad students and young academics—Dohrn advocated releasing massive populations of inmates from U.S. prisons, which she called "dungeons." Did Dohrn receive a standing ovation because of what she said that day—or because of her status as a living relic of a past her audience aches to inhabit?

With so many '60s Hall of Famers now holding top posts in education and the media, that recycled radicalism largely determines what is taught and learned in classrooms now, what is presented as news, and thus what the public talks about. So many films glorify the '60s with that same lockstep reverence that their cumulative message pins you in the past without your even realizing that this, too, is political.

So are those rebels turned professors calculatedly striving to pull the young—and thus the future—into their part of the past as the latest front in the same old revolution?

Or, like the crime writer Carol Anne Davis's fridgeless parents, are these holdovers just creatures of habit, doing what they've always done, too stuck to realize the effects?

Or are they opportunists, cashing in at last on stuckness in the past? Are they—as scions of the first youth culture—merchandising it for a new generation? Manufacturing and packaging their past in Che T-shirts at twenty bucks a pop?

The Time Tunnel was a 1966–1967 television series about a machine devised by U.S. government scientists that can fling its users into the future and the past. Unfortunately, not all the kinks have been worked out of this top-secret enterprise, dubbed Project Tic-Toc, before two men attempt to use it. They swirl away down the machine's spiral-patterned maw and can't come back. In episode after episode, valiant attempts to adjust the controls only lurch the castaways from era to era—from the Battle of Gettysburg to the SS *Ti-*

tanic to outer space. The show ended abruptly after one season, its heroes remaining stranded forever in pasts (and occasional futures) not their own.

Some of us enter pasts not our own on purpose. Unlike the characters on that show, we choose these destinations eagerly, studying them beforehand and booking virtual passage. If we get stuck there—well, that's exactly what we want. The only thing we would want more is to be back there for real.

Armchair history buffs know this yearning. It stirs as we read *Pride and Prejudice* (or *Treasure Island*, or the *Aeneid*, or *Tom Sawyer*, or *The Tale of Genji*) or watch *Excalibur* (or *Braveheart*, or *Casablanca*, or *Gidget*, or *La Dolce Vita*) or peruse a museum's collection of shields (or censers, or sabots, or sarcophagi, or tomahawks). Then it grows: that backward yank. That *wish*.

The hero of Miguel de Cervantes Saavedra's classic seventeenth-century novel *Don Quixote* is a fiftyish retiree named Alonso Quixano. A dreamy romantic, Quixano reads so many tales of bygone chivalry that he becomes convinced he is a medieval knight errant. Assembling a suit of armor and a helmet, renaming himself Don Quixote, Quixano wanders the Spanish countryside, mistaking inns for castles and windmills for giants.

The unhappy wannabe time traveler in Edward Arlington Robinson's 1910 poem "Miniver Cheevy" strains against the confines of an an all-too-real present. "Born too late," Cheevy "loved the days of old," nursing "the vision of a warrior bold":

> *He missed the mediæval grace*
> *Of iron clothing. . . .*
> *And kept on drinking.*

Latter-day Miniver Cheevys have it easier. When she's striding in a tight-bodiced, full-skirted frock across the deck of a tall ship docked at a Southern California port, or when she's leading a salty song at a city park festival as the hot inland sun bakes her wavy brown hair and glints off the brocade and feathers on her wide-brimmed hat, Christine Lampe calls herself Jamaica Rose. One of the West Coast's most active and avid reenactors, she portrays a pirate—as do her husband, Michael Lampe, whom she met aboard a pirate recreation cruise, and their two grown children. Lampe edits and publishes *No Quarter Given*, a bimonthly "publickation for the swashbucklin' type," as she writes, because "the printed word, regularly sent out, can be the best way to get a bunch o' independent-thinkin', scurrilous knaves into workin' together, and accomplishin' great adventures. . . . If we might be able to knit together a small band of sea-rovers, might we not be able to bring together even more of those with salt-water fer blood in their veins, and a lust for gold in their eye?" The magazine goes out to hundreds of subscribers "interested in the lore o' the sea, the tales of fearsome sea wolves, the recountin' o' fierce battles, and willin' ta send us 12 doubloons o' their plunder (or $12 American)."

A high school science teacher in regular life, Lampe says the lure of reenactment is obvious.

"The more technological society gets, the more we delve into fantasy. We imagine that we're going back to an easier time, a simpler and less complicated time when you wouldn't have phone calls and e-mails nipping at your rear."

You'd have plague germs and marauding hordes instead, but okay.

Young people in the sixteenth and seventeenth centuries "had fewer choices" careerwise, Lampe points out. Many youths were press-ganged into service at sea, where on merchant or military ships "they were treated very badly. An escape from that existence was to join the pirates—with whom they would get better food and better water and rum as long as it lasted." She admires pirates' ingenuity and, pillaging notwithstanding, their humanity: "They had a lot of clever ways of doing things. They had rotisseries. And the pirates were one of the first democratic groups. They actually voted in their captains. It wasn't necessarily the biggest, baddest guy who got to be captain."

With the success of the *Pirates of the Caribbean* films and novelties such as National Talk Like a Pirate Day—it's September 19 and it has its own website, talklikeapirate.com—piracy has bloomed into one of the world's top reenactment themes, right up there with the Renaissance, the Middle Ages, and the American Civil War.

But Lampe limits her immersion. It's "edutainment" for her, and only that. "I'm more interested in knowing about and talking about the pirates than in *being* the pirate." When writing articles for *No Quarter Given*, she notes, "I always have to remind myself" to use piratical-sounding slang. She is not stuck, she says. She comes and goes.

"But I know a few who really think they're pirates—who, because of this, don't think they need to abide by laws or use common courtesy. Part of the fun of playing pirate is that you can get away with a lot of stuff. You can abscond with their ladies and pretend that you're taking their gold. But some people aren't playing. It's real to them, and you have to step back and say, 'Oookaaaay.' "

Among these are the ones whom insiders call the "costume Nazis," who "have to have every last button be historically correct. They won't wear anything machine-stitched. Come on—the public doesn't care. They're not going to get down on their knees and look at your stitches.

"I've always felt that it was fun to play in another universe as long as you can come back," Lampe says. But in the reenactment community, "there are those who forget to come back. They forget that *this* universe exists."

At first glance, I am a prime candidate for some historical-reenactment society. I'm a history buff. I used to sob in history museums, gazing at log cabin dioramas, mock-up wigwams whose faux campfires were crinkled cellophane deftly lit. Peering at nineteenth-century Japanese prints upon which tiny figures in kimonos crossed minuscule bridges, I shuddered with longing to be there. On a cross-country summer bus tour of the United States at sixteen, I fell into a silent funk that our tour leader mistook for rebellion. "Look," she whispered, pulling me aside one night in Mississippi as fireflies darted under Spanish moss, behind which a white-columned house loomed in the humid, moonlit haze. "I know you hate this trip, but your parents paid for it."

What? I loved the trip. I loved it *too much*. Every day another fort, another trading post, another rutted wagon trail, another famous historical person's preserved home. As our TeenTours bus prowled Biloxi, I was still trying to process the Grand Canyon, the Painted Desert, and Bourbon Street—process their bigness, a momentousness my teenage mind interpreted as holy, as well as the fact that I could see them but not really *enter*. We in the present are forever blessed and cursed to be the past's spectators. That's what I was learning on the bus. That history is infinite, every moment infinite because it was different for everyone who lived it. The same instant—say, 6:44 a.m. in Houston on July 9, 1881—was ecstasy for one, pure torture for another.

You had to be there.

Guided tours tend to give the same message, that history is a theme park or a show—or at least a scenario whose horrors you can think about, then leave behind as you go. To *really* have been back there would have meant being unable to escape. Unable to avoid the inconvenient truths. Woe if we went back there wanting to be cowboys or kings and were, instead, captured and sold as slaves.

Role-playing helps us learn about the past. But in the guise of discipline and passion it is really only *play*. And that's why reenactment bothers me: It's a seductive game, narcotic for its fun and fires and fustian skirts and burnt-sage smell, its authenticity up to the point that it is not authentic. If I let myself play, I will jolt awake someday and see it isn't real, heartbroken as I was at four, at six, discovering that mermaids did not exist.

I envy reenactors as I do most hobbyists—because their focused love for a single pursuit seems more fruitful than my fickle scattered romances with a thousand different places, times, and things. I would like to be excellent at something odd: a champion plastic fruit collector, a renowned expert on Hayley Mills. When others invest their time and money in costumes and equipment, I laud their commitment. But I have never been good at fantasy without embarrassment. Pretending to be back there is the next best thing to being there, but *it's not being there*. And for the life of me I can't forget this, that time's portals work only one way and once they close behind us, we cannot return. The past is not a twenty-four-hour supermarket with perpetually sliding doors that part at our command. The past does not care how desperately we want it to.

Others don't share this view. Millions worldwide feel as if they were born much, much too late, not merely as regards religion or technology or politics but culture, everything. They anguish, sure that their presence in the present is a mistake, which they strive to correct. There are thousands of historical reenactment societies, spanning a huge range of historical periods—though the Middle Ages and the American Civil War era are the most popular. The U.K.–based Wychwood Warriors announces on its home page: "We have battle practice every week using swords, shields, seaxes and spears." The Jomsviking Brotherhood, also U.K.-based, declares: "Our warriors train intensively in the established Jomsviking Fighting System using authentic Viking-age steel weapons. We are *the* internationally respected fighting force; the most spectacular, dynamic, and striking Vikings alive today!" By 2006, an estimated 20,000 Britons belonged to living-history groups such as the Dark Ages Society, the English Civil War Society, the Medieval Siege Society, the Plantagenet Medieval Archery and Combat Society, the British Plate Armour Society, the Far Isles Medieval Society, the Viking Experience, and the Feudal Archers.

Organized with clockwork precision, the American Civil War Society's Union and Confederate "armies" are "composed of infantry, artillery, mounted and dismounted cavalry. We boast such units as the 69th NYSV (Irish Brigade), the 20th Maine, the 6th Wisconsin (Iron Brigade), Battery B Artillery, the 2nd U.S. Cavalry, the 8th Illinois Volunteer Cavalry, the 2nd Kentucky Dismounted Cavalry, McGowen's Brigade Battalion of Sharpshooters 1st Co., the 1st Louisiana Special Battalion, Company B , 'Wheat's Tigers,' the 8th Louisiana Infantry, Moody's Battery, the 8th Alabama Infantry, the Washington Artillery of New Orleans, and the Sussex Light Dragoons to name a few." Intriguingly and ironically, the society is based in Southern California, far from the battlegrounds of the real Civil War. For the true time tunneler, location is no barrier.

A pirate-themed "all-female privateer crew" calling itself The Ladies of the Salty Kiss is based in Oklahoma. The Blue Gryphon Pioneers—"Welcome all ye scoundrels, rogues, wenches and land-lubbers. . . . Within these pages ye'll be findin' a host o' information 'bout our band o' bucco's"—operates in landlocked South Dakota.

Sometimes you wake up, look around, and realize—in surprise, dismay, or shock—*I'm in a box*.

This box has a familiar shape, color, and texture: so familiar, in fact, and so almost comfortable that it was clearly built to order, just for you. But it's not comfortable anymore. It chafes your skin a bit or digs into your gut or cramps a limb. It clearly fit you once, but now you have outgrown it. Claustrophobia and panic rise as you ask: *How long have I been in here?*

Our boxes were constructed based on how we previously saw ourselves and how a certain set of people in a certain place and time saw us or thought they did: These boxes are personas—our roles in families, communities, relationships, careers. Outgrowing them is painful. And it's scary to emerge. We're so accustomed to that size and shape, even if it is now uncomfortable, that we feel awkward on our own. We know its contours oh so well. It might be cutting off our circulation, but others expect to find us tucked up inside where we were when last they checked. Breaking out of a box— breaking the box—is an act of rebellion, of rejection.

And we don't want to hurt those who helped us build it.

We're afraid of what they'll do when they find we've escaped. Along with those stories of honor killings and murdered ex-lovers, we've all heard about gang members who tried to leave a life of crime, only to be hunted down by former cronies. Coming unstuck doesn't always have a fairy-tale ending.

But when we cramp and cannot breathe, we search for hack-saws, then doubt whether we can wield them.

Carina, a Miami radio station manager, grew up in a large, devoutly Christian family. Her parents trained their nine kids to proselytize at school, at birthday parties, on the bus, and at the park. In the pockets of the homemade, always-out-of-fashion clothes that were passed down from sibling to sibling, they always carried pamphlets.

"One had a picture of Jesus on the cover," says Carina. "He was dialing a phone. It said, 'Christ knows your number.' "

Carina and her siblings never drank or swore. They were forbidden to date or wear makeup before they turned seventeen.

"The other kids," Carina says, "called us the God Squad." But at home and church, she adds, "We were peas in a pod. We looked alike, we talked alike, we thought alike—or so I thought."

In twelfth grade, after witnessing a fatal accident in which a young friend was killed, Carina started questioning her faith. "How could a loving God let Joey Ryan die? It struck me then," she says, "that I'd never believed in God or Jesus really but in our close-ness as a family, our love for each other—which I *associated* with God and Jesus but which *weren't* God and Jesus. After the accident I still believed in that—but I gave up on even talking about God and Jesus."

All that last year of high school, she found herself stuck in a box shaped like "a perfect church girl, listening to Debby Boone." She summoned the courage to tell her family about her change of heart. They wept, held prayer meetings for her.

She left.

She went to a small liberal-arts college in another state. Her mind and body felt new: "raw," she says. "Like cookie dough." For four years she worked her way through cliques, styles, friends, boyfriends. On school holiday breaks she always went home: "I missed my family. But it was hard for them. I think I went over the top in my attempts to prove to them that I was different—arriving in cutoffs and fishnets, with a shaved head. Showing off, the way kids do at that age."

These days, Carina says, "some of my sibs accept me. Others don't. It's not just the religious thing, not just that they think I'm going to hell. It's a little of that. But it's mostly that because they're still the way they used to be, they want me to be the way I used to be—the way they thought I *was*. We don't even talk anymore, and sometimes I feel sad about that and sometimes I don't. To them, until I get back in my box, I am invisible."

This predicament is the basis of the film *Five Easy Pieces*, whose protagonist becomes a freewheeling oil worker as a way of rejecting his elitist family and their determination to make him into a concert pianist. In the film *My Own Private Idaho*, the son of a big-city mayor is heir to a large inheritance. Yet in a desperate attempt not to inhabit the rich-kid persona his father envisions for him, Scott chooses to be a homeless street prostitute.

We can be typecast in our own lives, even by those who love us most and want the best for us.

Renae, a Washington State biologist, remembers childhood Christmases and family vacations that appeared jolly to the outside observer but which she spent feeling frozen, terrified to utter a sound, lest her father erupt into one of his rages.

"I have felt pinned down by other people's anger and unable to escape," Renae says. "My father had a volatile temper. He is a very intelligent, much admired professional with a charmingly casual social manner. But he had a hair trigger with his wife and children, exploding in barrages of angry invective when his concentration was interrupted, or his plans were spoiled, or he didn't get the degree of effusive gratitude that he expected. We all walked on eggshells around him, and developed amazing talents for tact, diplomacy, and apology in order to soothe him. Of course, I married a man with very similar characteristics: intelligence, accomplishment, charm— and a tendency to explode in anger, except in my husband's case the anger is usually directed at himself, not at me or our kids."

Growing up with her hot-tempered father, Renae became accustomed to that sort of behavior. The only sort of male head-of-household figure she had ever known was one who flew into rages. So when her husband began exhibiting the same behavior, Renae didn't react as some women would—she didn't walk out or insist that he stop. Preprogrammed in her childhood to quietly endure raging husbands and fathers, that's what she continued to do.

"My fallback strategy was dissociation—to simply grow still and wait for the storm to pass. This has not been a rewarding strategy. During my drinking years, I used alcohol to muffle my fear and outrage. That worked for a while, but eventually the drinking began to cause other, more soul-destroying problems. Since I've become sober, I've been able to recognize these repeated experiences as part of a pattern."

Renae's father and husband were stuck in their own pasts. Her dad had subsisted on such a rich diet of praise and recognition since childhood that by middle age he still inhabited the role of the spoiled and pampered prodigy. Her husband, raised by demanding and achievement-minded parents, continued as an adult to replay their harsh criticisms, castigating himself for even the slightest errors.

"It was a real breakthrough," Renae remembers, "the day that I noticed that my dog and I were reacting to my husband's angry outburst in exactly the same way: hunkering down, shivering, darting our eyes, and wondering when it would be safe to slink out of the room. That day, I decided to try something: I told my husband how his outburst made me feel. And when I did that, suddenly I could breathe again. I became a person again, present and active and alive. He was still angry"—still stuck, Renae says—"but I had choices."

And she chose to stay with her husband, to ride out his outbursts while reminding herself that she is an adult.

"This is a pattern I continue to struggle with, but I feel like the spell has been broken because I tried something—anything, one little thing—different. I'm not a powerless child or a drunk or a dog, doomed to repeat my droning lament over and over and over again. I still have the same problems, but my story has lost its monotony. I finally have a narrative with an arc."

Climbing out of the past doesn't have to end in estrangement. Showing others that we have changed, that we cherish the times we shared with them but have entered the present, can be hard—often as hard as the climb itself. And sometimes the sense of guilt or fear at leaving behind those who can't or won't climb out with you is so strong that you stay.

You remain in the past, *for them*.

What hurts worse than wanting a do-over when you know you can't have one?

Both the good thing about history and the bad thing about history is that you know how it went. Knowing that it's over, we must live with the fact that just the tiniest thing done differently somewhere back there would have changed the present entirely. One yes instead of no. One "wait" instead of "go." One push of a button, one phone call, one step. In retrospect, it seems so random and we want to fix it, smooth it, rearrange its parts as we might move dolls in a dollhouse. Because one word, one call, one step seem so slight, we tell ourselves that this fix that would make us feel all better should take . . . just . . . one . . . *tweak!*

But it does not. So we stay and stay, jousting with ghosts.

In principle, donning a pirate costume or dreaming of an Electric Prunes reunion harms no one. In principle, those pursuits are fun, imaginative, creative, culturally enriching. But if two weeks and several thousand dollars spent reenacting the Siege of Orleans— or countless hours spent online at fan forums arguing about which bootleg was best—means neglecting loved ones, then those pursuits are no nobler than hanging out in bars.

The trouble with being stuck in retrospect is that it cannot be done without pretty much abandoning the present and future. And when we muck around back there and refuse to let anything end, even though we know in our heart of hearts that it ended and how—sometimes we even have pictures to prove it—we're cheating. We are playing God, if we believe in Him: unraveling the tapestry he wove. Or we are playing Cronos. Severing the Moving Finger. Disclaiming physics.

Some would call that anathema.

2.

SEMIAUTOMATIC

Stuck in the Present

The first degree of stupidity is to think only
of the present and of bodily wants.

— VOLTAIRE

In the wake of World War II, a small coterie of American intellectuals took an interest in a 1,200-year-old sect of Buddhism called Zen. Few worldviews could be further from that of the postwar West. Anticonsumerist, minimalist, foreign, and godless, emphasizing nature, spontaneity, the random, and the unrehearsed, Zen was a veritable kick in Western theology's butt. In contrast to Judeo-Christian prescribed guilt and shame, sin and self-sacrifice, long hauls and promised heavens, Zen was all bold brush strokes and abrupt retorts. And not only had Zen originated in China, which was newly emerging as a major political opponent of the West in those postwar years, it also possessed the edgy counterculture élan of being most closely identified with Japan, the West's latest archenemy. So it appeared quadruply cool.

And it was all about inhabiting the instant.

The present.

"I'll tell you a secret," wrote the eighteenth-century Zen poet Ryokan. "All things are impermanent. . . . If you want to find meaning, stop chasing after so many things." It's hard for us now to imagine such a message seeming radical. But in a materialistic, white-picket-fence, gray-flannel-suit, nest-egging mid-twentieth-century America, it was.

This coterie of intellectuals, which came to be called the Beat Generation, had as its figureheads Gary Snyder, Allen Ginsberg, Jack Kerouac, and the transplanted Briton Alan Watts. In their writings and public speaking engagements, these eager bohemians vaunted Zen, injecting its exoticism and name-dropping its poets and patriarchs into their narratives about their urban and suburban lives. They were avant-garde superstars to millions of fans who swooned, reading about their new idols taking wine-drunk, wee-hour barefoot strolls, shouting haiku at strangers. In his 1958 novel *The Dharma Bums*, Kerouac described a Berkeley grad student's apartment transformed into an exotic "Japanese teahouse" via boulders, crates, and mats, its eloquent tenant exhorting friends to doff their shoes beside the door, then launching into monologues about Buddhist sages.

A thinly disguised Snyder, that fictional student is Japhy Ryder, a rangy anarchistic poet who, Kerouac tells us, had "discovered the greatest Dharma Bums of them all, the Zen Lunatics of China and Japan." Ryder is irresistible to pretty girls who arrive at his flat for spontaneous and semipublic—thus, Zen—sex.

Ryder quickly establishes his opposition to gray-flannel-suit Western society:

"When I was a little kid in Oregon," he avows, "I didn't feel that I was an American at all, with all that suburban ideal and sex repression." Rhapsodizing over sutras and bodhisattvas, he ridicules "America where nobody has any fun or believes in anything, especially freedom."

Despite their putative pacifism, those were fightin' words. A world war had just been fought and won, at huge cost, for what its victors said was freedom. Yet here was this new sex god telling Americans that America *wasn't* free.

Ryder was redefining freedom. To him, freedom didn't mean democracy or those liberties defined in the Bill of Rights. The freedom he craved was personal, sensual: the leisure to do whatever one likes, whenever one likes, whatever the consequences and no matter what others think. This was Zen with a hedonistic, narcissistic California twist. Urge? Satisfy it!

Rrrrrrrrrright *now*.

The Dharma Bums was published before I was born. But its influence on American popular culture was so strong that in the midst of the punk era, after the book had been around for decades, I went to UC Berkeley precisely because Japhy Ryder had. Pretentiously name-dropping haiku poets and spouting trivia about Japan, which I had never visited, I was a Dharma Bumette. A Dharma Bumpkin. The book's lure was so potent that, even then, loving it didn't really feel retro. I remember writing urgently in my journal the summer before junior year: "*I WANT A ZEN APARTMENT.*" I drew a sketch: sparse, low-slung furniture, books in a crate, one bowl and cup, pine sprig in a Japanese vase. But just by writing "I want," I was being un-Zen. Real Buddhism, of course, compels one to shed worldly desires. But here's what happens when exotic doctrines are cherry-picked and plopped into Western suburbia: Zen was a style to me, a look, like my friend Dee's pink spiked hair. Not that I would ever have said so then. But some years later I discarded it like an outdated raincoat, selling my Kerouac and Watts books at the secondhand shop.

Looking back at it now, I see the seeds of everything. The slogans, buzzwords, images, protocols, themes that would suffuse the '60s, then suffuse everything since. It's all there in those Beat books. Free love. Anarchism. Antiauthoritarianism. Anti-Americanism. Multiculturalism. Exotic spiritualities. Casual sex and alternative sexualities—orgies, arcane positions, partner sharing. Shabby chic. Talkfests fomenting revolution. Drugs.

What does this have to do with stuckness in the present?

Western faiths demand self-sacrifice: the self as sublimated, sinful wretch. Western faiths make you wait. By contrast, Zen vaunts hyper self-awareness. "Settle the self," goes the classic Zen injunction, "on the self." Japhy Ryder and his cohorts drink and smoke and loll and leap naked on mountainsides and have sex with near strangers while friends watch. They praise themselves, pontificate. Some might call this self-indulgence, gluttony, instant gratification. The Beats preferred to call it Zen.

Every avalanche starts with a single stone. Every social shift starts with a single word, a book, a charismatic character. What began in a few seedy San Francisco taverns and cheap flats went bigtime as Kerouac became a sensation—not for *The Dharma Bums*, but for *On the Road*, in 1957. He had discovered Buddhism by then; its influence infused popular culture as he became the toast of talk shows and magazines, thronged by groupies and would-be clones. Zen, watered down into a hip permission slip for instant gratification, soared suddenly from obscure foreign sect to cocktail-party fare. It's hard to imagine now, but scattering haiku books on your coffee table was a sure way to be suave in 1960.

In actual practice, Zen doesn't vaunt being *stuck* in the present. Its whole point is to never be stuck anywhere, on anything: to be fluid, lithe, and aware. Yanked out of context, hurled around the world and given a corporate and capitalist glaze, however, Zen becomes—not for those who take it up in earnest, but for the clamoring multitudes who continue to spread the fad—a compressed amalgam of those fragments we find fun. Omit the predawn meditation and the chores that real Zen monks endure. But oh:

The self.

The sensuality.

The sex.

The hungry, horny, incredibly impatient *self*.

Plopped into a land of plenty, Zen arguably informed every movement that came next in the West, leading in circuitous ways to good things but also to obesity, addiction, debt, STD epidemics—the generalized, diffused fallout of stuckness in the present.

Funny what a few haiku can do.

At a 1966 press conference, psychologist Timothy Leary urged his listeners to "Turn on, tune in, drop out." It had a Beat echo—and almost instantly became a generation's motto. Many interpreted the last of its three exhortations as "drop out of school," and they did—as Leary himself had done three years earlier, more or less, after being fired from Harvard for failing to teach his classes. Many more interpreted the phrase to mean "drop out of the rat race." It was the Japhy Ryder rhetoric reprised: Dharma Bummery with a Beatles soundtrack and love beads. It was permission from a counterculture icon—Leary was authoritarian and smart, with a Berkeley Ph.D.—to stop acting Calvinist. Stop studying. Stop working. Stop the long-term plans and deferred pleasure that go with those. For a public primed on Zen Incorporated, this was appealing indeed. Within a year, the Grass Roots paraphrased Leary's injunction in a Top 40 hit that went "Sha la la la la la, live for today." "Turn off your mind," the Beatles sang, "and float downstream." Nearly everything cool was a quick fix, instant karma: Psychedelics. Sit-ins. Squats. Hitchhiking. Splatter art. In those days, you could show up at the local commune and get fed, get sex, get high for free, no questions asked.

Which begged the questions: Want something? Why wait?

The result, according to philosopher John Searle, who taught at Berkeley in the 1960s, was a "set of totally dreadful vulgarizations of culture." In the '60s, Searle remembers, "people had a whole lot of really quite stupid theories about life. They thought you get immediate gratification through drugs, and indeed if you can't get immediate gratification through drugs, then you get it through some other equally instantaneous form of gratification. The idea that satisfactions in life normally take a lot of work, [that] you have to do years of preparation to do anything worthwhile—in the sixties," Searle recalls sadly, "it was very hard to convince people of that."

Clearly, even at the height of that era, *most* people remained in the rat race. They were building the roads and performing the dentistry and stocking the stores. The number of Westerners who took Leary literally was relatively small. That's why things continued to function and productivity continued apace. Yet the rhetoric, the look and style that presaged widespread stuckness in the present infused every social stratum. You didn't have to be a hippie to enjoy that nude scene in *Hair*.

The quick fix has evolved.

"I am a compulsive spender," Arizona newspaper publisher Greg Bruns tells me. "I buy lots and lots of things I don't need, will never wear, won't eat, will not give as gifts"—though he might initially have bought them for that purpose—and "won't have time to read. Sometimes there is an 'inner voice' that tells me I am making an unwise purchase," says Bruns. "I usually quell the inner voice with something sparkly." Newness itself exudes a "sparkle," he says, that excites him.

Bruns's home office is crowded with gadgets whose attractions have paled since he bought them—in some cases, since he ordered them—even before they arrived or appeared on his credit-card bills. These include $500 PDA/cell phones: "There are two that are currently in the pile of cast-off electronics that no longer excite me. I now have the Q phone, which is *okay*, but Samsung is coming out with a new PDA/phone"—new in March 2007, when we discussed this—"and I can't *wait* to see what features *that* thing will have," he says. "Once that comes out, if it is sparkly enough, I will buy it—price is not usually a factor—and cast the Q into the pile, as it will no longer excite me."

He owns five digital cameras. It used to be six.

"One of them I was just bored with, so I threw it in the water at Lake Havasu when I was up there. One of the cameras was the top-of-the-line Nikon—five megapixels . . . *wow*—when I bought it. It cost me over two thousand dollars. Three years later, I bought the top-of-the-line Nikon—ten megapixels . . . *wow*—spending an additional three thousand on the camera and accessories." At that point, he says, the "old" Nikon, perfectly functional and an excellent camera, was shunned like a leper.

"Multiple computers, computer equipment, and unused software are stacked in the closet," Bruns says. "I go through things quickly. I buy into marketing hype and purchase stuff I just don't need. I never know for sure whether I will keep or use whatever object I'm buying. I am just filling some deep well of desire for the latest cool things. I believe this deep well will not be filled completely in my lifetime. When something gets dumped in the well, whether it's a pint of ice cream or a kick-ass Nikon, I feel a sense of satisfaction and fulfillment, as if I have *finally* quenched my thirst."

Until the next time.

Bruns tells me that he accepts, even relishes, this aspect of himself. He's stuck, but knows the currents of his stuckness, its twists and turns, so well that he feels he has it more or less under control.

My friend Megan used to impulse shop, just as Bruns does. But unlike Bruns, Megan felt totally out of control when the shopping urge seized her. As if sucked by invisible forces into stores, she went on jags: Right *now*, she *had* to have three copies in assorted colors of something she had seen in a movie or read about in a book. Tiger-striped cushions. Crème-de-menthe-laced cream puffs. The boots from *Kill Bill*.

When she first brought them home, she displayed her new purchases atop an altar she had made from a glass end table draped with a sequinned scarf. She loved new things as few can love them. She knew what looked good on her light cocoa skin, her slim-hipped body, her long straight hair that was brown but which Kristin at the salon, for $100 a pop, dyed Thai Sapphire and Golden Shine and Frosted Wine.

Kneeling before the altar, Megan would show me her purchases with a halting flourish and shaky smile, already knowing what would happen, already feeling the first waves of postjag ennui, postjag regret. Megan owed $7,000 on her credit cards. She cried about this, called me sometimes in the middle of the night begging me to make her stop shopping. I scolded, pleaded, counseled, harped, sounding sometimes like a drill sergeant, sometimes like a grandma—*Who needs cream puffs? Dye your own hair at home like the rest of us!*—and sometimes, only sometimes, like her friend. I could never relate to her need-it-now urgency, had no patience for her impatience.

She would stroke the beaded lampshade or the pasta maker or the leather skirt, its other-colored duplicates lined up like a rebuke. Tears gleamed in her lavender-contact-lensed eyes under those lowered lids dusted with imported French kohl. Biting her lip, Megan would say: "I waaaaanted it."

She had been bankrupt once. She was veering toward twice. She worked at home, freelance, low pay, no benefits. Her folks sent checks to tide her over, but they made the zeroes into frowny faces.

"You just need," I said, "to learn to wait for things."

She wound a lock of hair around her thumb. "I waaaaaanted it."

Her voice high-pitched, trembling, like an electric bird.

I always tell myself I'm stuck on lots of things, but not the present. Whew. Forever slipping back (into regret) and forward (into fear), I seldom am here now. I am the one to whom you say: You seem a million miles away. I am a deferrer. Conserver. Reserver. Refrainer. A saver in piggy banks. At once a consummate planner and a space-cadet flake. An escape artist. One who asks for doggy bags. Putting things off—saving the best for last, then later, later, later—feels like victory to me. I am not sure that my needs will or should ever be met, much less instantly. I always have to remind myself that I even exist. Irked at Megan when she did not heed my advice, I would think: *At least that's one problem I don't have.*

I'm not stuck in the present. Nope. Not me.

Oh, really?

Who spends hours each day surfing the Net seeking "information"? Who thinks *I vaguely remember a theme park called Marineland* and, seconds later, is reading online about its sharks, its walrus, and Bubbles, its whale? Who should be working right now but would rather be in Hong Kong or strolling a beach on Martinique and, for the next hour at YouTube, will virtually be?

That would be me.

So there is more than one way to get stuck in the present. Even those of us who defer pleasure, those of us who pride ourselves on not being instant-gratification types, are seduced into it regardless by the Internet. This is the genie in the bottle anyone can summon and command. It answers questions and delivers entertainment, information, interpersonal communication, friendship, sex, plane tickets, hotel reservations, merchandise, and comfort at a touch with consummate speed and omnipotent servility. Not by mistake was that early search engine called Ask Jeeves, taking its name from fiction's most perfect valet. The Net exists to serve, *right now*—to obey but not judge its masters' whims. Accustomed to this, suckled on it, we become sultans and silly fops and spoiled kids, demanding service, pleasure, ease, and lightning speed. And that is all of us.

Desires met instantly—without work, without waiting, without judgment and without apparent cost—is no longer merely a fantasy or moral quandary. The issue of whether sensual urges should be battled or indulged is no longer merely the stuff of hagiographies, in which sexy demons bearing platters of victuals torment celibate fasting saints.

We have lost the meaning of time.

Grin and bear it, our ancestors said.

Whistle while you work, they said.

Another day, another dollar, came their singsong chant.

Back to the salt mines.

And that's how, hour upon hour and century upon century, civilization happened. Countless workdays were whistled through, countless pains grinned through and borne. Countless pleasures were deferred. Rewards were delayed, sometimes for a lifetime, as innumerable strivers, soldiers, slaves, and scholars said, age after age:

Someday.

Pleasure deferrers resemble the ant in Aesop's fable who works hard all summer and sets aside food to last through the winter while the indolent, live-for-today grasshopper sings and plays the summer away, then starves. Throughout history, pleasure deferrers were the ones who, like Aesop's ant, survived through one winter and then the next and lived long enough and well enough to reproduce and raise their young, who took after them physically and mentally and learned these same values. Reinforced thusly by natural selection, the ability to defer pleasure evolved into a prominent human skill. Our ancestors got so good at *not* living in the moment that—some might say—they almost forgot there was any other way to live. In their world, living in the moment (and being stuck in the present) was alien, foreign, dangerous, the province of infants and "Oriental" sages and the insane.

Along with its other merits, planning for the future is a healthy methodology for surviving trauma and for moving beyond bad memories, according to psychologist Boris Cyrulnik, whose parents died in the Holocaust and who is a world expert on human resilience. When—as was traditional for much of history—adults sacrifice personal comfort in order to supply their children with better future opportunities, this deferment amounts to "a consecration," Cyrulnik writes, "since each individual's renunciation of a small, immediate pleasure brings a great deal of happiness to the family as a whole when their dreams are realized."

By these lights, resisting stuckness in the present is an act of altruism, a conscious contribution to the continuity not just of one's own clan but of human society. It demonstrates a willingness to work for the greater good. In this sense, what Japhy Ryder types would decry as repressive is actually *progressive*. With its live-for-today irresponsibility, stuckness in the present is *more primitive* than behaving like Aesop's ant: less civilized.

The grasshopper would call the ant repressive.

And the ant would call the grasshopper regressive.

When the children of deferrers succeed, Cyrulnik declares, they "glorify their parents' courage." He imagines such children telling such parents: "Your suffering was worth it, since, thanks to you, I'm going to have a wonderful life." Consequently, it's a strong motivation not to be stuck in the present but to keep past and future forever in mind.

The flush, plush post–World War II years ushered in a relaxation revolution. A sensuality insurgency. A meditation nation. This bold shift toward living in the present pleased—and profited— millions of scenesters and squares alike. For the Beats and their disciples, that Zen mien meant wine-fueled orgies. But for ex-G.I. Dad and panty-girdled Mom, for crewcutted Junior and ponytailed Sis behind their white picket fence, new labor-saving inventions that poured into the postwar market made them feel like lucky clever consumers freed from boredom and backbreaking effort by sprinkler systems, cake mixes, TVs, and speedy new cars. No longer required to devote themselves to the war effort, U.S. industries concentrated on new inventions aimed at making life easier and more fun. The microwave oven was invented in 1946; Polaroid cameras, the transistor, and Tupperware in 1947. Jukeboxes appeared in 1948, cake mixes in 1949. The first TV remote control, introduced in 1950, was Zenith's "Lazy Bones." That year, too, saw the debut of the world's first charge card, the Diners Club card. Velcro was patented in 1951, Saran Wrap and TV dinners in 1953, oral contraceptives in 1954. The advertising campaigns for most of these products cast inertia as a thrilling novelty—showing people reclining, feet up, arms folded behind their heads. *Relax*, the commercial jingles urged.

It was a halcyon moment for capitalists—and for their virtual opposites, the counterculture. Both stood to gain. So both did.

And suddenly everyone was living in the moment. Suddenly one did not need to wait so long for so many things anymore. We take ease and immediacy for granted now, but the relaxation revolution happened then in one big burst largely because, for the first time in human history, *it could*. For the first time, so much had already been accomplished by so many hardworking Homo sapiens over so many centuries (and so much was still being accomplished by a certain sector) that large swaths of the populace could simply . . . stop.

And smell the roses.

And survive, even thrive, without worrying too much about future or past. For the first time in human history, those initial postwar decades allowed millions to rest, literally, on their predecessors' laurels. In the wake of a bloody war, it felt well-deserved.

Living in the moment isn't fun by definition. Ideally, one would choose one's moments. Vowing to savor each one, actual Zen-style, come what may, sounds bold but might prove you a hypocrite during the next typhus epidemic, drought, or mugging. Because epidemics, droughts, and highway robbery are less common than in previous eras, for most of us living in the moment is a luxury. Savoring each moment becomes a safe bet when you can do so with fair certainty that no army will raid your land, co-opt your house, and maul and kill your kin. No virus will wipe out your whole neighborhood overnight. At that magical moment in the lee of World War II, such horrors appeared almost obsolete.

So the West began its first coffee break.

Which stretched and stre-e-e-e-etched.

Right up to now. We are still basking.

This is the Someday of which our ancestors dreamed.

And the moment, the present, is where we are now pressured to stay.

It's a spiritual, social, cultural, and technological turnaround that would have astounded our ancestors—who toiled away, nurturing their nest eggs, as they intoned "All good things come to those who wait." By contrast, we are surrounded with persuasive reasons *not* to wait, inducements:

Go for it.

Just do it.

Take it easy.

Get this party started.

If the most prestigious marvel is the fastest marvel, speed will matter most. If the marvel's purpose is to extinguish waiting, time shrinks. Patience atrophies and becomes obsolete. If at a click marvels deliver entertainment, merchandise, and sex and all the rest, then we come to mock and despise whatever takes more than an instant and a click. As speed proliferates, we see marvels not as marvels but staples. Speed becomes a basic human right. In 2002, Verizon Wireless debuted a service called Get It Now. This allowed subscribers to download music, videos, and other entertainment onto their cell phones: "Watch sports clips, comedy, news and weather from major networks and indie favorites—all on your phone, on demand," the promo urged. "Express yourself with colorful and stylish images. . . . Fight boredom with fun games."

But by the time you read this, such technology will already be ancient history. And I will look the fool for citing it, like an old rube in a cartoon trying to feed hay to a car. Cutting edges are disposable blades now, replaced incessantly. We watch, twitching and restless. That our truncated attention spans have been pathologized— as Attention Deficit Disorder and Attention Deficit Hyperactivity Disorder—transforms stuckness in the present into a disease. The influential *Diagnostic and Statistical Manual of Mental Disorders*, published by the American Psychiatric Association, suggests an ADD or ADHD diagnosis for someone who "has trouble keeping attention on tasks or play activities"; who "does not follow instructions and fails to finish schoolwork, chores, or duties in the workplace"; who "avoids, dislikes, or doesn't want to do things that take a lot of mental effort for a long period of time"; who "often loses things needed for tasks and activities (e.g., toys, school assignments, pencils, books, or tools)"; who "is often easily distracted"; who is "often forgetful in daily activities"; who "blurts out answers before questions have been finished"; who "has trouble waiting [his or her] turn"; and who "often interrupts or intrudes on others (e.g., butts into conversations or games)."

Those symptoms reflect stuckness in the present and fit many of us, diagnosed or not: The drug companies that produce Ritalin, Adderall, Strattera, and other drugs commonly prescribed for ADHD might very well prefer that more of us were. But mainstream American culture itself, its values and commodities and methodologies, seems calculated to induce those symptoms on a massive scale, to make us all stuck in the present, chanting: Get it now!

Fight boredom!

The get-it-now headspace, so primitive and reductive, makes thinking back and/or ahead seem needless. When a phone is in your pocket, you need neither plan ahead nor keep appointments: you can cancel abruptly, at the last minute, or change plans, because whomever you were going to meet has a phone, too. Phones in our pockets, we need never be prepared. We can forever call for help: I'm lost, I'm tired, I'm hungry, I forgot my coat, bring it to me. Phones in pockets save lives. But they also blur the definition of an emergency. They free us from responsibility, transforming us at once into infants and dictators.

When a culture lives entirely in the present, the future becomes abstract at best, an enemy at worst, the past a strange sentimentality.

We are induced to spoil our children, spoil ourselves. We call it self-esteem and running with the wolves. We make greed cute. The other day, I saw an attractive young mother with a little girl about six years old. The child wore a pink T-shirt that said in glittery letters:

1. I want it.
2. You buy it for me.
   Any questions?

Self-help gurus build their careers on advising grown-ups to indulge themselves. With all solemnity, they tell us to take bubble baths, send ourselves Valentines and bouquets, demand what we want. Ingesting their liturgies, we use plastic cards to buy stuff with money that we do not actually have and are appalled when bills arrive in present moments that were futures past.

Bred on speed, we lose touch with time. We think we have conquered time, but time always has the last laugh. Our supposed win has weakened us. Lazy, we loll. Even children remain remarkably inert. "Everybody is glued to the computer, on Facebook or MySpace, and they're texting all the time," a fifteen-year-old boy declared in a 2007 *San Francisco Chronicle* article about how kids today have little interest in physical activities or the outdoors. Another fifteen-year-old said he would rather go to a shopping mall than to Yosemite. "These kids are becoming so acculturated to very fancy devices that do fifty things at one time that they can't grasp" any reason to put these devices down, fretted a high school principal. "To go on a hike, to participate in nature, to just look at the beauty is foreign to them." According to a Kaiser Family Foundation report, kids age eight to eighteen spend an average of six and a half hours a day engaging with some form of electronic media. More than half of American teenagers owned cell phones in 2005. Some owned more than one. This statistic crossed class lines. At one California high school, although 75 percent of the student body owned cell phones, 75 percent of that student body also came from such low-income households as to qualify for free or discounted lunches.

The very nature of how we work and play has changed irrevocably in the last decade, becoming ever more present-focused. Listening to the radio—an archaic pastime these days—means wishing and hoping and waiting, with no guarantee, for your favorite songs to play. Sometimes they don't, forcing you to endure songs you dislike (which teaches tolerance) and forcing you to hear songs you have never heard before (expanding your horizons to potential new favorite songs). Compare that to the iPod. Songs down-loaded online—and you know which songs, in which order—begin at your command. Other technologies have similar effects. Voice-mail, e-mail, and caller ID liberate us from real-time conversations. We need not conform to schedules imposed by others. We need no longer care when shops and libraries open and close. The Web is "open" twenty-four hours a day. We teleconference, telecommute. How much time did your grandparents spend on the ferry, street-car, subway, highway?

We take for granted this collapse of time. As victors disrespect losers and masters disrespect slaves, we have lost respect for time: its length, its heft, the rewards of merely enduring it. Again, our outlook is begotten by luxury. We trust that we will never be time's captives, that we will never farm fields, sail seas, walk miles for trivialities such as advice or milk or mail. We know that we need never spend years learning trades from martinets, wait years for praise or frills or sex.

The more sophisticated our devices become, the more brilliant they are and the less they make us do, the stronger the perverse re-verse effect they wield. The more grown-up our devices become, the more childish we get. Infantile. Coddled. Look. Point. Click. The ringtone is your favorite song. We call our accessories *toys*, even the ones for sex.

And the more infantile we are, the more we are stuck in the present. Like babies, we bask in free time. Our machines take care of us, feed us, clothe us, move us, and amuse us. Fast, living on baby time: Want. Get.

When actual babies see what they want, they seize it, bite it, hug it, suck on it. If they cannot reach it right this minute, they wail—because the only time that babies understand is *now*.

This is one main reason we love babies: because they live wholly in the moment, as honest as soiled diapers or snores.

We admire that.

In principle.

Maria von Trapp, stepmother to the singing *Sound of Music* family, marveled in her memoir that infants "do not worry because they have no past and no future. They live only in the present moment. If they play, they play! And they don't notice anything that is going on around them."

Writing for *Hinduism Today*, an Indian guru advises from her forest ashram: "You have to be like a baby infant who has no thoughts at all."

Zen Buddhists strive to sustain what they call *shoshin*, or "beginner's mind": the wide-eyed, optimistic, every-minute-an-adventure wonder of early childhood.

"There is nothing other than this present moment," writes Zen teacher Charlotte Joko Beck. "There is no past, there is no future; there is nothing but this."

That these ideas influence the way Westerners think today is evinced by the mainstreaming of mindfulness brokers such as Thich Nhat Hanh, a Vietnamese-born Buddhist monk whom Martin Luther King Jr. nominated for the Nobel Peace Prize in 1967. A lecture-circuit staple, Hanh has captivated millions of readers with nearly two dozen books and his trademark mantra, *Present moment, wonderful moment*, which we are urged to recite as a prompt throughout our days.

It's valid advice now and then—and certainly for those Action Jacksons who really do forget to stop and smell the roses. Then again, the whole human race would starve itself into extinction within a matter of months if *everyone* followed those precepts and lived solely for the present.

Buddhist monks and babies live in the present. But if all of us were Buddhist monks or babies, who would feed us? Who would buckle down and build the roads and haul the trash and perform neurosurgery?

Babies and Buddhist monks have special dispensations. Both are taken care of. Babies are protected by adults who realize that this arrangement is temporary, that this sweet helplessness will be outgrown. In fact, maturity begins when children learn there *is* a present and a past, that their actions have repercussions. Too much candy *now* makes my tummy ache *later.* Buddhist monks are shielded by the institutions managing their temples and by the devout, who donate food. In Japan and Thailand, where monks beg door-to-door or walking along the road, such donations connote good citizenship. In some societies, farmers consciously grow crops whose yield will be partly allotted to the monks, and the governments protect monks from danger and interference. Everyone in this system *besides* the monks must plan for long-term goals, thereby actually living in the *future*, not the present.

Our troubles start when we merge Eastern ideas such as mindfulness with huge Western twenty-first-century appetites, devouring free time won for us by other people's work and brilliance.

During the voyage described in *The Odyssey*, Odysseus and his crew encounter the Lotophagi, or Lotus-eaters, a strange people whose main foodstuff is a narcotic plant that, when ingested, induces a euphoric amnesia. Sampled by some of the sailors, "the lotus . . . was so delicious that those who ate of it left off caring about home, and did not even want to go back and say what had happened to them," Homer tells us, "but were for staying and munching lotus with the Lotus-eaters without thinking further of their return." Odysseus rouses the besotted sailors: "Though they wept bitterly I forced them back to the ships, and made them fast under the benches. Then I told the rest to go on board at once, lest any of them should taste of the lotus and leave off wanting to get home, so they took their places and smote the grey sea with their oars."

Odysseus knew that his crew had work to do and loved ones waiting at home for them. Homer was reminding us that, as tempting as amnesia is, someone or something is probably depending on us. We have to go home.

Danger is always lurking, even if we cannot see it. Trash gathers. Bank accounts dwindle. Enemies surveil. As the Boy Scouts say: be prepared. As veterans say: never forget. Mindfulness en masse remains a luxury.

And those who cannot afford to be stuck in the present subsidize those who are.

The good news about time is that it flows. The bad news about time is that it flows.

All that hard work, completed long before we were born, won us free time. Acres and acres of free time. But can you say without shame how you spend your saved time?

One way would be to reinvest those hours in creativity and productivity to make things *even better* for society.

Yet most of us do not. We simply soak it up. The inventions we treasure, like the tasty lotus, make us lazy. We save time to waste it.

Instant gratification was already making an appearance by the time Ralph Waldo Emerson wrote, in 1870, "I hate this shallow Americanism which hopes to get rich by credit, to get knowledge by raps on midnight tables"—he was referring to the fad for seances—"to learn the economy of the mind by phrenology"—he was referring to the fad for linking personality traits with the contours of the head—"or skill without study, or mastery without apprenticeship." Shortcuts were becoming national trends and infusing the national character. "Excellence is lost sight of," Emerson wrote, "in the hunger for sudden performance and praise." Today, this hunger is more alive than ever. The public still embraces get-rich-quick schemes such as *The Secret*, a mega-best-selling book and film whose premise is that a cosmic "Law of Attraction" will deliver to us the objects of our desire if we wish for them hard enough.

The United States might currently be the world's instant-gratification capital, but it was neither invented here nor is it ours alone. A person named Aesop might never have actually existed— Herodotus claimed that Aesop was a freed slave who died in the sixth century BCE at Delphi, though scholars still debate this—but the tale of the grasshopper and the ant is among the most famous of the fables attributed to him. The moral rivalry between "grasshoppers" and "ants" was already clearly underway 2,600 years ago.

That's because instant gratification is the automatic urge of every living thing. Resisting that urge is perhaps life's greatest challenge. What creature would expend effort if food and shelter were attainable without it? Being stuck in the present boils down to choosing leisure over work. Not *preferring* leisure, which is only natural and goes without saying, but *choosing* leisure to the extent that you are systematically unwilling to wait for it.

And by work we don't have to mean jobs or labor. Work means any effort aimed at achieving a distant goal. Study. Rehearsal. Practice. Research. Exercise. Eating right. Taking health precautions. Starting and building relationships.

If we mature personally by recognizing the future and past, and thus by learning to defer pleasure for later, better rewards—praise rather than scoldings, As rather than Fs—then it's the same for cultures. Those who make a practice of deferring pleasure are the most productive. This is one observation, a rare one, on which theologians and scientists agree. Fight if you will over the meaning of "maturity," but cultures oriented toward work rather than leisure are the superpowers.

In the Old Testament, Adam and Eve are banished from the Garden of Eden—where pleasures were plentiful and immediate. Learning to defer pleasure was their punishment. An angry God declares: "Because you have . . . eaten from the tree of which I commanded you, saying, 'You shall not eat of it,' cursed is the ground for your sake; in toil you shall eat of it all the days of your life" (Genesis 3:17, NKJV). The early Hebrews came to revere work as a form of sacred expiation. "Great is labor," the Talmud asserts, "for it honors the workman." The Talmud is peppered with commentary on the importance of work and workers, declaring that even the lowliest paid labor is better than being supported by others and/or accepting charity.

"Skin a carcass in the street and receive wages," reads one passage, "and do not say, 'I am an important person and this type of work is beneath my dignity.'" Idleness, it was believed, caused madness.

Stuckness in the present, in that view, is sacrilege.

The traditional Jewish emphasis on scholarship and mitzvoth, or good deeds, further vaunted the virtues of deferred gratification. On a freezing day, you might not *feel* like spending four hours in shul or at a hospice visiting the sick. And Torah study takes *so much time*. Sigmund Freud called Judaism "a religion of instinctual renunciation."

Early Christians, too, scorned laziness. Proverbs 13:4 warns: "The soul of the sluggard craves and gets nothing. But the soul of the diligent is richly supplied." Proverbs 14:23 sharpens the point: "In all toil there is profit, but mere talk"—such as the Beats' beloved gabfests—"leads only to want." Paul warns: "If anyone will not work, let him not eat" (2 Thessalonians 3:10).

When Martin Luther and John Calvin set out to reform Christianity in the sixteenth century, one of their main objectives was to increase the public's reverence for work. In their view, one should work not just to survive and to stay away from sin, but because work was a holy duty owed to God, a way to display oneself as a candidate for heaven. Slackers, on the other hand, were damned.

Spending eternity in heaven was the whole point, of course—the *ultimate* ultimate goal. So this Protestant view was the definitive rejection of stuckness in the present.

By working hard, one could emulate God Himself—who, Calvin wrote, "is not the vain, indolent, slumbering omnipotence which sophists feign, but vigilant, efficacious, energetic and ever active." Good Christians, Calvin felt, should strive to earn maximum profits and not spend them on pleasure but invest them in future business ventures. Luther favored the German word *beruf*, denoting dedication to a "secular vocation."

By the dawn of the twentieth century, these attitudes had gelled into what sociologist Max Weber dubbed the "Protestant work ethic." This de rigueur deferral of gratification he described as "a systematic method of rational conduct with the purpose of overcoming the *status naturae*, to free man from the power of irrational impulses." The Protestant work ethic "attempted to subject man to the supremacy of a purposeful will to bring his actions under constant self-control with a careful consideration of their ethical consequences." And its "most urgent task," Weber wrote, was "the destruction of spontaneous, impulsive enjoyment."

Weber pointed out that Catholic nations were less productive, less economically successful, than Protestant ones. Surely, he speculated, this was because Catholics by nature were less diligent workers, because they were not ideologically driven to defer gratification. This, he theorized, was at least partly because their opulent cathedrals gave them so strong a taste for the lavish and sensual, which drove them to waste money and luxuriate. Then they could wash away their sloth and self-indulgence (as he saw it) with convenient trips to the confessional.

As a result of the Protestant work ethic, the northern European nations that adopted Protestantism starting in the sixteenth century began to grow more prosperous than the former superpowers, the Catholic countries of southern Europe: Italy, Spain, and Portugal. Over the next several centuries, the locus of power shifted northward, a shift that many historians have attributed to the hyperproductivity of the newly Protestant nations. So history seems to indicate that while deferring gratification is no fun for the individual doing the deferment, if a whole nation defers it collectively, then eventually the nation's whole populace benefits.

Groups that traditionally defer gratification have inspired a great deal of loathing and resentment over the centuries, becoming stereotypes, the butts of predictable jokes. These are familiar: the dour puritan, the Japanese salaryman, the Jewish or Asian student skipping the party, cracking the books. The success of social and cultural groups that defer gratification, statistically, makes stuckness in the present seem the province of weaklings, losers, and fools.

Not everyone agrees with those scientists and theologians who posit that pleasure-deferring cultures are the most mature cultures. Another school of thought holds that the opposite is true.

The idea of the "noble savage" was spawned and promoted by eighteenth-century European Romanticists who lamented that human beings living in modern societies were cut off from nature—and their own true natures—because modern societal protocols, such as deferred gratification, were artificial constructs. Drawing upon the narratives of Captain James Cook and other explorers whose journals idealizing indigenous peoples in faraway climes were Enlightenment-era best sellers, Romanticists such as Jean-Jacques Rousseau wrote feelingly of "noble savages"—portraying them as peaceful, sensual, honest, egalitarian, and free. By contrast, the Romanticists portrayed their own peers as perfidious, shallow, belligerent, and false. Predating that movement by a century but setting the tone for its gushing exuberance, British philosopher Anthony Ashley-Cooper, the first Earl of Shaftesbury, praised "that simplicity of manners and innocence of behaviour which has been often known among mere savages; ere they were corrupted by our commerce."

The Romanticists based their claims largely on their own wishful thinking and on explorers' fanciful, much-embroidered accounts

of their faraway adventures. Violence, privation, and repressive social systems were common in indigenous societies long before they
had any contact with the West. The real-life hunter-gatherer is often cold in the present, or hungry or hot or wet or sick, or impaled
on the weapon of a rival. Evidence abounds of wars, torture, infan-
ticide, class disparities, oppression, starvation, and criminality in
preindustrial cultures. Yet such facts were ignored as anthropologists and artists became enraptured with the ideal of the noble savage. How tempting, especially after the debacle of World War I,
when the field of anthropology was burgeoning, to believe that
Western society was a mistake. And all its precepts, too—about sex,
work, planning, war . . . and time.

"From the Disneyfication of *Pocahontas* to Kevin Costner's eco-
pacifist Native Americans in *Dances with Wolves*," writes the science historian Michael Shermer in *Skeptic* magazine, "and from
postmodern accusations of corruptive modernity to modern anthropological theories that indigenous people's wars are just ritualized games, the noble savage remains one of the last epic creation
myths of our time."

In his book *Constant Battles*, Harvard archaeologist Steven Le-
Blanc confesses that while doing fieldwork among Anasazi ruins in
the American Southwest, he and his colleagues discovered "clear
evidence for warfare." Some buildings had almost certainly been
fortresses. Others included defensive architectural features such as
lookout posts. Yet because these findings contradicted their "noble
savage" ideals, the scholars patently ignored them.

"It took more than twenty-five years, and a great deal of additional fieldwork and library research," LeBlanc admits a generation later, "for me finally to change my initial naive view of the past
and of humans in general." As for the evidence, "we were simply

not conditioned to see it. The idea that all was peaceful . . . in the ancient past was, and is, how most archaeologists and anthropologists see the world," LeBlanc laments. He adds, "Academics are not the only ones with these views . . . almost everybody seems to be preoccupied with the idea that all was peaceful in the hundreds of millennia of the human past. . . . Archaeologists and ethnologists have an audience. The audience wants to hear about peace and not about warfare."

And they also want to hear—because this is part of the same package—that those happy pacifists lived their sexy lives wholly in the moment, proving stuckness in the present as a good thing.

The idea of the noble savage will not die, because the self-loathing of Western society has grown apace. And if the genocidal Western warmongers amassed their empires by deferring gratification, by living in the future and the past, well—let's pledge allegiance to whoever does not.

Yet if industrialism turns us into spiritless drones marching in lockstep, *this very same system* is the one that also spawned an exponential array of ecstasies, many of them ironically instant. It is the deferrers, deferring away in labs and offices and factories, who create our means of living longer into the future *and* better archiving the past *and* getting stuck in the I-want-it-right-now present. Mock the Big Mac if you will, but behold the phone, video recorder, pacemaker, medicine, car. As products of a nation founded by Puritans, Americans are hyperconscious of workers and work. Inevitably, driven in equal parts by greed and sympathy, a certain portion of our work would be devoted to creating products and conditions freeing us from work.

Little did those products' inventors or consumers imagine that taking the "relax, have fun" spirit to a new level would result in a social shift so major that, soon, inertia would be not just a treat or a lark. It would be *the whole point*.

A goal. A lifestyle. A philosophy.

Après the Dawn of the Diners Club, the Beat Generation was waiting in the wings. The Beat ethos was ostensibly anticivilization: Kerouac rhapsodized about cave-dwelling Tang Dynasty poets and fellaheen, injecting this Arabic word for "peasantry" into the pop-culture lexicon. (In the '70s, my high school boyfriend would drum his English-class desk with his fingers, wristwatch glinting, and sigh urgently, "I want to be fellaheen.") Ditto the "turn on, tune in, drop out" wave that followed in its sandaled footsteps. Yet both movements were made possible by deferrers and thrived on deferrers' backs. By the late '70s, pop-cultural tides had changed: products and producers were no longer seen as the enemy. If *The Dharma Bums'* Zen-riffing Japhy Ryder was a sensualist anticonsumerist whose message spent twenty years being commodified by capitalists, the culture-wide result was sensualist consumerists.

I Want It All Now was a landmark 1978 NBC-TV documentary about life in wealthy, avant-garde Marin County, California. At one point in the film, a woman pays two masseurs $180—a lot of money in those days—to stroke her body lightly with peacock feathers. At another point, a golden-skinned Marinite tells the camera: "I want everything. *Everything*. Nothing less."

Hedonism had become an anthem.

In 1979, historian Christopher Lasch wrote of "the new narcissist," an emerging true-life archetype that filled him with horror. Vanishing before his eyes, Lasch lamented, was "the culture of competitive individualism" that had built the West; as seen in *I Want It All Now* and American society at large, "the pursuit of happiness" was being driven "to the dead end of a narcissistic pre-occupation with the self." Incurious about either future or past or the wider world, Americans had "retreated to purely personal pre-occupations."

What could be more symptomatic of a society stuck in the present than seeing getting what one wants as a new virtue, an end in itself? Stuckness in the present is a common symptom of narcissism. I want it all. Now.

"Acquisitive in the sense that his cravings have no limits," Lasch wrote, the new narcissist "does not accumulate goods and provisions against the future . . . but demands immediate gratification and lives in a state of restless, perpetually unsatisfied desire."

Decades before the advent of the personal webcam, Lasch observed that his fellow Americans behaved as if they were perpetually on camera, posing and vamping. *Look at me*. Today, many of us behave as if life were a nonstop reality show. At least in our own minds, we are always at center stage, always pontificating, expecting bouquets and applause.

How did we come to see ourselves as stars?

"The Most Important Person" was an educational cartoon series produced in 1972 by the Sutherland Learning Associates, funded by a U.S. Department of Health, Education, and Welfare, Office of Child Development grant, and screened regularly on the popular kiddie show *Captain Kangaroo*. Featuring an animated cast of birds and kids, the series explored aspects of childhood from dental care to friendship to helping others. Each episode was accompanied by the same theme song, which went:

The most important person in the whole wide world is YOU.

In principle, a nice heartwarming boost. In practice, overkill. A new generation was learning to look out for Number One.

In the 1980s, test scores were sagging at California schools. State assemblyman John Vasconcellos thought he knew why. Vasconcellos was a longtime client of psychologist Carl Rogers, the creator of what is now known as Person-Centered Therapy. Its main premise is that all people are inherently good, that our goal should be complete "self-actualization," and that what often bars us from this goal is low self-esteem. The person-centered therapist displays a totally positive attitude toward clients, never judging or even advising them, and reflects complete empathy for the client's feelings. Inspired by his own therapeutic progress, Vasconcellos decided that California's students were low achievers because they hadn't self-actualized, because they didn't love themselves enough. The way to raise their grades, he thought, was to raise their self-esteem. In 1986, he spurred state legislators to sponsor the California Task Force to Promote Self-Esteem and Personal and Social Responsibility.

Three years later, the task force issued its report confirming Vasconcellos's claims. Going even further, the report promoted high self-esteem not only as a remedy for low test scores but also as a "social vaccine" to cure delinquency.

"Most personal and social ills plaguing our state and nation" result from low self-esteem," the report read. But if teachers studied techniques for raising self-esteem and implemented these at all California schools, prisons, and welfare offices, the report promised, crime rates would plunge. Moreover, "young people who are self-esteeming . . . are less likely to become pregnant as teen-agers."

The report concluded with a firm mandate: "Make self-esteem-enhancing childcare available to all."

It also mandated that a media campaign be mounted based on its claims. The media eagerly embraced the report and its cool, Japhy Ryderesque message that kids didn't need to study harder or endure stricter discipline—as Confucius would have urged 2,500 years before—but needed only to *feel better*.

Vasconcellos was delighted. The report, he wrote, "signals a revolutionary cultural reversal" in which self-esteem enhancement would now be modern education's "major task."

Self-esteem curricula was the next big thing, not just in California but nationwide. In ubiquitous classroom "lessons" and exercises, kids were asked to complete, one after the other, aloud, sentences beginning with "The best thing about me is . . ." and "I love me because . . ." Kids who attended elementary school during the 1980s remember making "me" flags and filling scrapbooks with pictures of themselves. One can only imagine the effects of such activities on very shy children, or those raised in homes where modesty was hailed as a virtue. Exhorted to boast and strut, afraid of getting low grades for not doing so, a self-effacing child would be considered weird, a freak.

And if Kerouac's oeuvre was largely an exercise in stream-of-consciousness self-aggrandizement—he was famous for refusing to let his work be edited—then classroom bragging lessons were its progeny.

It was a project to create a certain kind of child.

"We create a 'socially constructed reality' in our classes by what we do and say and what we instruct our students to do and say," education associate John Shindler of California State University, Los Angeles, explained in a paper instructing teachers on self-esteem enhancement. "That reality has a profound influence on our students. In the short term, the fruits of creating a psychology of success in students are often difficult to see, but . . . we cannot afford not to make self-esteem development a primary focus. Talented people will not always succeed in life, but people with genuinely high self-esteems will find ways to."

In an injunction straight out of China's Cultural Revolution, Shindler urged: "Find ways to *make the students the teacher.*" This could be achieved via "leadership of daily activities, jigsaw instruction, etc." All assessments of all students, Shindler declared, must be upbeat and optimistic. Under no circumstances are students permitted to doubt themselves: "Do not accept low self-estimations." And because honest competition results in hierarchies with both winners and losers, teachers should "*never force students to compete,*" Shindler warned—using italics—"for 'real' rewards (i.e., your love, grades, status, privileges, or any tangible rewards)."

So, uh—don't force them to compete for grades?

It was not only a new kind of child but even a new kind of self-esteem. It was rewarded automatically, whether or not one had done anything to earn it. Traditionally, one derived satisfaction and pride, the building blocks of self-esteem, from one's actual achievements: hard work or victory or good deeds or demonstrable success. It's like promising yourself a cup of hot cocoa after—but *only* after—you walk Spot or shovel snow. Pride is a potent motivator. For our ancestors, it shimmered like a golden prize at the end of difficult tasks: pleasure earned, a delicious future toward which one worked through the present. Throughout most of history, this was the reason almost everything got done.

Our ancestors believed that they didn't deserve to feel really good about themselves until they'd built that aqueduct, tilled that field, defended that fortress, put away that nest egg, passed that test.

With the new kind of self-esteem, why bother shoveling snow? Each and every moment is now a hot-cocoa moment.

Analysts have spent the past twenty years debunking the California self-esteem report. American schools still hawk self-esteem as fervently as ever, yet academic studies continue to show no viable correlations between self-esteem and scholastic performance. In fact, some of these studies suggest the opposite of what Vasconcellos imagined. They find that the students with the highest self-esteem often have the lowest grades.

"There are no long-term studies that show the efficacy of widely used methods for enhancing self-esteem," sociologist John Hewitt notes. As for self-esteem being a social vaccine, in 2003 a Brown University task force found that high self-esteem does not prevent children from smoking, drinking, or having early unprotected sex.

That's a no-brainer. Unearned high self-esteem makes you believe that you deserve constant instant pleasures. It also makes you believe that you must not be blamed for anything you do. Hence: smoking, drinking, unprotected sex. For those who are stuck in the present this way, the future (that vague point at which the cumulative results of these practices might kill you) and the past (during which these practices were proven to harm others) are meaningless.

Grade inflation—now euphemistically called "supportive grading"—increasingly lowers the bar. In 2004, 48 percent of American students reported earning an A average in high school, compared to 18 percent in 1968. Unnervingly, SAT scores *decreased* nationwide during this same period.

In her book about the children of baby boomers, *Generation Me*, psychologist Jean Twenge describes an "army of little narcissists," of "kids who can't take criticism" and who display "extraordinary thin-skinnedness."

They also demonstrate a wide gap between reality and self-image. In one 1989 study, students in eight different countries were tested for math skills. While the contingent of Korean students scored the highest, their American counterparts came in last. After taking the test but before learning the results, the students were polled on how well they believed they had done. The American students displayed the highest confidence of any group.

In experiments performed by University of Michigan psychology professor Brad J. Bushman and Case Western Reserve University psychology professor Roy Baumeister, subjects with high self-esteem displayed a quicker and more violent response to criticism than did their counterparts with lower self-esteem. This leads to an interesting point: when someone with unearned high self-esteem confronts something unpleasant, in this case criticism, he or she reacts *in the way that those who are stuck in the present usually react*—that is, impulsively, heedless of repercussions.

After systematically surveying all major self-esteem studies with a team of colleagues, Baumeister addressed the American Association for the Advancement of Sciences in 2004. High self-esteem, he told his colleagues, does not in and of itself "make young people perform better in school, obey the law, stay out of trouble, get along better with their fellows or respect the rights of others." Classroom self-esteem programs "developed a momentum" and were popular, Baumeister theorized, because they were fun and easy for teachers and students alike: "The exercises, e.g., going around the room and letting everybody say what is special about himself or herself, feel good to all concerned. Certainly it is a more enjoyable way to pass some hours in the school day than, say, doing math."

Baby boomers were dubbed "the Me Generation" years before Jean Twenge reshuffled that catchphrase as the title of her book about their offspring. "GenMe"-ers, as she calls them, include her thirtysomething self and the students she teaches at San Diego State University. As children, she and her peers were taught "that our own needs and desires were paramount."

This is the generation that auditions for *American Idol* without being able to carry a tune, insisting in all earnestness that not only *can* they win, they *must*.

Today's youth, Twenge tells us, arrive at college having been so praised and coddled all their lives and cut off from cause and effect—thus from past and future and the reality of time—that they are truly shocked at receiving any grade lower than A, and indignantly demand that their professors raise their grades. They not only fantasize about being superstars someday rather than waiters or even dentists, they really believe they *can* and *will* be superstars. Siphoning these unfounded dreams, the further product of inflated self-esteem, companies get rich selling cut-your-own-CD software and studio rental time. "Pop-star camps" are ubiquitous at community centers, dance studios, and even churches. The promo of one such camp in Massachusetts warns: "Watch out Hilary Duff, here come the Pop Stars! This camp is sure to keep that rockin' kid of yours on her toes. . . . The week will end with the girls performing in their own musical video." In 2006, Minnesota hopefuls could attend not only "Pop Star Camp" but also "Princess Camp." ("Learn to dance like a princess!")

From instant cake to instant karma to instant stardom. *The Dharma Bums'* egotism, its characters' sense of themselves as "giving visions of eternal freedom to everybody," trickles down into de rigueur delusions of grandeur.

Being above criticism means never having to learn from mistakes we think we did not make.

"Materialism," Twenge writes, "is the most obvious outcome of a straightforward, practical focus on the self: You want more things for yourself. You feel entitled to get the best in life: the best clothes, the best house, the best car." Yet the real world, with its inconvenient impingencies of future and past, is "like a cruel joke—we've been raised to expect riches, and can barely afford a condo and a crappy health care plan."

That's because those with no sense of the future or past never learn how to save.

"I am twenty-four years old, and I was born into a broke generation," writes journalist Anya Kamenetz in her book *Generation Debt*. Metaphors for immobility pepper Kamenetz's elegy, published in 2006, about "why now is a terrible time to be young." Twentysomethings "stall out on the first uphill slope," Kamenetz laments. Stuck in the present, "they're on a treadmill of debt scheduled to last from thirty years to eternity." Their predicament resembles "being stuck in an elevator that doesn't even go to the top floor. It's the inability to make plans.

"The common thread joining all members of this generation is a sense of permanent impermanence," she writes. "It's hard to commit."

This, she claims, is because they don't have enough money. (And for this she blames not limitless expectations or egos or demands for instant gratification but shrinking opportunities and selfish boomers Mom and Dad.)

Over 90 percent of American college students use credit cards. The average undergraduate carries over $2,200 in credit-card debt, the average grad student twice as much.

What are they buying with money they don't have?

Momentary pleasure.

According to a Harris Poll, college students were spending $474 million on CDs and other music-related items annually by 2004, $341 million on video games, $600 million on DVD purchases, and another $326 million on DVD rentals. That year, the poll found, 74 percent of college students owned DVD players and 55 percent owned gaming systems.

Many young people are already in debt by the time they graduate from high school, and many have gone into debt not out of necessity: They haven't been borrowing cash, say, to buy needed food or secondhand textbooks—but rather they've plunged into the red via an endless string of whims, spending money they don't have on overpriced amusements and entertainment-related products that they don't need.

That's because credit-card companies, banking on the greed and impatience and sense of entitlement inculcated in the self-esteem crowd from the cradle onward, now target the most vulnerable demographic of all. Preteens and high school kids can acquire, created especially for them, the Wired Plastic Prepaid Visa, the Baby Phat Prepaid Visa RushCard, the hypnotically named Eufora-Prepaid MasterCard, the Visa-Buxx Card, and the American Express Gift Card, whose promo declares: "Only teens know what teens want. Whether it's a funky pair of jeans, something very hi-tech, or the hottest concert ticket in town, the American Express Gift Card *Especially for Teens* is just for them."

Like other prepaid debit cards, Mastercard's MYplash is a cash card that parents can reload at will. "MYplash—the Card for Fans," announces the card's official website as a multicultural animated teen boy and girl dance to electronic sounds. "Rock the Plastic. You don't have to be 18 to use it. Just have a parent sign up with you," the text directs. Of course, to further feed the inner neo-Japhy, these cards can be "personalized." Users can choose from a range of images to adorn them, categorized into "Rock," "Pop," "Urban," "Lifestyle," "Action Sports," and "Brands." They show surfers, skateboarders, concertgoers and, in 2007, a span of performers including Clay Aiken, the Backstreet Boys, Chingy, and Avril Lavigne. "Pick a card," the page urges, "and get it now." Now. Now. *Now*.

Preteens and high schoolers live at home, where their parents provide food, shelter, transportation, and clothing for free. Yet in 2003, the average twelve- to nineteen-year-old American spent $103 a week.

On *what*?

Spending too much money, especially money *that you do not actually have*, is the quickest formula for getting stuck. Not just in the present, as every moment becomes devoted to discerning your desires and sating them, but also stuck in bad habits or even addictions and, of course, debt.

This is hardly a predicament unique to youth. Americans in general cannot and/or will not save. In 2006, the average household carried over $9,000 in credit-card debt. This figure had risen from around $8,000 in 2000, and had tripled since 1986.

Americans spent $11 billion on 8.3 billion gallons of bottled water in 2006. They spent $5 billion celebrating Halloween.

But kids are bellwethers. They are our future.

That's especially scary when they seem neither to know nor care about the future.

Sages praise babies for living entirely in the *now*. Yet criminals live there, too. Theft is instant cash. Rape is instant sex. Violence is an instant way to manifest rage, pain, or desire. Rather than wait or accept fate, "some people resort to homicide when they feel stuck in their current situation," prolific true-crime author Diane Fanning tells me, "and they envision the death of another individual to be the only palatable alternative to extricate themselves from their predicament."

Countless murders come down to the quick fix. Fanning's book *Written in Blood* is about a North Carolina novelist convicted in 2003 of murdering his wife in 2001. "Michael Peterson was in a financial bind," Fanning says. "His wife was the major breadwinner, but with the declining value of her stock options, the security she provided was ebbing away. He realized he could lose his million-dollar home." Michael Peterson shattered Kathleen Peterson's skull with a fireplace implement, claiming she had tripped while descending a staircase.

"He thought he would solve his problems," Fanning says, "with a fresh infusion of half a million dollars in cash" from a life-insurance policy.

Just as software and cell phones get streamlined to work ever faster, making gratification ever more instantaneous, crime too has been overhauled to produce its own version of the super-quick fix: the drive-by shooting.

Like most versions of stuckness in the present, nearly all crime boils down to a lack of self-control. As does much debt. But if we've been learning anything for the past fifty-plus years, it's how to lose control. From Kerouac to acid trips to "me" flags to cool video-TV phones, culprits throughout the culture and the economy vie to vaporize the components of self-control and get us all stuck in the present.

With every Big Mac, every cell-phone call, we are devaluing, unlearning, another survival skill. Bit by bit we erase from Homo sapiens' evolutionary package skills by which what one does in the present based on knowledge accrued from the past ensures that one will exist in the future.

And when we have lost all such skills, when so many of us are so stuck in the present that no one can remember the past or fret about the future, we will have lost paradise.

That long Someday will end.

And who will come to bail us out or wipe us out?

OOPS! I DID IT AGAIN

Stuck on Habits

> The chains of habit are too weak to be felt until
> they are too strong to be broken.
>
> —Samuel Johnson

One night when he was twenty-one, Ron Saxen zapped a whole jar of Hershey's hot fudge sauce in the microwave and emptied it onto a half gallon of Häagen-Dazs ice cream: "Which left only my half-pound bag of plain M&M's and my half-pound bag of peanut M&M's; I poured them both on top," Saxen remembers. Eating every drop, he took a break halfway through the giant sundae to consume a palate-cleansing bowl of cereal with milk. After the ice cream, he ate four Snickers bars and two Reese's peanut butter cups—and still felt restless.

"McDonald's is open until eleven-thirty," he told himself, reaching for his keys. "Why not add in a couple of Big Macs . . . *and* a cherry pie?" He weighed 260 pounds, his binge eating alternating with brief stints of anorexia. The more he ate, the more he hated himself. The more he hated himself, the more he ate.

Kate Holden was a smart little girl, often called a geek. In college, she socialized with a cool, artistic crowd: "my happy group of friends," she calls them. Getting high with them made Holden feel less geeky. Smoking pot "seemed like progress, to be able to loosen my stern grip on myself. I liked to keep a cask of wine beside my bed." When the group progressed to heroin, Holden responded to "an inductive pressure, a sense that if I didn't, I would lose. And so I thought perhaps I should try it. Just once, to know." Once led to twice, then lots more, and then she was a street prostitute, turning tricks in the rain to fund an addiction she calls "grinding slavery." Two stints in rehab failed to free her; both times Holden was back at her dealer's flat within hours of completing the program.

After shooting up, "there would be a heady sense of glow for the first five or ten minutes. . . . Then I had the relief of having scored, of having achieved what I wanted above all else, of having managed it yet again." Heroin, Holden remembers, "is satisfaction you can hold in your hand." Other, healthier forms of "fulfillment, contentment, pride . . . are feelings that a person can derive from being a good person, an able parent, a successful worker, an inspired artist. They are inchoate, invisible, ineffable feelings." But, she adds, "they are abstract. Heroin is a satisfaction you can pursue, it's concrete. . . .

"It was winter when I started. It was winter for a long time."

Oops. You did it again.

You know that feeling: buzz, a sigh, regret. Okay, it felt good for a second there. An hour. That rush. Relief—then *damn*.

I shouldn't have.

It could be anything, from shoe shopping to shooting black-tar heroin. Support groups thrive worldwide. Debtors Anonymous. Compulsive Eaters Anonymous. Crystal Meth Anonymous. Clutterers Anonymous. Vulgarity Anonymous, for those who cuss a lot. And hundreds more.

What is a habit boiled down to its bones? You do something over and over. Most habits are harmless. Some aren't.

Where do we draw the lines between habit and hobby and compulsion, solace and self-destruction and crime?

When you don't stop, you're stuck.

Stuck on repeat.

A friend of mine always arrives several hours late to family functions, if she comes at all. She always vows she will be on time the next time but never is.

The rest of the family, numbering a dozen or so, arrive on time from all directions. Some drive several hours. The meal is buffet-style because of her, because buffets are open-ended. They always delay eating a while past the appointed time, saying: *Give her a chance*.

Her father always calls Penny once, twice, leaving "where are you?" messages. The family waits. Sometimes his phone rings and they jump. It's never her.

They eat, feeling a bit guilty because what if this time she's not just late but had an accident en route, is lying hurt or dead as we butter corn on the cob without her?

When she arrives, *if* she does, some of her relatives have left already. Some are leaving. The meal sits congealed. Tossing her purse onto the couch, she gets a plate and fills it ceremoniously, offering explanations that would be wrenching were they not similar in their surreality. *My dog ate mothballs and I had to take him to the vet.*

I had to help a friend wash gum out of her hair. I bought you something nice but it broke as I was leaving today so I went to buy you another one but they were all sold out.

She tucks into her food. Those who were leaving sit and stay. Penny chats on.

I asked Penny once why she has this habit. She wrinkled her nose:

"Time always slips away."

Tricky word, *always*. It means that we know something is more than likely to occur. Thus we can see it coming. Yet it has a sad, inevitable air. If we factor in the causes of the certain effect, we can change the equation. My hand always blisters when I stick it into fires. Doughnuts always dissolve in swimming pools. Thus I keep my hands out of fires and doughnuts far from pools.

Voilà: unstuck.

But if we do no such thing, if we know that something "always" happens yet let it happen, we *make it happen*, more or less. This is a choice. We pretend it is not. That is, we dodge responsibility. We say *it always happens* in various tones. Airheaded: *Oops!* Passive: *Oh well!* Aggrieved: *Damn that thing! It always just goes and . . . happens!*

I asked Penny to describe the hours leading up to her arrival one night. She listed a litany starting at one that afternoon involving laundry, pumice, iMacs, and a bird feeder. Altogether, they occupied two hours.

"Then what took up the other three?" I asked.

She said she'd bought an ice-cream pop and cigarettes and driven to the pier.

And then?

"Well," Penny said, "I ate and smoked."

"For three hours?"

"Two. Then I drove over here. Traffic," she said.

Penny enters a kind of state, I am sure, fueled by ancient resentments, memories of dramas too long undiscussed. Her habit is a punishment. It punishes her relatives. But it punishes her, too, because she hates standing out as the family fuckup. And she sort of knows this and sort of does not.

Me? Habits?

I bluster about the possibility of change, then do the same things every day. I eat the same breakfast. Look at the same websites. Start working at the same time. Wrestle the same fears. My habits harm no one, but make me as predictable as an automaton. Once, as a child, I read a story about a boy who refused to eat anything except cheese, peas, and chocolate pudding. I dread that others will find out how much I resemble that boy.

For ten years I hardly ate anything. I woke up in my nice bed in my nice apartment next to my nice boyfriend and thought every day: *I will not eat.* Ah, that same never-ending tiresome tournament-of-one my generation honed to a dumb art.

How did it end? Three weeks after he had a stroke, my dad died. After years of hunger, I gorged on his favorites: ice cream, candy, cake. Starved bodies overreact. I hated the way this made me look, then hated hating it, hated the back and forth. Someone gave me the fine idea of exercise: the clean science of heartbeat, repetitions, speed. The new new math of other numerals besides those on a scale. I became: medium.

Wait, so you can eat like a normal person if you move like a normal person, as much as but no more or less than we were built to move?

Well, duh.

Another habit: I dress like a slob. I cannot stop. Blue jeans several sizes too big and faded, patched, washed, and worn chamois-soft. Sneakers, no socks. Cotton tops, jewelry even. But always these massive threadbare pants. This is not politics. This is not rage, though some find it insulting: *She couldn't be bothered, eh?*

My dad always said I dressed like a pig. And onlookers cannot assess the size and shape of my behind. But these pants feel too good to give up just for that. I do not care.

This, like all habits, like much in life, is an equation. Reasons, factors, denials. Prices to pay. Somehow, I need this raggedness, this softness, and this size.

Because I believe I deserve no better?

Kinda.

Because, still a child inside, I dress like one?

Uh-huh.

Because I shun the oppressive, manipulative retail cycle?

Yup.

Because life is hard, so pants should be soft?

Mmhmm.

In a looks-mean-everything world, my habit is arguably bad.

Not bad enough to make me stop.

Granted, changing wardrobes is easier than quitting cigarettes or meth. It's not even on the same scale. That's a funny thing about habits: because we all have them, because the having of habits is a universal condition, we can all relate to this topic. We all know how not-quitting feels. We all grasp that anguish, desire, regret. And even as we fret over our lateness, way too many lattes, late-night-each-night Internet chats, little white lies, tattered pants, we know that at the far end of this same habit continuum stand crack addicts, still-smoking heart patients, and anorexics weighing forty pounds. We laugh at some habits. Some kill. We're only human, after all.

Habits are instinctual, an evolutionary legacy. Creatures find safe and easy ways of doing things and repeat them rather than reassess or renegotiate at every turn. Through the forest, the doe knows its optimal route. The bat knows where to catch the best insects. Autopilot saves time, trouble, and thought. Shortcuts are second nature, great for daily chores such as brewing coffee and tying shoes. Imagine having brain damage that left you unable to do those tasks without extensive thinking, that left you unable to internalize any routine. Imagine the exhaustion, the risk. Habits streamline life.

But sometimes what we've internalized hurts us.

Or hurts others.

And/or turns us into dupes. Drones. Criminals.

What have you programmed yourself to perform?

Is it any wonder that we think and act like a nation of addicts?

Even if our habits have nothing to do with illegal activities or dangerous substances or out-and-out self-injury, even if our habits are as seemingly harmless as lateness or lying, we are taught from infancy onward—by the media, by marketers, and by the medical industry—that life is fraught with cravings that we are powerless to resist, that only dorks and fundamentalists resist. In an identity-fixated culture, we are taught that habits help define us, "brand" us. *I procrastinate. I smoke. I shop.*

This chapter makes no pretense of conclusively solving serious addiction problems, the kind that kill. And although you might say

I'll never be an alcoholic or a meth addict so this has nothing to do with me, it does, because even our mildest and most harmless habits are addictions in miniature. Our reasons for adopting them, the manner in which we got stuck and stay stuck on our habits, the language we use to describe and explain and excuse them—are all reflected in the patterns of serious addiction and in our society's approach to serious addiction.

As a tiny but telling example, addiction language infuses even our casual conversations. We append the suffix "-holic" or "-oholic" onto virtually any English verb or noun, taking upon ourselves the addict persona. One website asks: "Are you a cat addict?" Elsewhere on the Web, users proclaim: "I'm a yarn addict." "I'm a Wii addict." "I'm a Court TV addict." "I'm a blogoholic." "I'm a chile relleno addict." "I'm a fantasy football addict." "I'm a sushi-holic." "I'm a sock-a-holic." "I'm a charm addict," laments a woman at a jewelry site. "I'm a horsepower-holic," a driver confesses.

In July 2007, Michael and Iana Straw pleaded guilty to two counts each of child neglect after social workers discovered the couple's two babies severely malnourished and dehydrated in their Nevada home. Treated for starvation and a genital infection, the twenty-two-month-old boy could not walk properly because his muscles were insufficiently developed. Hospital staff shaved the eleven-month-old girl's head because her hair was clotted with foul substances, including cat urine. At trial, a prosecutor claimed that although plenty of food was in the house, the young parents were too distracted by online video games to feed or tend to the kids. Michael Straw, who was jobless, had spent a $50,000 inheritance on computer equipment and a large TV.

Just about anything can be habit-forming. Habits sneak up on us in the middle of our ordinary lives, and by the time we realize that we're at their mercy, we feel helpless and ashamed to have let this happen. Shame and a sense of helplessness make any habit harder to quit.

"When I'm working," says LaShawn, a Tennessee software designer, "I like—okay, I *need*—something to nibble. I can't concentrate if I don't nibble. But if I'm going to nibble, I want to nibble something good. Sorry to sound like a jerk, but I feel like I deserve the best." When she started at her current company four years ago, LaShawn chose to nibble on Belgian chocolate truffles.

"I'd sit here tapping away with a little box of truffles next to my keyboard," she says. "I was just taking teensy-weensy bites, so it might take me a whole hour to eat a single truffle—but by the end of an average day, I'd have polished off five or six." Over three years, she gained almost forty pounds and her doctor was warning her about diabetes, which runs in LaShawn's family. "I was all woe-is-me because other than the truffles, I generally eat pretty healthy food. But I didn't think of the truffles as food. I thought of them as—well, an office supply.

"At the doctor's office one day I had to admit that these yummy little things were hurting me. But when I tried to work without eating them I couldn't think straight."

She tried other snacks instead: "First, baby carrots. Yuck! Next, olives. Too oily, even with toothpicks." Finally, she settled on a deluxe brand of dried cranberries—and unlimited cups of lavender tea.

"The idea of looking better and avoiding diabetes is another way of pampering myself," says LaShawn. "Why not choose this way?"

We all have behaviors we wish we could stop, but say we can't.

We have to want to stop to stop.

We have to *have to* stop to stop.

On a summer trip to Thailand, my college classmate Sarah was stranded for two weeks on an uninhabited islet after her kayak sank. She survived on rainwater, kelp, and toothpaste.

Those of us raised in the lap of luxury can scarcely even picture deprivation. Before her ordeal, Sarah had scarcely missed a meal. She was a Valley Girl, your average upper-middle-class American coed. Deprivation was an abstraction to Sarah, anathema, as it is to most of us: deprivation is a filmstrip about Darfur, a fairy tale about a hungry little match girl. (For anorexics, self-imposed deprivation is a perverse, grotesque, self-indulgent kind of luxury.)

To us who grew up in the lap of luxury, the idea of quitting a habit feels impossible, because we have been raised to believe that our wants should never be denied.

"Want" is a loaded word. Where do we draw the lines between craving and need, will and persuasion? Does what we are brainwashed to want count as want?

Stuck on habits, we let ourselves be controlled by substances, people, and actions. Life becomes occupied territory, our bodies become colonies of Coca-Cola or Medellín or *Vogue* or Visa. Stuck on a habit, you become unable to defend anything larger than yourself because you refuse to defend yourself. You are ovverun. You are owned.

A bad habit is an abdication of autonomy masquerading as desire.

How did that happen? Where and when did you give yourself away?

You went there. Bought that. Smoked, ate, snorted, injected that. Did that.

Your choice. Yours.

What could be clearer? I put on my tattered pants. Penny is late. She also visits liquor stores where she hands clerks cash in exchange for slim French cigarettes. Her neighbor is a drug dealer. Customers ring his doorbell, come inside, and hand him cash in exchange for small packages. For her last birthday, someone gave Penny a funny cartoon book about trying to quit smoking. It's called *These Things Ain't Gonna Smoke Themselves*.

They ain't.

And all this action, this volition, the gymnastics routine of want, get, then want and get again suggests that our bad habits are our own doing. And yet . . .

The dominant paradigm right now is pretty much the opposite. The dominant paradigm right now is that bad habits are not personal choices but diseases. Clinical disorders. Illnesses. Sicknesses on par, the paradigm goes, with cancer or colitis.

In that worldview, habits are *not your fault*. Over them, *you have no control*.

Do you consume eight thousand calories daily? Your redneck pals call it pigging out. The U.S. government calls it "binge eating disorder," which, according to the National Institutes of Health, "is a condition that millions of Americans may have. People with binge eating disorder often eat large amounts of food and feel that they can't control their eating." The NIH recommends psychotherapy and antidepressant medications.

Do you recognize yourself in that *Simpsons* episode in which Marge plays slot machines compulsively, neglecting her kids? Homer rages to the kids about "the gambling monster that has enslaved your mother. I call him Gamblor, and it's time to snatch your mother from his neon claws!" Funny. But how much funnier is Homer's made-up monster than "pathologic gambling disorder," which looks so pompous and proper in the *Diagnostic and Statistical Manual of Mental Disorders*, the world's most influential mental health sourcebook. It joins hundreds more behaviors, not all of them substance-related, now classified as maladies.

Is alcoholism a disease? Yes, the American Academy of Family Physicians informs us. "Most experts agree that alcoholism is a disease just as high blood pressure, diabetes and arthritis are diseases. Like these other diseases, alcoholism tends to run in families."

But you don't need to go out to the toolshed and bash your own knuckles with a hammer in order to get arthritis. Getting arthritis requires no action or initiative on your part and is generally truly beyond your control. Alcoholism, on the other hand, would be nothing more than an innocuous and unacted-upon urge—no different from a million other urges we resist every day—if we did not pick up those bottles and put them to our lips. Even high blood pressure and diabetes, which can be exacerbated by poor diet, are quantifiable biological ailments that you can intensify via certain behaviors. But the act of eating a sugary diet is not itself a "disease." The action and the ailment are different. Yet in the case of alcoholism, for example, the "experts" seem to have intentionally confused an array of physical symptoms with the self-directed actions that might have caused those symptoms. It's like diagnosing a broken leg as "skiing-accident syndrome."

Not that we should begin to minimize the hell of actual addiction. Not that we should be such Pollyannas as to suggest that addiction isn't deadly serious. It is. Nor should we think that addicts can halt their addictions *just like that*, like flicking on and off a switch. We know—*I know*—the vise grip of the unrelenting urge. When the urge, sated once, rises again to mock us and to master us, we know the true meaning of helplessness and hopelessness and shame. What do we call a choice that engulfs everything around it? A habit, a condition. A state. But sickness? How much of the word "disease" in this context is medicine; how much is metaphor?

What favors do we do ourselves to say we're sick?

"Like any other addiction, genuine compulsive online shopping is a disease," announces an article in *Entertainment Weekly* magazine (albeit hardly a medical-industry or government mouthpiece), which includes quotes from psychotherapists. "The important thing . . . is to remember that the condition can—and should—be treated," the reporter tells us, with "medications like Luvox, an inhibitor used to treat compulsive gamblers."

"Smoking is a pediatric disease. It's addictive and it kills," declared Dr. Jeffrey Wigand at an American Cancer Society forum in 2000.

Not: smoking *causes* diseases. But: smoking *is* a disease.

We've been pathologized.

"Addiction is a brain disease," said Alan Leshner, a psychologist and former National Institute on Drug Abuse director, during a PBS interview with Bill Moyers. "We need to conceptualize this disease . . . in the same way that you would think about diabetes."

During this interview, Leshner told Moyers: "Addiction is not a voluntary circumstance. It's not a voluntary behavior."

Moyers felt moved to ask: "So the addict has no choice?"

"That's right," Leshner replied.

"But the first time is a choice," Moyers queried, "surely?"

Leshner agreed, but asserted that "at some point when you move over into addiction, it's no longer voluntary."

This change, he said, is characterized less by physical reactions to withdrawal than psychological ones.

"The physical symptoms can be managed relatively easily, and in fact for many drugs like crack and methamphetamine, there are no dramatic physical withdrawal symptoms. Two of the most addicting substances ever known to humankind really have very few physical withdrawal symptoms. . . . On the other hand, crack and methamphetamine produce unbelievable craving, unbelievable compulsion to use them, and that's really the essence of addiction: the psychological part."

The professional nickname for binge eating disorder is BED. For pathologic gambling disorder it is PGD. Clinical trials have proposed the ADHD prescription drug Atomoxetine as a BED medicine and, for PGD, the opioid receptor antagonist Naltrexone, previously used in treating alcoholism.

Does Penny suffer from Punctuality Occlusion Disorder (POD)? Poor Penny! Do I have Wardrobe Aesthetic Disorder (WAD)? Take me to the pharmacy.

This question of whether bad habits are diseases should be a flash point for fierce debate, raging worldwide. It should, because the answer to that question reveals how we view accountability, responsibility for what we eat and drink and buy—in fact, *for whatever we do*. But when no one was looking, the debate was skipped entirely, and now it's accepted wisdom that bad habits are diseases. For most of those doing the talking on this topic, the matter is settled.

And it sounds like this: *It's not your fault. You're sick.*

In a society that reveres medicine, those words wield such power.

Disease is not something you do but something that befalls you.

It afflicts you and disempowers you.

It's involuntary. Beyond your control.

Disease is science—complicated, overwhelming science, neuro this and bio this and pharma that. As such, it is for experts and professionals to understand, not you.

The ill merit care. Sympathy. Patience.

And treatment, of course.

Intervention.

Medicine.

There, there.

The "bad habits are diseases" meme is commonly known as the disease model or the disease theory. And while it should be a flash point or at the very least a topic still open to discussion, it's pretty much a fait accompli, accorded and endorsed by an unlikely coalition comprising doctors, lawyers, filmmakers, reporters, counselors, celebrities, and others. Hop aboard.

Who loves the disease theory? Government agencies do. The website of "Drug Czar" General Barry McCaffrey when he headed the White House Office of National Drug Control Policy declared: "Chronic, hardcore drug use is a disease, and anyone suffering from a disease needs treatment."

"Addiction is similar to other diseases, such as heart disease," asserts a typical National Institutes of Health booklet. Another NIH booklet is titled "Drug Addiction: A Treatable Disease."

Other major disease-theory endorsers are—unsurprisingly—clinics and medical associations and pharmaceutical firms. For them, every newly named addiction-cum-disorder is a gold mine, yielding lucrative opportunities for research, development, mass production, marketing, and sales.

And the disease theory is the meat and potatoes of Alcoholics Anonymous and other twelve-step recovery groups. In his *Big Book*, the manual for Alcoholics Anonymous members, Bill Wilson called alcoholism a "progressive illness."

"If a person has cancer," Wilson wrote, "all are sorry for him and no one is angry or hurt. But not so with the alcoholic illness"— at least not in the 1930s, when he wrote the *Big Book*.

The disease theory is also popular with activists, who never met a victim they didn't like. Of course it's also tops with lawyers, who whip it out in court to excuse criminal behavior: *Ye-e-es, my client starved her baby nearly to death, but that's because she has video-game disorder! She's a very sick woman!*

Media venues love it, too, competing to debut new diseases that raise the scare factor: "Work phobia an anxiety disorder, not laziness," declares a typical headline in London's *Telegraph*. "Always online? Beware of Internet addiction disorder," warns another the same day in the *Jerusalem Post*. Addicts love the disease theory, too. It's so much easier to say *I'm sick* than *I'm screwing up my life*.

And yours.

Which is not to say that the disease theory doesn't liberate a lot of people from devastating addictions. That mind-set works for them, giving them a strength they perhaps couldn't summon as long as they blamed themselves for their actions—and self-blame, for them, would be yet another form of stuckness. For a long while, being told—and telling others, in the grave, solemn tone with which one discusses illness—that I had an eating disorder gave me comfort. I relished the shift I felt, deep down, from me the willful refuser-of-meds to me the hapless patient. I had skipped meals for years, driving my boyfriend crazy, rejecting delicious treats around the world, making a self-indulgent silly mockery of all who ever died of hunger in famines and wars. I had a *disorder*. This sounds serious. "Disorder" is a generously one-size-fits-all word, implying however much in the way of medical overtones might suit its user. I embraced the sickness side of it for years. Now I am not so eager. Yes, my caloric intake was disordered, was out of order. And yet this was not some fever visited upon me but a way I chose to live, committing to it anew every day. At its height, no, I would not be talked out of it and refused to see reason, but I could have stopped and knew I could have stopped and every day decided not to stop.

Pneumonia gives me no such liberty.

The disease theory, dictated from on high as our end-all and be-all approach to addiction treatment, could very well damage and weaken us as a society over time, in ways that this chapter will explore.

Not all of the disease-theory proponents have sinister, under-handed, or mercenary motives. A primary rationale for promoting the disease theory—a rationale accepted earnestly by many—is that its main purpose is to *help* addicts and others in trouble. The reasoning goes like this: self-destructive behavior is the result of low self-esteem, and if we can raise people's self-esteem, their misbehavior will cease of its own accord. Even many who readily assert that addiction is not a disease in the strictly scientific sense feel that the idea should be promoted anyway, that professionals and the public should promote it as a united front, because only in that way can we deliver a credible blame-absolving message, and thus fix the problem—which, after all, is society's problem as well. All it takes is one coldhearted naysayer to break the spell, and all the world's recovering addicts and other troubled souls will chorus, "Wait—you mean that was a *trick*? You mean I'm *not* a victim?" At which point their self-esteem will dissolve and they'll all relapse and society will go to hell.

So the theory goes.

You wouldn't want that on your hands, would you?

The disease theory is hardly a new idea. In a 1784 pamphlet titled "Inquiry into the Effects of Ardent Spirits on the Human Mind and Body," Philadelphia physician Benjamin Rush called habitual drunkenness an "odious disease" and a "disease induced by a vice." The temperance movement maintained that stance. "Drunkenness is a physical, as well as moral disease," wrote Salvation Army cofounder Catherine Booth in 1879.

But it is only recently—since the close of the twentieth century—that the disease theory attained almost universal approval and acceptance. For all its potential benefits, it is also a perfect fit for our narcissistic, passive, lazy, trauma-obsessed, blame-dodging, "I didn't do it, boo-hoo I'm a victim" times.

But still, you might ask: Who would want to be told, *You're ill*?

Well, consider the alternatives. Smoking or shopping or starving yourself or shooting up—you vow to stop, yet don't. So are you selfish? Spoiled? Suicidal? Weak?

Stop saying that!

Are you lazy?

Shut up!

A leech?

Shut up!

Are you simply not trying hard enough to stop?

I said shut UP!

Should you change your priorities? Your friends?

Don't tell me what to do!

Or . . . are you simply sick?

Ahhh. Yes.

When we are sick, we are allowed to snuggle under blankets, having soup and ice cream, watching videos, absolved from work and chores and from needing to pay close attention to anything or anyone. Every few hours we take our medicine.

Even with the blankets and soup, being actually sick feels terrible.

But our culture has a fantasy version: sickness as a respite, as somewhat romantic.

Add this affliction aesthetic to a culture that also embraces an addiction aesthetic—from stoner chic to smoker chic to the fashion industry favorite, heroin chic—and getting stuck on bad habits appears, to the consumer and casual observer, not like a mistake but almost an ambition. Bad habits are diseases we can't help catching. But if you catch one . . . *hey, you might look like a supermodel!*

Promoters of the disease theory accept that we begin bad habits voluntarily: that the first time we engage in certain substances and behaviors, we do so by choice. But almost immediately, they assert, we become biological slaves to our habits as these substances and behaviors physically alter the cellular and molecular structures of our brains, flooding our frontal lobes with excessive amounts of the feel-good neurotransmitter dopamine. Under normal circumstances, regular surges of dopamine are triggered naturally by quotidian pleasures such as kissing or laughing or satisfying thirst. The disease theory holds that certain substances and behaviors feel *sooo* good that they unleash *sooo* much dopamine into the system that the brain's dopamine receptors become overwhelmed by these influxes and defend themselves by shutting down. This means that we need more of the substance or behavior in order to feel the same buzz we felt the first time. Tolerance raised, we crave more, now, again. At this point, the disease theory avers, we are beyond the power of reason, now powerless over the substance or behavior: just as powerless over crack or gambling, say, as diabetics are powerless over their blood glucose.

The first of the twelve steps says: "We admitted we were powerless over alcohol."

An upstart faction of scientists and other scholars scorns the disease theory. They argue that the alleged causality is still scientifically shaky, that links between behaviors and substances and brain biology and genetic predisposition have not yet been proven decisively. They contend that of course every new scientific study we read about in the papers supports the disease theory—because the entities funding research projects stand to gain from the spread of the disease theory, so the projects chosen to receive funding are the ones most likely to produce pro-disease-theory results.

"The conventional wisdom is that there is some power in the drug that makes people keep using the drug," states psychologist and American University law professor Jeffrey Schaler, whose book *Addiction Is a Choice* skewers the disease theory. "Another part of that argument is that once you use the drug, something changes in your body. And that change—*which has never been identified, only hypothesized*—causes you to keep using the drug" . . . or keep doing the unpleasant behavior, as the disease theory now embraces far more than drug use.

"However," Schaler asserts, "drug use and addiction doesn't have to do with what drugs do to the body, but how drugs get into the body. If you take a drug like cocaine, obviously something changes in your body." But proof of bodily changes is in itself virtually meaningless, he argues. "Every time you think any thought, your body changes. There's always a physiological change associated with whatever you do. Now the question is, 'Does that physiological change make you do what you're doing, or do you choose to do that?' If you have epilepsy, and you have a seizure, of course there's a physical change in your body that makes you go into convulsions . . . that's clearly not a volitional act. But whether you're going to reach for another cigarette or not *is* a volitional act."

Schaler contends that the disease theory is bad science that undermines our culture and character. But even if you believe the science is rock solid, what are the widespread, long-term effects of believing ourselves to be powerless over our own behavior? Of accepting the idea that we have no choice and can't stop of our own volition, even if we say we want to?

If bad habits make us feel less autonomous, the disease theory makes us feel even less autonomous by saying: Yes, you are helplessly dependent on your habits and the only possible solution is to become dependent on something else that is also not yourself—that is, dependent on the system, on institutions and prescriptions.

Yes, bad habits feel bad. Physically. Mentally. It's so, so, so hard to quit, especially if your family history predisposes you, either environmentally or genetically or both: Forty percent of alcoholics have at least one alcoholic parent, for example. Native Americans are five times likelier than other ethnicities in the United States to die of alcohol-related causes, according to the National Institute on Alcohol Abuse and Alcoholism. Among other factors, genetic differences in two enzymes—alcohol dehydrogenase (ADH) and aldehyde dehydrogenase (ALDH)—have been studied extensively in an effort to explain why various groups have higher or lower rates of alcohol-related issues.

But to say alcoholism *and* gambling *and* shopping are diseases? It's hard, so hard, to walk that line.

Stanton Peele is another skeptic. In his book *Diseasing of America*, this psychologist and addiction consultant calls the disease theory "the marketing of loss-of-control ideas and treatments," and warns: "Once we treat alcoholism and addiction as diseases, we cannot rule out that anything people do but shouldn't is a disease." Peele acknowledges that certain substances indeed spur biological reactions, but charges that the word "disease" is subjective and reductive and vague enough to be used as a grab bag for social and personal crises that have more to do with priorities, values, and culture than the disease theory wants us to realize. Why, Peele demands, do we embrace "the idea that we are so impotent and helpless?" Why have we "decided that we—and our children—cannot control even our own emotions and behavior?"

Stuck on habits, we call in sick to life itself.

Peele deplores what he sees as a plague of passivity leveling the land: all of us limp, lacking initiative, defaulting on responsibility. He calls the disease theory a "cultural delusion." Another delusion, he claims, is the notion that we're helpless victims. Although he acknowledges that addiction can create bodily effects, he refuses to deem addiction "a specific biological syndrome." The "biochemical aspects of addiction are only half the story," he contends.

And the other half matters more to him, because in it resides our hopes and dreams, our willpower.

Our power.

Every habit tells a story that has to do with much more than a specific substance or behavior, illegal or not. It has to do with personal details: friends, moods, conversations, fashions, fears, and priorities. Peele argues that to accept the disease theory is to reject the importance of these highly personal details, which ultimately, if studied closely enough, can help us come unstuck. In his view, the fact that you started smoking crack because everyone on your street was smoking crack is a primary factor in your crack habit, reflecting the fact that you prioritize peer-group acceptance over, say, your health and ability to hold a job. In which case, moving off that street is a prime step in breaking that habit.

It hurts sometimes to admit our priorities. It's much easier to say "I'm sick" than "I am selfish, I am shallow, I am sneaky and conniving and I disrespect my relatives."

This is the crux of stuckness: all stuckness, whether it's about habits or beliefs or relationships. *The problem with change is that it requires self-awareness, courage, and effort.* Doing nothing is always easier, even if by doing nothing, by coasting, you get more and more stuck and slip inch by inch into misery. Poverty. Illness. Loneliness. Staying stuck takes no effort at all, and so although we might not not like the destination, the bus ride to hell is at least free, with air-conditioned seating and a restroom. Who has the gumption to leap from the moving vehicle and crawl, bruised and humiliated, back to freedom?

However, Schaler and Peele are voices in the wilderness. Such views are far outnumbered.

In a society as heavily invested in science and medicine as ours is, "disease" is a potent word. It's a grisly word, sure. But it's also seductive, because we want easy answers right here, right now. And *You're sick* is an easy answer. It's final, official, and clinical: a diagnosis. And the reason we develop bad habits in the first place is because we love quick fixes.

In eras past, the sick were stigmatized. The most obvious example involves the infectious condition long called leprosy but now known as Hansen's disease. In medieval Europe, those displaying the disease's classic symptoms—sores, large nodules, disfigured noses, and missing digits—were systematically reviled, as it was believed that their condition was a divine punishment. In England, Hansen's disease sufferers were forced to wear identifying cloaks and hats, ring bells or clappers signaling their approach, and submit to the so-called Mass of Separation, recited over them by priests who intoned:

> I forbid you to ever enter a church, a monastery, a fair, a mill, a market or an assembly of people. I forbid you to leave your house unless dressed in your recognizable garb. . . . I forbid you to wash your hands or to launder anything or to drink at any stream or fountain. . . . I forbid you to enter any tavern. . . . I forbid you to touch any child.

Not satisfied with merely censuring the sick, our ancestors also cast a harsh judgmental eye on certain personal habits, even criminalizing some of these. The village glutton, sleepyhead, and slut were objects of mockery. Village gossips in pre-nineteenth-century England were often forced to wear stifling headgear known as "scolds' bridles." Well into the nineteenth century in England and America, habitual gamblers and drunkards were locked in the stocks for days on end, publicly humiliated.

Centuries of social reform and scientific understanding have wrought great improvements in attitudes. But in striving to prove ourselves far superior to our superstitious, reactionary forebears, we have convinced ourselves that it is anathema to stigmatize just about anyone or anything. We no longer stigmatize the sick, of course, but now we hesitate even to stigmatize those whose behavior actually bothers us—or, being self-destructive, bothers them. Striving to prove ourselves ethically evolved, we withhold judgment entirely.

The more we let ourselves be diagnosed as ill, the less willing we are to sit still with ourselves and think about how and why we got stuck—because we've come to believe that it's out of our hands. Bad habits might or might not become molecular and cellular, but as disease-theory dissidents such as Peele and Schaler point out, each habit starts with a single thought.

What was yours?

It must have been pretty persuasive. Or did it catch you at a vulnerable moment, dazed and confused? The moment a habit begins is not necessarily the first time you ever try whatever it is. That's not a habit yet. That's curiosity, adventure, desperation, experimentation, stupidity, convenience ("Well, since it's right here") or politeness ("Well, if you insist"). The habit starts when you—conscious, awake, eyes open—decide to do it again. Or the third time, the fourth, or the fifth. A transition happens in which you decide, usually silently and secretly, maybe giddily or vengefully or shamefully, that this activity is now part of your life, a facet of the complex creature that is you. Of all the actions in the world to repeat, you picked this. Something about it appeals to you: even if those closest to you find it horrible, perhaps *because* they do, something in it said *Choose me* and you did. Bad habits are like boyfriends: we love our own but cannot expect others to stop scowling and understand.

That commitment—*Okay! Do it again!*—is what we later won't want to admit, because in retrospect it might seem so random and so small.

Freshman year, my college roommate had unlimited access to free cocaine. That would be a pretty big deal to a significant proportion of college freshmen anytime, but this was the late '70s in Southern California, which was time- and placewise the apex of cocaine chic, a halcyon age before all those news reports came out about the deleterious effects of extended usage: the nasal necrosis and septal perforations, the increased heart-attack risk. Back then, coke had preponderantly clean, exciting connotations, symbolized on T-shirts by snowflakes and angels. My roommate, Dawn, made a swirly pastel poster for our dorm-room wall bearing just one word: ENERGY. It was her euphemism for cocaine. Her favorite T-shirt bore the image of a bright white angel blowing a horn from which issued the word TOOT: another euphemism. That's the kind of time and place it was. A guy Dawn knew back home in San Francisco sent cocaine in ziplock plastic pouches tucked inside fat decorative greeting cards whose pop-up clowns and sateen poufs and lace obscured the extra bulge. *Happy 3rd Birthday to a Special Little Boy. Happy Anniversary, My Dear.*

The cards arrived nearly every day. Whenever Dawn or I came back to our dorm from the campus mailroom, a small crowd would soon gather at our door. There was always enough coke for four or five takers. Dawn cut it into lines on a mirror that said COKE. Music was always playing, Fleetwood Mac or Joni Mitchell. The people who gathered in our room were slim and beautiful and, like Dawn, getting Cs. She always offered me a line. "Want some? Come on."

And I always refused. Not that I was a Miss Priss. I drank Orange Crush with Southern Comfort (though my parents never drank) and cussed like a Marine. But cocaine scared me. It was too attractive, too expensive, and would not always be free, so if I liked it, someday I would have to pay for it. I am cheap. The last habit I wanted was an expensive one.

But then—

There is always a *then*.

So random and so slight. A good idea at the time.

My best college friend Wendy was planning to see Elvis Costello with me but decided at the last minute to go with Jim from down the hall. I could have gone alone or with some other kids, but sat around sulking instead.

The razor blade went *klik, crunch, klik*.

"Want some?" said Dawn.

I nodded.

And.

Wow.

I mean.

Just. Wow.

I ran for hours on the beach, alone. I watched the sun come up.

A few days later I tried it again, loved it again.

But then I stopped.

Forever. Cocaine still came almost every day. *(Congratulations on Your Confirmation, Grandson.)* Dawn still offered me the straw. I did not decide pompously *Never again!* or struggle to resist. I just thought, the next time she asked and the next and the next, *I can't because I have to study for a midterm* and *I can't because I have a dinner date* and *I can't because I don't really like you* . . . and I never snorted coke again. My moment came and then it went.

It's just an anecdote, just me, but true.

If someone as weak-willed as I was back then, someone with no strong moral convictions, hardly any self-esteem or self-awareness—if *I* calmly turned my back on what felt like paradise after trying it twice, then surely almost anyone can. *I turned down free cocaine*.

In Southern California in the '70s.

You might ask where I found the strength and courage to do it, but the fact is, I had no special strength and courage. I'm nobody special. Every day I regret my decisions, question my desires, and allow my emotions to run roughshod over my attempts at logic. My weakness and cowardice are proven over and over again every day. So if a weakling like me could resist, why do others find it so difficult? And at what point, after how many visits to paradise, would resistance have felt harder, felt impossible?

Common sense would seem to say that resisting the temptation to do dangerous, too-good-to-be-true things is the effortless default position for all intelligent creatures: a survival strategy.

Yet some among us find resistance difficult . . . sometimes killingly so.

Why?

We all know by now that addictions and other bad habits can lead to illness, bankruptcy, death. And even if we temporarily forget, our watchdogs keep reminding us. For example, a disturbingly graphic 2007 British public-service ad campaign shows smokers impaled through their mouths on authentic-looking giant fishhooks and dragged painfully around.

Even the average child could recognize the warning signs by now and stay away.

So why don't we?

Because habits fill holes.

In our days. In our souls.

Baleful even in their jubilance, punk songs proclaimed this.

"I belong to the blank generation," Richard Hell and the Voidoids sang in 1977.

"We're pretty—pretty vacant," the Sex Pistols sang that same year, "and we don't care."

Living in the lap of luxury, surrounded by stuff, we nonetheless have lots of caesuras in our lives. Gaps. Chasms that we don't dare contemplate and instead rush to hide with . . . more stuff. Or substances or repetitive behaviors that keep us distracted from what's missing.

This is partly (but only partly) because we have come to rely on machines to do so much for us: give pleasure, products, information, entertainment, companionship in a click, performing tasks whose strenuosity used to remind us that we were alive. To the extent that we no longer perform these tasks ourselves, we are no longer human.

Not that I want to go back to a bygone age and ride a donkey to the nearest music hall—I spend most of every day online—but we have worked it so that we no longer have to walk, talk, read whole books to extract information, assess strangers by sight and sound, create something from nothing, entertain ourselves or wait. Occupants of our brave new narcissistic electronic world are, as media critic Lee Siegel observes in a café, "bent into their screens and toward their self-interest. My attention, too, is turned toward my ego. . . . I am opening e-mail sent to me, writing e-mail expressing one or another desire that belongs to me, clicking on Google looking for information to be used by me. Ten years ago, the space in a coffeehouse abounded in experience. Now that social space has been contracted into isolated points of wanting."

Machines have made our dreams come true while filling us with inchoate despair. Is it any wonder that so many young people self-mutilate, slicing their flesh habitually with razor blades and knives? "Cutters," as they call themselves, literalize the other holes in their lives—the boredom, the pain, the failed connections—by making holes in themselves. Cutting appeals to cutters because of its brutal physicality, which seems the only way they can remind themselves they are alive.

This is evinced by postings at SIARI.co.uk—whose name stands for Self-Injury and Related Issues and which bills itself as "the largest self-injury site on the Web." A cutter named Betsy writes: "I have a fascination with the blood, it is from within me." Linelle adds: "The sight of the injury has a calming effect. But so does looking at the scars. When they begin to fade, I get anxious. If I can't see them anymore, I have to put them back." Deja explains: "When I see my blood, it does several things for me. One is that I can tell that I'm alive." Karina asserts: "Seeing my blood has a big significance to me. It makes me feel real. Makes me feel alive." Sinead expresses it in a poem:

> *I do it to feel . . .*
> *Or to make myself real . . .*
> *Why do I do it?*
> *I do it to live!*

What horrible things do we get stuck on for fear of turning into robots otherwise?

As if those holes in our mechanized lives were not already worrisome enough, they are torn wider—then propped open with sticks—by the nihilism that fuels much of our culture today.

Nihilists believe that everything is meaningless. Popularized in its current form by the nineteenth-century German philosopher Friedrich Nietzsche—who defined it as the belief that "our existence (action, suffering, willing, feeling) has no meaning"—nihilism is at the same time incredibly liberating and incredibly depressing. If everything is meaningless, then nothing is either inherently bad or good, so everything's permissible. But if everything is meaning-less, then nothing is worth loving, fighting against, or fighting for. If everything is meaningless, no habit can be conclusively called "bad," and being addicted to anything is no better or worse than not being addicted.

Nihilism infuses postmodernism, poststructuralism, and decon-structionism, which in turn dominate current academia, the arts, and social discourse. We embrace it as the ultimate in deadpan cool *and* brash rebellion, a stunning smackdown in any debate. *Nothing matters!*

Nihilism's watchword is *Whatever.*

Brainwashed to believe that nothing is actually bad, we are powerless to resist.

Texas A&M University education professor James Scheurich, a postmodernist himself, devised a glossary of postmodern terminol-ogy, which he distributes to his students. It defines poststructural-ism as "the study of phenomena as systems, with the assumption that these systems have no inherent meaning." Postmodernism is "a broad social and philosophical movement that questions the ratio-nality of human action, the use of positivist epistemology, and any human endeavor (e.g., science) that claims a privileged position with respect to the search for truth or that claims progress in its search for truth." In other words: nothing is true.

French philosopher Jacques Derrida, considered the father of deconstructionism, declared that words themselves hold no fixed meanings. He preferred to call any assemblage of words a "text"—a preference now ubiquitous among many academics, including English professors, who say the classics are not inherently "better" than cereal-box blurbs and that what matters most about a text, be it the *Aeneid* or a sugar packet, is not what its author might have meant (because words have no set meanings) but what a reader feels while reading it, and no two readers will or should feel the same way.

Generations suckled on these theories grow up stuck in the murk of moral relativism, their passivity reinforced as they fear looking too closely or too hard at anything, lest they declare— "judge" is a cussword now—anything or anyone better than anything or anyone else. Generations grow up believing that declaring anything to be a fact would be the act of a fascist.

That such a grim mentality could become cool attests to the strength of the takeover. Pat Santy, a Michigan psychologist concerned about her daughter's education, notes on her blog: "These children were raised on postmodern milk; and their brain development has reached a point of no return and is functioning now for the sole purpose of blocking out the real world, rather than trying to understand it. Reality, truth and reason are far too dangerous. . . . If you can convince children that objective reality is an illusion, that A does not equal A, that black is white, and that good is bad, if you can make them accept that everything is subjective and relative, then you own them. They will believe any drivel."

That drivel might spurt from the mouth of the advertiser, the sleazebag on the corner, or the friend who says, "Try this."

Cutters and other self-injurers would love Mikhail Bakunin. "The passion for destruction is also a creative passion," wrote this nineteenth-century Russian anarchist often credited alongside Nietzsche with launching nihilism as a social movement.

Bakunin was writing during a wrenchingly transformative time in history. The Industrial Revolution taking place all around him—

as millions fled their villages and traditional trades to labor in urban factories—was the first in a series of upheavals that wrought
lasting wounds on the Western psyche. These new urban masses
became faceless, losing their old bonds with nature; the new machines already dehumanizing them, as depicted in Fritz Lang's
1927 film *Metropolis*, one of whose most memorable characters is a
robot woman, the *Maschinenmensch*.

The soul, acclimating itself to concrete and steel, becomes cal-
loused. World War I was another awful blow, a purposeless debacle
that decimated an entire generation. Further hardened—because
how else to survive such inhumanity?—the West then endured the
Great Depression, then the Holocaust, and then more wars. Despite all the achievements and progress and joys of these last two
hundred years, it's no secret why cynicism and disillusionment
crept into the collective heart.

As for why cynicism and disillusionment became trendy, it's because nihilism suits many agendas. After stating outright that nothing means anything and nothing is true, the loser in any given
argument or conflict can declare: "Your victory is not a victory. Because nothing is true, the narrative on which you based your strategies cannot be true. Since everything is meaningless, the principles
you purport to uphold are meaningless."

See how convenient that is? Nihilism is the only means by which
losers can "win."

With the rise of victim chic and affliction chic and addiction
chic, nihilism has become the worldview du jour. Every underdog
is the loser in some arena, and at this point in history every underdog has mastered nihilistic rhetoric.

The general effect is to abolish not meaning but the public's belief in meaning: a malaise clearly illustrated—to choose just two

current examples—by the creationism/evolution debates and the claims that the World Trade Center attacks were an inside job engineered by the U.S. government.

Art and popular culture always siphon the strongest latest social currents, charting the state of the heart. Artists and creators of popular culture must continually push the envelope, creating ever more extreme renditions of the worldview du jour. Thus, an ambient nihilism built up over centuries of urbanization and dehumanization and war is supersized on-screen and on the page and through the microphone. The turn of the last millennium was a heyday for critically acclaimed, frankly nihilistic films such as *Fight Club*, *Natural Born Killers*, *Se7en*, and *Pulp Fiction*. Technical and artistic merits notwithstanding, these films display and rhapsodize moral wastelands. No character emerges as a real hero. All are compromised composites of brutal and brilliant qualities: These mixtures, we understand, are meant to keep us from defining anyone or anything as definitively good or bad and to punish us for even contemplating such definitions. We are instead to sit back passively and nonjudgmentally, simply letting the sexy gorgeous ultraviolence and confusion wash over us. (That these characters often also glamorize addiction is another piece of the puzzle, as we'll see later in this chapter.) This is the ethos of the twenty-first-century audience: lumpen. And, in our refusal to condemn any behavior, resolute.

In this burgeoning genre, protagonists are no more virtuous than antagonists. Kindness and care go unrewarded. Cruelty goes unpunished. It's all clever and wry and rebellious and ugly-beautiful and at some point in almost all films of this type, someone vomits graphically—just to prove that there are no longer any limits to what is acceptable, much less entertaining. Ugly is the new, new black.

In eras past, humanity defined itself by its quests: for love or knowledge, freedom or victory. Hip nihilism also renders obsolete even the concept of a quest. It mocks all grails and those who hunt them, tells us rainbows end only in air.

If nothing is magnificent enough to merit quests, then what are we to seek these days but chemical adventures and cheap thrills, again, again, again?

Bad habits fill our holes.

Bad habits fill the spaces that might otherwise be occupied by hopes, dreams, ambitions, beliefs. Bad habits bandage unhealed wounds. Bad habits fill those scary gaps left by what we *do not have and do not know and do not do and do not realize we miss.*

What is your habit filling in for?

Kate Holden was an intelligent, educated, energetic, attractive middle-class young woman whose heroin addiction was her version of a quest, repeated at least once a day: "You must get the money"—which meant, in her case, sex work—"find the dealer, arrange the equipment. Then you take the little grain of promise, and you dissolve it, and you draw it up into a needle; you hold it in your hand, and you push it into your flesh."

My starvation habit served a purpose, too, though not the one I believed it served then. I thought I did it to stay thin. But what it really was was my version of victory. I was a coddled only child from a suburban paradise where everyone made everything easy for me, because of love and to salve their own fears. And what they could not shield me from, they warned, would kill me, and thus kill them, too: they'd die of grief. This is how I avoided challenges and risks and never knew what I was made of, what I could take on, what I could take. Yet humanity burns to know, testing itself with harsh initiations, imitation horrors. Having none, I felt fetal, unformed. Starvation in a land of luxury was my test, false yet all too real. Anorexia was my boot camp.

In my family, Penny's lateness fills in for the confrontations, even ordinary conversations, she wanted yet never had with those closest to her at crucial phases in her life: during her dad's affair, perhaps, or her parents' divorce or when a friend's father made advances to her or when she moved out of the family home forever at age fourteen. Besides brief bursts of invective and tears, they never talked about it meaningfully at the time or afterwards. Twenty years hence, everyone acts as if none of it ever happened. Just under the surface, barely covered, those conversations that never were still fester, gape, and sear.

Empty bed? Empty wallet? Empty hours? Bad habits can be found to fill them all. Bad habits are surrogate spouses, surrogate pals, surrogate religions and places to go. They are surrogate jobs: they look and feel like work, as Holden's to-do list reveals. *See how busy I am?*

Belonging to the blank generation, we begin our bad habits. Why not, we ask, when nothing is definitively good or bad? We seem decisive doing the tasks our habits require. They go from double-dare to hobby to identity.

And then we say we cannot stop.

And then they say we're sick.

The world's leading mental-health reference guide is the *Diagnostic and Statistical Manual of Mental Disorders*. The *DSM-IV*, as its fourth edition is familiarly called, is published by the American Psychiatric Association in collaboration with nine other officially sanctioned organizations, including the American Academy of Pediatrics and the American Medical Association. Its criteria serve as virtual medical gospel for millions of professionals worldwide.

When a set of symptoms is classified and named as a disorder in the *DSM*, it becomes official. Patients can be diagnosed with it and defined as sick, eligible for treatment.

The *DSM-IV* defines hundreds of ailments related to intoxicants, repetitive behaviors, and other bad habits. Even a single inebriant offers the diagnostician a wide range of potential diagnoses. For example, someone who has an alcohol habit might be diagnosed with Alcohol-Induced Anxiety Disorder. Then again, if she is forgetful, she might be tagged with Alcohol-Induced Persisting Amnestic Disorder. She might alternatively be diagnosed with Alcohol-Induced Mood Disorder, Alcohol-Induced Persisting Dementia, Alcohol-Induced Psychotic Disorder, Alcohol-Induced Sexual Dysfunction, or Alcohol-Induced Sleep Disorder. She might also be diagnosed with several of the aforementioned disorders at once. What you call coffee jitters could be tagged Caffeine-Induced Anxiety Disorder and/or Caffeine-Induced Sleep Disorder.

To aid in the diagnosis of Pathologic Gambling Disorder, mental-health professionals have devised a mnemonic, based on symptoms cited in the *DSM-IV*. It's based on the acronym WAGER OFTEN:

Withdrawal (characterized by restlessness upon trying to quit)
Affects Relationships (e.g., with spouse, job, career)
Goal is to get even (e.g., compensate for losses by gambling again)

Escape (e.g., one "gambles as a way to escape problems or
relieve dysphoric mood, helplessness, guilt, anxiety, or
depression")

Rescue (e.g., requires financial bailing out by others)

Outside the law (e.g., has broken it)

Failure to control

Tolerance (e.g., raised tolerance as one gambles with increasing
amounts of money).

Evades telling the truth.

Needs to think about next gambling venture.

So—does that sound like a disease to you? Or rather a personality trait, and a list of the social consequences resulting from repetitive behavior? Can you measure "affects relationships" with an X-ray, or view the molecular structure of "evades telling the truth" with an electron microscope?

Addiction is one of the fastest-growing medical specialties. Addiction clinics proliferate like mushrooms worldwide and the word "addiction," in the same manner as "disease," is being applied to a soaring number of habits that have nothing to do with substances. In 2007, the world's first residential clinic for online game addicts, Gamesterdam, opened in Amsterdam. It was a brainchild of the twelve-step-based Smith & Jones Addiction Consultancy, which calls itself a "lifestyle coaching company." A promo explains: "Xbox, Counter Strike, Quake and EverQuest are names that many of us have never heard. . . . For many young people these names have become an obsession. Computer and video games can be fun and innocent. . . . However, 20% of all gamers can develop a dependency." This affliction, we are warned, can grip kids as young as eight.

"When an alcoholic in denial is brought [in] for an intervention," the Smith & Jones website explains, "our staff is trained to ask the individual certain questions in order to look for evidence of disease symptoms. When we started asking these same questions to compulsive gamers, we were surprised to hear many of the same responses. Things like obsessive thinking, health problems, long-term damage to personal relationships, education, and careers were all classic signs of a serious addiction."

So that's their definition of disease. Cancer creates "health problems," certainly. And cancer can do "long-term damage to personal relationships, education, and careers." Cancer can lead to obsessive thinking, such as *Why me?*

Same with online gaming, of course.

The definitions of the words "addiction" and "dependency" have been in flux for decades (although Jacques Derrida would say they mean nothing at all), with some professionals decreeing that addiction is uncontrolled, compulsive use or behavior, others flat-out calling it a medical disease, and others striving to differentiate between physical dependence and psychological dependence, then striving further for ways to measure compulsion. Is it an on-off situation, in which you're either compulsive or not . . . or can you be a little bit compulsive, just a tad—but not enough to be labeled an addict?

Obviously, physical dependency can be proven by the onset of withdrawal symptoms when one attempts to quit. But other factors are in play. Can cravings, like compulsion, be quantified, codified, and pathologized?

The definitions will change a hundred times again between the moment I write this and the moment you read this.

Standard addiction treatment in the West includes psycho-therapy, prescription medications, and twelve-step membership.

Doctors and psychotherapists strongly endorse the twelve-step model most famously associated with Alcoholics Anonymous, and the sentences of many convicted criminals stipulate that they join such programs. (In 1996, Arizona became the first state in which first- and second-time nonviolent drug offenders were systematically sentenced to mandatory treatment in lieu of incarceration.) Medications are prescribed in many treatment programs, even for addictions that are not substance-based. Antidepressants are commonly prescribed, but new medications targeting cravings and compulsions are in constant development for a burgeoning market. In 2001, fifty-five different medications were being developed at the medical branch of the U.S. National Institute on Drug Abuse— and that is just one branch at one institute among hundreds around the world. Since then, according to NIDA director Nora Volkow, the institute has been "investing in the development of new medications for methamphetamine addiction" and "pursuing the development of an immunization strategy based on monoclonal antibodies for the treatment of methamphetamine overdose." New drugs are being created to control our lack of control over . . . drugs.

With the growing acceptance of the disease theory, bad habits are increasingly presented in courtrooms as mitigating circumstances that could be interpreted as "My client couldn't help it—he's sick!" Matthew Knippenberg was charged in 2005 with sexual battery and impersonating a police officer after he fondled a group of children at an Indiana playground. According to the official court document, Knippenberg claimed he had groped the children "because he was under the influence of methadone and Xanax." He told the court that "his substance abuse problems led to the present offenses,

and [that] such problems 'explain' these offenses and warrant a reduced sentence." Of course, the crushing irony is that he was being
prescribed methadone and Xanax to control his other addictions.
Not only is addiction a valid excuse for misbehavior but even the
treatment for addiction is an excuse now, too.

Tennessee teacher Pamela Rogers served jail time for having
had sexual relations with a thirteen-year-old student. Then she vio-
lated her probation by e-mailing nude photos of herself to the boy.
Her plea to avoid being sent back to jail in 2006 included a psycho-
therapist's testimony that Rogers was a sex addict. At a 2001 trial in
Chicago, Elizabeth Roach claimed that a shopping addiction led
her to embezzle nearly $250,000 from her employer. During one of
many sprees, she bought a $7,000 belt buckle and a $3,000 pair of
earrings. Although theft of this magnitude normally carries a
prison sentence of at least a year, Judge Matthew Kennelly decreed
no prison time and only five years' probation for Roach, telling the
court that his ruling was based on his perception that "Ms. Roach
could not control her compulsion to shop" and "was not able to
fully control the things she did."

What kind of quicksand is this? Will a serial killer get off scot-
free someday after persuading a jury that he has an uncontrollable
"throat-slashing addiction" or "Uzi-shooting disease"?

Fox News legal analyst and New York University law professor
Lis Wiehl calls addiction "the new 'Twinkie defense'"—alluding
to the landmark 1979 case in which ex-firefighter Dan White, who
slew San Francisco mayor George Moscone and city supervisor
Harvey Milk, was convicted of manslaughter rather than murder
based on the claim that he had eaten sweets, which clouded his
mind and made him incapable of premeditating the crime.

"The next time you get caught doing something stupid," Wiehl writes, "whether it's speeding, faking an illness to avoid work, or literally getting caught with your hand in a cookie jar—don't just stand there foolishly accepting responsibility for what you've done. Simply explain that some addiction and/or Twinkies made you do it. It couldn't hurt—and who knows, it might even get you off the hook!"

As anthropologists and sociologists will tell you, humans tend to choose their behavior based on what, in any given time and place, is considered acceptable to their particular communities. In most human communities, we fear shame. We fear jeers. We fear blame, condemnation, ostracism, extradition, exile. In times past, as Hansen's disease sufferers and everyone who was ever tarred and feathered and run out of town on rails knew, banishment often amounted to a death sentence.

Each culture condemns a certain set of behaviors, but *what* each culture condemns changes from era to era, from place to place. Gambling, punching, public nudity: depending on where and when one lives, such habits are scorned, accepted, admired, or somewhere in between. (Multiple standards within cultures, such as on gender or class lines, further subdivide habits into "acceptable" and "unacceptable.") Some of our ancestors were locked in the stocks for drinking or branded with hot irons for blasphemy, but we won't be. On the other hand, most of our ancestors would not have lost their jobs for making racial slurs, but we probably would. "Animal Bordellos Draw Norwegians," reads a 2006 headline in Norway's *Aftenposten* newspaper about clubs in Scandinavia where humans have sex with dogs and other vertebrates. Yet in Massachusetts in 1642, a youth named Thomas Granger was hanged for having sexually penetrated "a mare, a cow, two goats, five sheep, two calves and a turkey," as Plymouth governor William Bradford reported in his diary. Bradford added that, as specified in Leviticus, these animals were "cast into a great and large pit that was digged for the purpose for them, and no use was made of any part of them."

Standards change. What was once forbidden is now permitted, what was once commonplace is now outlawed. Of what our forebears called the Seven Deadly Sins, we are absolved. If we could see just fifty years into the future, watch which habits will be commonplace and shunned, we would be stunned.

In seventh grade, I wanted and did not want to do drugs. I didn't want to, knowing what my dad would do if he found out. I didn't want to, because it might interfere with my straight As. I didn't want to, fearing that all drugs were truth serums and I would look the fool. But I wanted to, too. How could I not? It was the '70s. Being cool pretty much required either doing drugs or acting like you did.

Some choice.

We hummed along with catchy drug songs. "One toke over the line," sang Brewer and Shipley. "We're goin' to get high, high, high," sang Paul McCartney and Wings. The narrator of Steve Miller's "The Joker" called himself "a midnight toker" and we giggled as we sang along. "She don't lie, she don't lie, she don't lie: cocaine," chanted Eric Clapton. The Doobie Brothers had named their band after pot itself. We memorized Cheech and Chong routines, reciting riffs in fake stoner voices about joints, munchies, and narcs. We warned each other not to "bogart" diving boards and birthday cake and we smirked faux-knowingly when we heard, in any context, the words "grass," "acid," or "lid."

After-school TV was peppered with public-service announcements telling us not to do drugs: in one, a toothy monkey shrieked while clinging to a girl's back; in another, a voice intoned, "Why do you think they call it 'dope'?" But popular culture, which those ads were up against, had a far stronger pull. My favorite song in seventh grade was Black Sabbath's pot paean "Sweet Leaf." I had never smoked pot in my life. My stereo blared this anthem to something of which I knew nothing. My friends and I doodled pot leaves everywhere, reverently drawing jagged-edged foliage that we had never actually seen.

We were in training.

Wearing T-shirts that said STONED AGAIN and THINGS GO BETTER WITH COKE, we were walking advertisements, eager bearers of the emblems of an addict aesthetic, an addict attitude—*addictude*—that was becoming mainstream. Southern California, where I lived, might have been in the lead, but addictude advanced across the landscape as control of the arts, culture, and commerce transferred from the hands of squares to the hands of the hip. By the early '70s, marketers and screenwriters and journalists and the heads of major corporations were veterans of the '60s and its youth-culture boom. These new leaders had grown up with rock 'n' roll and rebellion. The new products, programs, movies, music, art, styles, icons, and lexicon they introduced and that flooded the market during my adolescence glamorized the very habits that just a few years earlier had been almost universally denounced. Having bad habits has been sexy ever since.

It is a confluence of convenience, of cashings in. When anyone anywhere lights up, shoots up, snorts, splurges, gorges, purges, or the thousand other things that humans do that become bad habits, hark and hear countless cash registers clang *ka-ching*—as dollar signs flash in countless corporate eyes.

Your bad habits might not involve drugs or alcohol or any other substance. Mine don't. Even so, do you have any idea how many factions stand to gain from your bad habit, your weakness, your treat, that thing you do? You think you're independent, an individual, autonomous. That is part of the trick.

You are a slave, not just to the activity itself but to countless strangers, companies, and institutions that you cannot see, a row of linked arms extending over hill and dale, commanding you and extracting your time, your mind, your cash.

Since the earliest days of cinema, movies have functioned as extended cigarette commercials. One could hardly fail to notice how many films prominently feature cool, sexy, savvy characters who smoke. All the best heroes, the sultriest temptresses, the suavest villains, the most lovable rebels smoked—not just smoked, but smoked as a part of their identity. Humphrey Bogart's Sam Spade character, Sean Connery's James Bond, James Dean's rebels—and many more, puffing away, saturating the film industry and our collective unconscious since the earliest days of talkies.

This propaganda was no accident. Until recently, it was standard practice for tobacco companies to pay filmmakers to ensure that characters in their productions would be shown smoking the companies' products. As one among countless examples, Philip Morris paid $350,000 to have its Lark brand featured in the 1989 James Bond film *Licence to Kill*. Although this practice was officially banned later that year, eleven years later a study funded by the National Cancer Institute found that tobacco was still very visible in films—in fact, it was even more visible than it had been before the ban. According to the 2000 report, 85 percent of the major releases included in the survey showed tobacco use, 28 percent showed cigarette-brand logos, and 11 percent showed characters openly endorsing certain brands. At a minimum, those 28 percent of films displaying cigarette logos were paid to do so, as part of what the industry calls "product placement." Logos virtually never appear in mainstream films by accident, or for free. If a film character is drinking a beer, for example, and you catch a glimpse of its brand name on the bottle, know that you have just seen an advertisement, embedded surreptitiously in the scene. If no beer company is willing to pony up cash for product placement, then the set designer will make sure the beer bottle is rotated in the character's hand so that no logo shows. No major film studio gives away free product placement.

As for the films that depict smoking but don't show specific brands: in some cases they were paid to do so by the tobacco industry as a group to promote smoking as a concept. In other cases, the producers—themselves influenced by previous decades of brainwashing—just think smoking looks cool and will thus render their movies cool.

Indie films are notorious for this. It's ironic. As *independent* productions, they purport to purvey . . . rugged independence. Yet the typical indie film includes harrowed, intense chain-smokers and/or other types of addicts. (Surprise, surprise: they're usually nihilists too.)

In May 2007, the Motion Picture Association of America announced plans to assign film ratings based on how much smoking was depicted in productions. According to an official MPAA statement, "depictions that glamorize smoking or movies that feature pervasive smoking outside of a historic or other mitigating context may receive a higher rating." The Harvard School of Public Health, commissioned by the MPAA to study the issue, recommended in February 2007 that studios "take substantive and effective action to eliminate the depiction of smoking from films accessible to children and youths." Knowing how skilled the powerful smoking and film industries are at diving through loopholes, some antismoking activists remained skeptical. University of California professor of medicine Stan Glantz, who heads the advocacy group Smoke Free Movies, called the MPAA announcement "just a placebo."

So much is invested in winning and keeping customers. And it's not just cigarettes. Fast-food chains, sugary breakfast cereals, and other foods also receive prominent product placement in a substantial percentage of contemporary films. Meanwhile, the number of obese viewers keeps rising. But perhaps the most ubiquitous—and problematic—product placement involves alcoholic beverages.

Young rap and hip-hop fans "are more likely to have problems with alcohol, drugs and violence than listeners of other types of music," according to a 2006 report by the Pacific Institute for Research and Evaluation. PIRE's researchers attributed their findings to "the alcohol industry's use of rap and hip-hop to market products." Even a quick immersion into that genre's lyrics and videos induces product-placement overload. It's sad—both to see kids targeted as suckers and to see kids acceding so eagerly, thinking they're dissing the Man, yet being such corporate dupes. Talk about shooting fish in a barrel.

"Pass the Hennessy," sang Tupac Shakur in "Hail Mary," boosting the cognac brand that is a hip-hop status symbol. "I'm drinking Hennessy while tryin' to make it last," he sang in "Life Goes On." "I'm sippin' Hennessy and Coke although addicted to weed smoke," he sang in "Heaven Ain't Hard 2 Find." "Let you get my last shot of Hennessy, ain't never had a friend like me," he sang in "Never Had a Friend Like Me." "Champagne, Hennessy, a favorite of my homies when we floss on our enemies," he sang in "How

Do U Want It." "Wanna know who's my role model? It's in the brown bottle—you know our motherfucking motto: Hennessy," he sang in "Hennessy." "Dip yo' dick in some Hennessy," sang Too Short in "Candy Paint." "I Like Hennessy and beer," sang Kurupt in "The Hardest Mutha Fuckaz." Recently I visited a makeshift Oakland street-corner memorial marking the spot where a young man had been shot to death the day before. In a place of honor alongside votive candles spelling out RIP NATE was a row of empty Hennessy bottles.

We think of our habits as ourselves.

At another online forum for "cutters"—that is, those who habitually and deliberately cut their own flesh—the user who calls himself gRaFFiTiDeKoRaTiOnS writes: "I self harm, and I have consistently done so since age twelve. . . . If a person has a problem with the fact that I self harm, or has a problem with any other aspect of my personality then . . . I dont want to associate with that person." At the same forum, rockergoddess explains that cutting is "a part of you . . . part of the package that makes up who you are. It is important to me to find people who can accept the entire package that is me." Another user, Benningasm, adds: "My arms are fucked from the scars, which I'm [having] surgery for." Yet "my scars, to me, are the most beautiful thing ever." Behold the legacy of false autonomy.

That same sensibility characterizes the thriving "pro-ana" movement, whose adherents embrace their anorexia. Pro-ana websites such as Houseofthin.com, Proanamia.com, and Anafriends.com offer "thinspiration"—pictures of thin celebrities, tips on how not to eat, lists of songs containing overt or covert "be thin" messages (such as Pulp's "Anorexic Beauty," which praises a woman's "feather-weight perfection"). Anafriends includes "Fasts and Competitions" and forums on "Fave Food That Isn't Really Food"—including black coffee, chipped ice, sugar-free gum, and sugar-free Red Bull.

My habit makes me beautiful and makes me me.

Describing her site's name, Houseofthin's creator writes that its acronym is "pretty awesome too. H.O.T."

We start learning addiction the minute we start watching TV or being pushed along supermarket aisles in strollers.

Children learn languages early and at warp speed, and the language of advertising is no exception. Until the middle of the twentieth century, kids weren't considered a viable consumer demographic. In the old days, ads for toys and children's food products were aimed exclusively at parents. *Your little ones will love our nutritious, delicious cereal.* By the 1960s, kids were becoming a major market sector. Soon they were revealed as a virtual gold mine. By the 1990s, ads were targeting toddlers. The latest demographic is the prespeech set. Attracted by logos and color schemes, infants have shown an ability to discern between brands by the age of eighteen months and can demand brands by name by age two, according to investigative journalist Susan Gregory Thomas, author of *Buy, Buy Baby*. She laments that these "youngest consumers in American history" are being manipulated to get stuck not only on unhealthy foods but also on the "ills that rampant materialism used to visit only on adults—from anxiety to hypercompetitiveness to depression."

Also credulity. Dependency. Lack of restraint. Impatience. Bad-habit building blocks.

Many child-advocacy groups agree, working to outlaw ads aimed at kids. Such ads have been banned in Sweden since 1991, based on the notion that they are "unfair" in principle, as studies have shown that while children younger than age ten certainly discern between brands, they cannot clearly tell the difference between advertising and programming. (Swedish broadcasts of the Japanese cartoon show *Pokémon* are edited to exclude its standard tagline "Gotta catch 'em all," which sounds like—and is—an inducement to buy Pokémon products.) Junk-food ads were banned from British children's programming in 2006. But kiddie advertising in the United States remains rampant. The Federal Trade Commission proposed banning such ads in the 1970s, but Congress overruled the measure. And now a steady stream of popular cartoon characters are pressed into service as product pitchmen.

It's as easy as selling candy to a baby, because it *is* selling candy to babies.

Spider-Man hawks Nesquik chocolate-flavored cereal. To coincide with the release of *Shrek 2* in 2004, General Mills launched a new Shrek cereal, its sugary morsels shaped like characters in the film. "We're so excited to bring the *Shrek* experience to life in a new way," General Mills promotion planner Andrea Arlich said at the time. "Shrek and his friends are so popular with kids . . . these products offer a new opportunity to interact with the lovable DreamWorks characters." In other words: we can sell a few cents' worth of flour, oil and sweeteners for several dollars if we just mold it into little globules that vaguely resemble familiar characters from another corporate product, a major-studio movie. More themed products were released to coincide with the third film in the *Shrek* series, *Shrek the Third*, in 2007—including green Shrek Cheetos, Shrek Pez dispensers, Shrek M&M's, and Shrek-related toy offers advertised on over sixty different Kellogg's-brand breakfast foods, from Rice Krispies to Eggo Flip Flop Choco-'Nilla waffles to Mini Swirlz Cinnamon Bun cereal to Yogos Bits Strawberry Slam. When McDonald's introduced a Shrek-themed Happy Meal, the pop-culture gossip blog defamer.com joked that it should have a "Puss 'n Boots My First Glucose Monitor and Donkey's Own Bodyfat Calibrator included with every purchase."

Child-development expert Susan Linn notes that a key message in marketing today "is that kids should not be satisfied with one of anything." Ads aimed at kids trigger what industry insiders call "the nag factor"—such that shopping trips "will be characterized by squeals of joy every time" the child sees the familiar character, product, or logo, "and cries of disappointment" if the parent fails to respond. This pattern reinforces not only stuckness in habits but also greed, impulsiveness, impatience, and brand loyalty—all of which "are antithetical," Linn asserts, "to those qualities necessary in a healthy democratic citizenry."

We fall into habits instinctively. As noted throughout this book, autopilot is a natural, usually neutral, coping device. Advertisers merely strive to use it toward their own ends. They figure that you're bound to get stuck on *some* form of footwear or refreshing beverage anyway. So let it be Nikes. Or Coors. The trouble lies not in our instincts but in how marketing warps our instincts with "more, now, again" desperation.

Our habits make strangers rich. If your habit leads eventually to your death, these rich strangers grieve only in having lost another customer-cum-slave, another source of income. But new ones are born every minute. Our masters love that.

They also love how bad habits make us behave. Docilely. Pre-dictably. Because even when we think we're misbehaving, those of us with bad habits are almost invariably following *someone's* orders, whether it's a corporation's or a pop-culture icon's or a false friend's, hup two three. Bad habits make us easy to trick. Easy to track. Easy to trap.

Our loss of control is their gain.

The language of advertising is the language of addiction.

In the '60s, Lay's potato-chip commercials taunted viewers with the slogan *Bet you can't eat just one*. (Funny, they were right.) Commercials for Coca-Cola's Dasani bottled water warn: *Can't live without it*. (Uh-oh. Really?) How do advertisements work? Usually by depicting human beings tormented by desire. Ravening. Drooling. Chewing their lips, whimpering. They overcome obstacles to acquire the objects of their desire. They beg. They plead. They undergo endurance tests. *I'd walk a mile for a Camel*. Then they get what they want, and they're in ecstasy.

We sympathize. We empathize. Watching that sizzling burger, that melting cheese, that sleek car rounding a curve, we come to see that desire is intolerably painful but reassuringly universal—we've all been there—and quenchable with a quick transfer of funds.

Ads magnify the trauma of desire. The angst of craving. The human-rights crime of deprivation. All day every day, ads reinforce this pain-acquisition-reward sequence in our minds.

My friend Megan, whose impulse shopping led to bankruptcy, used to glide around stores with an anguished look, jaw tense, hands shaking as she plucked items from shelves and flung them into her basket without looking at their prices. At the cash register, shaking worse, she would recoil as the sums added up.

"You don't need all this," I would say.

"Without it," Megan retorted, "I'd feel deprived."

A lot of money and talent go into making shoppers feel like this. Careers in marketing are forged perfecting the exact panic that Megan felt when she sat at home before a shopping spree, tapping her feet, craving candy or a new mascara, telling herself *I shouldn't*, then seizing her purse and car keys and scrambling to the door. Companies spend $30 billion every year advertising food products in the United States, $370 million on advertising electronic games. (Gamesterdam, take note.) The beverage industry's combined advertising budget was $3.5 billion in 2005. McDonald's currently spends over $1 billion a year on marketing.

Choose me.

Brand loyalty is stuckness on that product and that brand. Brand-logo clothing proclaims STUCK AND PROUD. Wearing brand-logo clothing, we are pushers, luring others to get stuck with us.

Surrounded as we are by ads, walled in by ads, mainlining ads, we are perpetually wired to feel a keening desire for objects, substances, speed, sensual thrills, and illusions of instant escape.

Watching ads, we do not learn to stop and think. We do not learn to wonder what we want. We do not learn to wait. Ads say: *Just do it*.

Now.

America's watchwords are freedom and democracy and independence. Those terms suit our consumption strategies as well. Choosing from a range of options gives us a sense of freedom and democracy and independence. It feeds our sense of power and luxury and autonomy. We shudder to think of other systems in which no choice is permitted, no options given. We shudder to think of one-style-only dress shops in the former USSR, of theocracies whose citizens are allowed to practice only one religion. Our wide range of choices makes us feel superior.

Yet while we bridle at the prospect of having no options, we cannot handle a multiplicity of options, either. Faced with more than a certain number of possibilities, we enter a panic state that researchers call "choice overload." In one experiment, Columbia's Sheena Iyengar and Stanford's Mark Lepper offered different-sized assortments of Godiva chocolates to successive groups of test subjects. One group was given no choices: each member simply received one piece not of his or her volition. Another group was offered an assortment of six candy varieties, from which they could select just one. Another was offered a range of thirty varieties and were also asked to select one piece from among the range of shapes and flavors. All the groups were then asked to report on their experiences.

The unhappiest group of all was the group offered no choices. The group that was permitted to choose from among six options had a better time: they felt calm and empowered. But the enjoyment level dropped in the group offered the widest assortment, thirty candy varieties. Although members of this group were excited to see the large range, after the selection process they were "more dissatisfied and regretful of the choices they made" than were members of the group offered only six options. "Choosers in extensive-choice contexts enjoy the choice-making process more," Iyengar and Lepper noted, "presumably because of the opportunities it affords—but also feel more responsible for the choices they make, resulting in frustration with the choice-making process and dissatisfaction." The prospect of "unlimited options" overwhelms and upsets choosers, the scholars noted.

If even thirty proves to be "many more choices than they can possibly handle," consider that the average supermarket offers over fifty thousand choices.

"How," Iyengar and Lepper wondered, "can there be so much dissatisfaction in the face of so much opportunity?"

In a world of infinite choices, we retreat into our shells, totally overwhelmed, and comfort ourselves with choosing the same exact thing over and over: getting stuck.

Choice overload expands beyond consumer products. Life in a complicated, crowded, busy world comprises "an endless series of choices," writes social theorist Barry Schwartz, author of *The Paradox of Choice: Why More Is Less*. "As choices proliferate, people have a harder and harder time making decisions. And they end up less satisfied with the decisions they make. They are filled with regret over those that turned out well but might have been better."

When choices disappoint, he adds, choosers "blame themselves. The result is stress, unhappiness, and in extreme cases, clinical depression."

We dodge the prospect of that pain by abdicating our autonomy. As our world becomes ever more glutted with options, our decision-making faculties freeze from the angst of choice overload. Habits and favorites become more than mere sorting tools. They become panic reactions: symptoms of systemic shock.

And, as such, harder to break.

Five thousand new books are released in the United States every month. Hundreds of TV channels beckon. TIVO and iPods and their offshoots "allow us to edit out every moment of every cultural object or event that doesn't suit us," Schwartz writes. Yet "there can be too much of a good thing," and "a point can be reached at which options paralyze rather than liberate."

And we get stuck "choosing" the same thing over and over.

Companies and technology further entrench this sameness—the mindless, relentness repetition that breeds habits—with "choice filters": artificial constructs that preselect and shrink the range of options available in any given situation. Again we trust machines more than we trust ourselves. Examples of choice filters at Amazon .com are those clickable "Recommended Based on Your Browsing History" and "Customers who bought this item also bought" lists: computer-generated presorts to "save" us the "trouble" of perusing the site's enormous inventory.

"There are now so many magazines narrowly tailored to particular interests that there is no need, ever, to read about something that lies outside your existing worldview," Schwartz observes. "We are more reliant on filters now than we ever were before. We couldn't get through a day without them." And the more options that arise, "the more driven most people will be to settle on the most choice-simplifying filters they can find." Those who continually "opt for the same old thing" and "rely on filters rather than on themselves," Schwartz warns, "become more passive."

Our struggle to maintain control spins us out of control—and into the grip of whatever forces we allow to do our choosing for us. It's a self-imposed totalitarianism: a dictatorship in which you get to personally select your very own dictator.

When we say "I know what I like," do we mean it? Or do we mean that we fear what we don't know and haven't tried?

The prospect of coming unstuck by changing ourselves—despite an endless flood of self-help books—has become yet another anathema in a culture that raises its children to believe themselves perfect. As we saw in the previous chapter, this message infuses academia from nursery school onward. It is mainly a product of the self-esteem movement that began in the 1970s and crystallized in the 1980s as educators decided that children who felt good about themselves—who neither judged themelves harshly nor allowed themselves to be judged harshly by others—would never misbehave, since misbehavior was seen as stemming from low self-esteem.

A seminal teachers' handbook in this movement, published in 1976, is Harold Wells and Jack Canfield's *100 Ways to Enhance Self-Concept in the Classroom*. Illustrated with pictures of happy children, it details lessons in which students create personal "me flags" and "me collages" and "me commercials." In one lesson, kids are exhorted to imagine themselves as "God of the universe." Several lessons teach kids to brag, urging them never to "disown the part of themselves that wants to brag and tell people how great they are." In several lessons devoted to bragging—one of these is called "Bragging"—teachers are instructed to have pupils take turns boasting to the rest of the class, "exaggerating by standing up proudly, throwing chests out, talking enthusiastically."

Canfield later became very successful as a motivational speaker and cocreator of the *Chicken Soup for the Soul* book series.

Lest you think that this was some kind of kook manual, too ludicrous to be taken seriously, please be aware that *100 Ways to Enhance Self-Concept in the Classroom* was a landmark text that has influenced American education ever since it was first released, and that the messages contained in it and in similar books have become nearly universal in classrooms. Adults born before 1964 who never had kids of their own might have no idea how much has changed since their schooldays. In my mid-'60s elementary-school classes, whenever any smart-alecky kid would show off or boast, our teachers would intone, "Nobody likes a braggart" and send the offender into a corner to think it over. Humility and modesty were not just considered virtues but enforced with a firm hand. (And that was public school, not Catholic school.) Now the poles have reversed. The boastful child would be awarded a trophy.

How does this relate to bad habits? Well, in *100 Ways* and similar books, children learn to dismiss criticism wholesale, no matter its context or content and no matter the critic. In a lesson called "Positive Mantram" in *100 Ways*, kids are asked "to imagine the face of someone who has put them down in some way in the past—a parent, teacher, coach, friend, fellow student, Girl Scout leader, policeman, etc."—and then to "close their eyes and repeat in unison . . . the chant: 'No matter what you say or do to me, I'm still a worthwhile person!'"

Worthwhile, sure. But young minds might well interpret that as "No matter what you say or do to me, fuck off."

You might at this point be scratching your head, wondering what conceivable purpose such indoctrination could serve. Wells and Canfield were advocating the theory that children with positive self-images would excel at learning and be uninclined to misbehave. But the real message is almost guaranteed to cause stuckness and sustain bad habits: a child who grows up believing that criticisms— even from loved ones and law-enforcement officers—are nothing but nasty put-downs to be distrusted, dismissed, and drowned out is a child uninclined to self-assess, much less to change.

Add this educational "mantram" to the abdication of adult responsibility engendered by our addiction-themed pop culture with its beloved disease theory and the result is a petri dish for stuckness.

You're soaking in it.

Coming unstuck can be bitter and sweet. Carmen is a Nebraska geology professor who stopped drinking two years ago with the help of Alcoholics Anonymous. She muses: "Lately, things have been hard for me. I have been feeling really stuck. I keep coming up against long-term, complex problems in my life and nothing seems to make them better. And while there are some things I could do that might or might not help, it's been really, really hard for me to take action. So I go blaming myself again and again for being in this situation.

"But then I stop—and I put things in perspective, and then I remember to feel grateful for the little things that are going well. For example, I'm grateful that I've been sober for this long, and that the reason things aren't going so well has *nothing*—for the first time in a long time—to do with my drinking. I mean, sometimes I make mistakes. Everybody makes mistakes. But at least now I know I didn't make the mistake because I was too drunk last night to remember what I promised to do today. These days, it was just an honest mistake. I live my life honestly, and I try to do my best, and when I make a mistake I try to put it right, and that's the end of it. And when I think about that, and how different I am now from who I used to be, I guess I can live for a little longer with the things that aren't fixed yet."

Twelve-steppers place their faith in a so-called higher power. Many interpret this as a deity, though some consider the organization itself their higher power, or the meetings themselves. The point is that the power is outside oneself. Conceding any and all control over their addictions, twelve-steppers "turn our will and our lives over to the care of God."

"Let go and let God," their bumper stickers say.

In a mea culpa way, twelve-steppers who want to break their bad habits (from drinking to swearing to shopping too much) confess defects that they are "ready to have God remove." Indeed, they do the hard and shocking self-assessments, but ask their higher powers to perform the transformations rather than transform themselves.

"I am Mike, and I am grateful to a loving God, who chose me to be an alcoholic," writes a man posting a review of AA founder Bill Wilson's *Big Book* at Amazon.com.

On a website maintained by Alateen—the youth division of the twelve-step Al-Anon organization founded in 1951 by AA founder Bill Wilson's wife, Lois Wilson—a member calling herself Kwen S. writes: "I can admit I'm stuck, and that my efforts are useless. . . . I can pray. Who knows how God may respond? Perhaps . . . human help will arrive. Perhaps an overlooked fact or idea will come. Perhaps a definite sense of God's presence will give me hope . . . when I get stuck in life I Let Go and Let God. When I do that, I discover that a way opens where there was no way before."

Most rehab centers and support groups follow the twelve steps, which have helped countless millions. Nonetheless, critics deride the method's emphasis on powerlessness. Critics also distrust the twelve-step premise that recovery never really ends: that one cannot simply quit and be free, that one will *always* be an addict and must *always* attend meetings and *always* keep the steps in mind, just as diabetics must always take insulin. A promo for the world-renowned rehab facility Hazelden avows its commitment to the twelve-step philosophy "for lifelong recovery."

This approach is endorsed by celebrities—by the rich and pow-

erful publicly calling themselves powerless. One night in 2003, superstar fashion designer Calvin Klein disrupted a New York Knicks
basketball game by touching and talking to a player. In an official
apology that Klein issued subsequently, he stated that he'd been under the influence of mind-altering substances: "For many years, I've
been able to successfully address my substance abuse issues, which
for anyone is a lifelong process, through strict adherence to counseling and regular attendance at meetings. However, when I recently stopped attending meetings regularly, I suffered a setback."

So . . . on his own, without counseling and meetings, this famous multimillionaire simply cannot resist certain substances? If
he can't, we wonder despairingly, how can we?

For believers, faith is potent. The jury is still out on whether
that's because God actually exists or because going through the mo-
tions of handing the task to a higher power is a brilliant trick by
which we heal ourselves without being burdened by the awesome
responsibility of healing ourselves. Does it even matter? The twelve
steps attract furious criticism, largely from atheists. But if a higher
power works for some—if that's the kind smile waiting for them,
or the strong arms throwing down a rope—would you begrudge
them that? We cannot all be our own Superman.

As for the long-term effects of a medicated nation, only time
will tell. Why are we so willing to experiment on ourselves, and on
society as a whole?

But we must stop pretending that habits are not choices. We can
choose to forgo clearly dangerous or destructive behaviors just as
we can choose to ignore commercials telling us we cannot resist lic-
orice twists.

As a rule, shit doesn't simply happen. We make it happen every time we pick up the bottle or lay down a bet or unzip our pants or take out the wallet.

These things ain't going to quit themselves.

What works? Shame works.

During his first interview in the documentary *Methadonia*, a heroin addict named Steve nods out. He is dirty and raggedly dressed. Drool sluices from his lips as he stands upright on a sunny New York City street corner, eyes sliding shut halfway through a sentence he cannot complete.

Later in the film, we meet Steve again. But now he is transformed: clean, neatly dressed. He has found an apartment and has reunited with his long-estranged parents.

"When I think about all the misery I caused people," Steve tells the interviewer, "all the pain . . ."

We learn that after Steve spent years on drugs and failed at least one attempt at rehab, one drugged-out day his girlfriend happened to pick up from the floor a pair of socks he had just removed. She held them to her nose.

Reenacting this small gesture for the camera, Steve shakes his head in utter horror. That seemingly trivial moment had fundamentally changed his life. Staring into the lens, his eyes widen with unmistakable, scathing shame.

"My socks," he groans. "I didn't mean for her to find 'em. She smelled 'em."

He shakes his now neatly combed head.

"*She threw up*, they were so stinkin'. She could've left me on the stink socks alone." Steve's mouth trembles. "She could've left my ass on the stink socks alone, they was so funky."

That day, through her, he saw himself.

And he thought: *I induce vomiting.*

Not in just anyone, which would be bad enough, but in someone I don't want to lose.

For Steve, that was enough.

But why did it have to take so long?

What will be *your* stink-socks moment?

What works? Reality works.

For years, my friend Gerard exercised compulsively and ate very little—subsisting mainly on egg whites and espresso. He beamed with pride whenever new boyfriends praised his lean, boyish looks. Then one night, Gerard was staying with friends whose bathroom had floor-to-ceiling mirrors. As he stepped into the shower, "I turned and caught a glimpse of myself," Gerard remembers. "I'd seen myself naked before, obviously, but—"

Mimicking his reaction to the sight that night, his jaw drops.

"I'd never seen myself from every angle all at once, from the back and the sides."

Every bone showed, Gerard says. Sideways, he was practically a straight line.

Gerard had lost friends to AIDS. He wasn't HIV-positive, but that night in the bathroom, he says, "I looked like I might as well have been. I looked like they did at the end."

For him, that was enough.

What works? Replacing a harmful habit with a harmless habit works. Fear works. Love works.

By his early thirties, Ron Saxen had been alternating between binge eating and self-starvation for more than half his life. His weight would soar, then plummet via harsh diets—even, at one point, the "crystal meth diet," as Saxen calls it wryly.

"I really started to doubt I'd ever pull out of it," he says now, in retrospect. "How many times can you say, 'Starting tomorrow I'll be perfect for the rest of my life'? I spent a lot of time lamenting that if people knew how good-looking I really was beneath my fat they would be shocked. 'Beautiful Ron' was stuck beneath what the world saw on the surface. If they only knew, they would envy me. I can remember sitting on a park bench one day asking myself: *Would I give up an arm to be thin if I could be thin for the rest of my life?* I remember thinking: *Maybe.*"

During one slim phase when Saxen was working as a fashion model, a colleague's offhand suggestion about losing another few pounds sent him into a panic. Frustrated at his inability to lose more weight fast enough, Saxen gave up and began eating one-gallon sundaes again. While he called his thin self "Beautiful Ron," he called his heavy self "the Wrong Ron." Veering between the two had caused him to lose a career, a stint in the military, and relationships with friends, relatives, and romantic partners. He was not just out of control about food, but also about money and sex.

Being told that his weight could kill him was not enough to make "the Wrong Ron" stop. Nor was being called a "fat-ass-ten-sandwich-eating-motherfucker"—as he was one day by a suspected shoplifter he was trying to catch in the store he managed.

Then a car accident left his younger sister comatose. Keeping vigil in the hospital, Saxen thought deeply about life's fragility. Normally, he would have distracted himself from such unnerving ideas with a binge. But this time, instead, he just sat, feeling besieged by "the magnitude of . . . sins I'd committed against myself by making dumb fuck decisions and not having the balls to change course. In my thirty-three years, I'd already done so much and lost so much."

As he watched a loved one hover between life and death, his priorities realigned.

His sister regained consciousness and recovered. Saxen returned to his life, but with new values: he ended a troubled relationship, moved in with friends, started exercising with one of them, went to therapy, went back to work, and thanked his boss for having granted him time off to spend at the hospital. That thank-you bloomed into a meaningful relationship. Within five years, they were husband and wife. Saxen no longer binge eats. When he craves a treat, he watches a movie while eating a single candy bar— not a whole bag of bars as he used to do.

"All eating disorders have an adaptive function," Saxen says. "Until you discover what function your disorder serves, you are stuck in your disorder and stunted emotionally." As a teen, he started overeating to comfort himself in the midst of a large incompatible family that refused to address its frictions openly. He remembers vividly his first of many after-school dozen-egg omelets:

"If I could've coped and handled anxiety then as I do now"— with exercise and reasonable conversations—"instead of with food, who knows what or where I'd be? Love gave me the strength I didn't have. Even when you're in hell, you need someplace to go to before you can leave, and my wife—before she was my wife— showed me the place."

"I can't" often means "I won't."

You say you "can't" give up smoking. But what if you were

shipwrecked on an island with plenty of food and water—and not a single cigarette? What would happen then? Would you just die on the spot, for lack of cigarettes? Would your craving magically enable you to swim across the ocean simply because you *needed* a cigarette that badly? No. You'd cope. You'd get used to it. You'd quit. But being marooned on that island is only marginally different from sitting on the couch today and realizing you're out of cigarettes. Is it really worthwhile to get up and drive to the store for a pack of smokes? If it takes being on a desert island to make you realize that you value life more than your addiction, why not have the same revelation in your living room?

We cannot fathom having no excuses.

Growing up in lands of luxury, forgiving lands, a sizable proportion of us know that we will always be bailed out. Our culture has obliterated the exigency of being forced, just as it has made deprivation seem intolerable.

Growing up in lands of luxury, a sizable proportion of us do not want to wait, work hard, or endure pain—or even the slightest discomfort. Machines help us with this. So do the powers that be, patting our heads and giving us handouts. Desert islands mandate toil, patience, pain. Not suicidal pop-song pain, but pain with a purpose. With hope.

If you feel stuck, you might need to maroon yourself on your own inner island for a while, with nothing. And say: "I will create a new life for myself here. I'll become self-sufficient."

If I must, I must.

4.

THE HORROR, THE HORROR

Stuck on Trauma

Scar tissue is stronger than regular tissue.
Realize the strength, move on.

—HENRY ROLLINS

M y father never met his aunts, uncles, cousins, and grandparents. He never met the paternal clan in Minsk or Pinsk—
he never could remember which—who lost touch when his dad
died, which was in Brooklyn and quickly, grin-to-grave in four
days, leaving a non-English-speaking wife and four kids, my dad
still in diapers.

Nor did he know any on his mother's side. She had sailed alone
to America at eighteen, with nothing (it was said) but a pair of gar-
net earrings. Growing up, Dad knew their names and the names of
their villages—but heck, how could he meet them when they were
so far away and even poorer than his mother? Widowed, diabetic,
going blind, she sewed to pay rent on a tenement apartment with
no toilet of its own. Dad and his sisters chanted childhood rhymes
about the cold communal bathroom down the hall. They were so
poor that a neighbor offered to buy—adopt, he said—the cutest of
my aunts. My grandmother refused. She sent a few dollars each
month to her parents and siblings in Ukraine. They wrote back,

thanking her. If she was late, they wrote and asked: Where is our cash? She cooked the cheapest meals: kasha, potatoes, gizzards, hearts. Fruit was a rare treat, ice cream laughably deluxe. My dad, in his hand-me-downs, was jumped weekly by toughs. When they broke his glasses, he had to spend months squinting through the cracks. At fifteen, Dad caught meningitis—the same sickness that had killed *his* father, fourteen years before. He spent weeks in a hospital with twelve beds to a room, watching men and boys die of what he had. He survived, but was partly deaf. Not so deaf that he couldn't ship out during World War II. During the war, when he was in the Philippines, his mother kept sending cash to her European relatives. But now she never heard from them. She never, ever heard from any one of them again.

Growing up in Los Angeles, I used to ask my dad about his traumas. In the sun-washed backyard of our ranch-style house, with its suburban patio and cactus garden on a slope along a panoramic coast a half hour's drive from where he made a comfortable living as an aerospace engineer, I begged for details: anecdotes about poverty, tenements, disease.

"Oy," he said. "Who wants to dwell on that bad stuff?"

In cutoffs and flip-flops, making him recite the names of relatives he never met, I hung my head and mourned what I called our ancestral loss. Dad flicked dirt from his gardening spade, sneering. "Who do you think you are? Anne fucking Frank?"

He grew up being told that big boys don't cry. Neither, his sisters heard, did big girls. Famished? Fatherless? Beaten up? At war? Widowed yourself, young, as two of his sisters were? *Don't cry.*

It was as Fred Astaire and Ginger Rogers sang in *Swing Time:* "Pick yourself up. Dust yourself off. And start all over again."

They did. They would have said they didn't have the luxury to lick their wounds: couldn't afford it; folks depended on them. Anyway, they would have asked, why cry when bad things happen all the time and the guy next to you might be enduring something even worse?

Until quite recently, an almost universal fact of life was that it was nasty, brutish, and short. Each day brought plagues, wars, inquisitions, persecutions, slavery, infant mortality, famines, and droughts. Realizing this, our forebears soldiered on. They told themselves *Get over it*.

Some groups ritualized the worst of their past collective traumas, turning shared horrible memories into pageants, memorials, fasts, feasts, and reenactments that said: *Mark our tragedy, give thanks for our recovery. Move on.* For millennia, those planned trauma remembrance rituals were at once spiritual, theatrical, emotional. Observed once only, or once a year, they were experienced collectively so as to further imprint their import and validate the victims while giving survivors and their surrounding culture permission to let go and live. The Haggadah, read aloud by observant Jews as Passover begins, asks: "Why is this night different from all other nights?" Then it declares: "On this night, we remember that we once were slaves." In other words, we set aside this night to focus on those horrendous days when our ancestors in bondage built the pyramids.

This is the purpose of rituals: to focus intense emotions on a specific, limited time and place and set of actions: one big bang. Calculatedly beautiful, even if its beauty is a brutal kind, a ritual is a finite capsule into which celebrants pour their panic, terror, hatred, rage—contained in this day, week, or month rather than flowing out in a constant, diffused, life-wrecking haze.

Before the advent of psychotherapy and other recent developments, notes Rachel Yehuda, director of the Traumatic Stress Studies Division at the Mount Sinai School of Medicine, "the pervasive feeling" was that, "with time, people ought to be able to 'get over' the effects of a traumatic experience and 'move on' without noticeable impairment."

In days of yore, those who failed to bounce back from trauma invited their own destruction—or so they were told.

That message permeated the earliest legends and holy books. In ancient Greek mythology, a chain of traumas haunted the royal House of Atreus, as interpreted by Homer, Aeschylus, Euripides, and Sophocles. Seeking fair winds to aid his ships during the Trojan War, King Agamemnon sacrificed his daughter Iphigenia to appease the goddess Artemis. Unable to forgive him, Agamemnon's wife, Clytemnestra, and her lover, Agamemnon's cousin Aegisthus, lay in wait and slew him. Clinging to their trauma, the royal couple's aggrieved daughter, Electra, and infant son, Orestes, grew up to avenge the murder by killing Aegisthus and their mother, shoving a sword down Clytemnestra's throat. Orestes was punished for carrying his grudge that far: chased by the Furies, he went mad. The moral of the story is: *Get over it*.

In Japanese mythology, the Shinto sun goddess Amaterasu radiated light and compassion. In a typical fit of wickedness her brother, the storm god Susanoo, destroyed Amaterasu's rice fields, offended her attendants with obscene gestures, flayed a heavenly colt, and flung its gory hide into her chamber. Shocked and dismayed, Amaterasu retreated into a dark cave. Ignoring the entreaties of humans and deities who formed a huge pleading crowd outside, the goddess refused to come out. The Earth lay in darkness, its crops and creatures dying. Finally Ama-no-Uzume, the goddess of revelry, began performing a risqué dance for the crowd assembled outside the cave. Their delighted roars drew a curious Amaterasu closer and closer to the entrance, where at last she was lured into emerging. Light returned.

The moral of the story was: *Get over it*.

Not anymore.

These days, heads of state sob on national TV. As do athletes. Cops. Lawyers. Stars. They mourn horrors remembered.

And we lap it up.

These days, trauma is a commodity. Pain is a status symbol. Suffering brings brownie points. Losers are winners now. We suckle on stories of suffering. Ours, theirs.

We wade through tales of pain, project ourselves into that hurricane, that hospital, that vestry with that pedophile of the cloth.

Victims are lionized celebrities, sobbing across the screen, the stage, the page. As displayed by the mainstream media, survivors are heroes today, less because they survived than because they almost did not. Their pain is the whole point, not their recovery. Their pain is what perverse consumers crave. We have made industries of pain. Trauma now dominates our discourse, infusing each aspect of our lives: news, entertainment, education, literature, with endless variations on *it hurts so bad*. This revved up in the early 1970s and shows no sign of slowing down.

We compete to see who hurts worst.

We polish scars to shine like stars.

We deluge each other with what used—in that callous past—to be called sob stories but are now called trauma narratives. Most are true. Some are not. Some blur the lines between the two. We have internalized the arc. Screams are the elevator music of the modern world. With every brand-new *Million Dollar Baby* (feisty cinematic female boxer, paralyzed, begs to be euthanized), with every tidal wave and war crime, we slurp suffering.

We have attuned ourselves to trauma so intently, so universally, so unquestioningly, and for so long that we are stuck on the screaming and no longer know how to stop.

My trauma narrative?

I was born without hip sockets. Racked with sobs, my mother learned this fact from a doctor to whom she brought me when, at the age when babies are supposed to crawl, I did not crawl. I lay on my back in his office like a distressed insect, flopping my legs. He said we were lucky to live in mid–twentieth century America with recourse to the best orthopedic science. In poorer countries and in the past, he said, my condition could not have been repaired. I never would have walked. My mother wept. But lo: he said that with long-term intervention, I would walk "like any other little girl" but could probably never ballet dance or do splits.

I wore a steel hip brace for five years. It had large clanking hinges and felt pads at certain contact points. Trousers would not fit over it. I wore full skirts, crinoline party dresses, puffy sunsuits, A-line tents. In photographs from infancy to kindergarten, I have been craftily posed to hide the steel. This is virtually all I remember about the brace beyond its noise: Mom sighing as she fluffed my skirts and slips around my knees and Dad, across the room squinting into the viewfinder, saying, "No, I still see it."

At six I walked just like any other little girl, pelvis almost imperceptibly tipped. But because I could neither skate nor cycle— told that these would undo the work of the hip brace, I was never taught, was not allowed—kids teased me ceaselessly. They called me Cripple, Ortho, and Deformo.

Other trauma narratives: My first-grade teacher smacked my

hands with a ruler for "acting smart." My fourth-grade teacher, whom everyone loved for her green vinyl miniskirts and matching boots, called me a showoff when I finished my classwork before anyone else. When I tried to defend myself, she laughed and told the class, "This girl has diarrhea of the mouth." One day she offered us a new vocabulary word but before telling us the word, she said she would define it first. The definition she gave was my name. The word was "arrogant."

When my room was messy, my dad called me a "fucking pig." He hit me with a plastic hairbrush once. It left a mark. My friends called me a "cheap Jew" for picking up pennies from the street. One night, in secret, in ninth grade, in black marker, two boys— I knew who, and I liked one—scrawled on my locker JESUS LOVES EVERYONE BUT HEEBS.

More traumas: Sudden deaths of relatives and friends. I had a traffic accident: flipped van, head injury. I am afraid of nearly everything. If fear showed on the skin as bruises, I would be 85 percent black-and-blue.

Now you know some of my traumas. Part of me wants to cry. Part of me says, "Why should you care?"

Granted, this world is full of suffering and always has been. All of us have had our share and some have had much more, and until we walk miles in their shoes it is not for us to question why those who cannot bounce back cannot.

But.

We *can* ask why we fetishize trauma. Ask why we, as a society, often envy the traumatized. Ask why it sometimes seems, given how hungrily we devour tales of woe, that we do not really want the traumatized to heal, but would rather that they picked and picked and picked their scabs for our perverse perpetual delight.

Given a panorama of possible topics, it is trauma that we choose to think about, read about, talk about, turn into entertainment. And the frisson we get from this is not always schadenfreude or sympathy but sometimes expiated guilt. Some of our hunger for the pain of others is the masochism of the privileged, who feel worried and ashamed that they have not suffered enough. Our insatiable hunger for past trauma turns it not into a horror to avoid or leave behind by any means necessary but a horror on which to dwell for the sake of its being horrid. For the sake of knowing that it hurt.

Someone, sometime.

We're stuck.

Don't believe me? Consider the star status of author Augusten Burroughs, whose trauma narrative tells us that he was twelve when his mother handed him over to grow up in what he describes as the feculent home of a psychiatrist who molested him: *Running with Scissors*, book in 2002, Golden Globe–nominated film in 2007. Trauma memoirs are a booming entertainment genre. Written when the author was in her early twenties, Marya Hornbacher's *Wasted: A Memoir of Anorexia and Bulimia* sold over a million copies and, in 1998, was nominated for a Pulitzer Prize. Published ten years later, her second memoir, *Madness: A Bipolar Life*, begins with vivid trauma as, with a blade, "I am cutting patterns in my arm. . . . Blood runs in rivers down my arm, wrapping around my wrists and dripping off my fingers. . . . I split my artery." As that first scene ends, Hornbacher is rushed to a hospital: "I am a steak. They are cutting me up to serve me."

Hello, talk-show circuit.

Which came first: the deluge of trauma narratives, or our desire to hear them? Which attracts us more: the glad-it-wasn't-me relief of hearing others' tales of woe, or the tingly communion of sharing our own?

And even if a small voice inside you whispers *Get over it*, society rewards you when you don't. Its ears prick up as it prods and pays you to spill. The ploy for sympathy is the key to the city now.

The mainstreaming of any true tale has a flattening effect. For all our claims to honor pain, clamor and mass production cheapen it. The details of one house on fire, one deadbeat dad, one war, are swirled into the twisted glamour of big-screen, best-selling, famous pain.

Which is not to suggest muzzling the traumatized. They are entitled to their pain.

But as with so much else, we have taken a perfectly reasonable premise to extremes and diluted the most useful part. Striving to compensate for past iniquities, for a sometimes blind triumphalism, Western culture realized after World War II: Victims have voices, too. Let's listen. That rush of long-overdue revelations was cathartic. It was something else as well, something we were less willing to admit. It was a thrill. Trauma tales are like the adventure tales of old, all fire, squalor, and gore but from a new perspective: not the voice of the hero but of the victim, the victim *as* hero, the voice of the doomed, the nearly dead. At the heart of this matter throbs thrill guilt, the masochistic lurch that happens when you hear a trauma tale and feel indicted. Taking blame for inflicting that awful pain: you, or *people like you*.

How did it get so muddled, this Moebius strip of shame and blame, self-flagellation and forgiveness? How did we start anointing—and wanting to be—so many different kinds of victim? Do all kinds deserve our equal sympathy—or, if we have to parcel it out, how?

During the Vietnam War, a new version of trauma narrative emerged: the trauma of the perpetrator, who by virtue of that trauma morphs into a victim. In previous wars and their aftermaths, warriors had not been viewed as victims. In fact, the opposite was generally true: Those males who had slain the most enemies the most forthrightly were seen as the most heroic—hailed as brave saviors. These warriors in days of yore saw blood and guts up close. Before the advent of modern artillery, battles were hands-on massacres where soldiers scalped and speared and dismembered and disemboweled each other from inches away, with recourse neither to long-distance weaponry nor medics in the field.

True, soldiers in days of yore had sometimes been portrayed, romantically, as victims. Ancient poetry yields elegies to young friends killed in battle. This theme permeated American Civil War songs such as "Just Before the Battle, Mother (I Am Thinking Most of You)." It fueled a burgeoning post–World War I peace movement in the grim, sad poetry of Siegfried Sassoon and his fellow soldier-bards.

But in those portrayals—from Homer's *Iliad* to Sassoon's "Suicide in the Trenches" ("pray you'll never know/The hell where youth and laughter go") to World War II–era films such as *The Best Years of Our Lives*—soldiers were believed to be traumatized by having witnessed and suffered injury and death, *not by having perpetrated them*. Soldiers in the Vietnam War were the first in the West to present themselves in a widespread, public way as having been traumatized specifically by the act of harming others. For the first time in history, guilt and shame were perceived to be the source of soldiers' trauma, along with—or even overwhelming or replacing—the standard war horrors.

This complicates matters considerably. If trauma transforms the traumatized into victims, then in this new scenario everyone affected by war becomes a victim: civilians on both sides, soldiers on both sides. If all are victims, then no one can confidently be called either a victor or an enemy.

The shift in our definitions of what constitutes victimhood affects our view of crime as well. A robust anti-incarceration crusade is one component of the growing belief that criminals are themselves victims: that they do what they do because of traumas they suffered earlier in life, that they break laws because of their own pain, and thus they deserve as much sympathy and consideration as those whom they have robbed, raped, injured, conned, or killed.

Overheard trauma's a twofer. Ache vicariously—or wallow in mea culpa shame. Both get us drunk. So we clamor for trauma tales. We find them everywhere, within us and without us, an artesian well of horrors piped into the atmosphere. Add to the entertainment factor the function of trauma tales as political tools, fulcrums for blame, and their appeal is irresistible. Trauma is now the vortex of an all-consuming fad. As such, it keeps us stuck: on our own traumas, those of others, those of individuals and groups, history as a panoply of traumas. Trauma is our idiom, our currency. Processing trauma often alters from a forward motion into a stalled or even a backward one. Festering feels bizarrely good.

The prospect of healing pales beside the rewards, or so it seems, for never letting go.

Martin Seligman finds this troubling. The University of Pennsylvania psychologist, a leading expert on learned helplessness, advises strongly against clinging to past trauma and to anything else that keeps us looking backward rather than forward.

"Contrary to popular belief, we are not prisoners of our past," Seligman asserts. He cites studies suggesting that events experienced early in life do not shape our personalities and attitudes as keenly as genes do, that being stuck on past traumas is not necessarily a given: "As adults, we are indeed free to change." Seligman describes life as a tapestry whose patterns we weave day by day, strands in hand. Although, having worked with former concentration-camp prisoners and prisoners of war, he readily acknowledges that some traumas wound beyond recovery, he believes that most traumas can and should be left behind, that it is our task in life to learn how. He believes that we too often choose to stay stuck on traumas, choose to keep reliving their horror—like picking a scab continually rather than letting it heal. "We look for consolation," then look no further, Seligman declares.

We seek sympathy as much as strength—or even more.

Oprah Winfrey has been called the world's most powerful woman. *Time* magazine named her one of the twentieth century's hundred most powerful individuals. *The Oprah Winfrey Show* is the highest-rated talk show in television history. So the topics it covers—the topics Oprah talks about—are the topics America hears about.

Oprah loves trauma narratives.

One typical show, which first aired on January 26, 2004, is summarized thus in the archives: "An inside look at bullying: a high school football player attacked by his own teammates. A girl who went undercover in a fat suit. And watch as the tables are turned on a bully."

Traumas are Oprah's bread and butter, literally. The show's archives read like the caption cards in a chamber of horrors: "Ricky

Martin Travels to Meet Tsunami Orphans." "When the One You Love Is a Pedophile." "A Father Faces the Teen Who Killed His Family." "From White House Intern to Crack Addict." The episode titled "A Pro Football Player's Secret Shame" focused on New York Jets wide receiver Laveranues Coles, who announced in 2005 that he had been molested for two years as a child by his stepfather. July 2007, to choose a month at random, was peppered with pain. The July 4 episode was "The Day Your World Falls Apart"— presidential candidate John Edwards's wife, Elizabeth, discussing her cancer diagnosis. July 5 was "When Your Husband Cheats with Your Best Friend." July 6: "Childhood Interrupted," about kids forced to assume adult responsibilities after family crises. July 13: "The Day I Found Out My Husband Was a Child Molester." (This was a completely different episode from "When the One You Love Is a Pedophile," which aired two years earlier.) July 17: "Confronting the Attacker," in which "a mother of five goes behind bars to confront the man who murdered her father. Then, what one guest has to say to the man who killed her mother."

Trauma was a virtual theme at the 2006 Sundance Film Festival. *A Lion in the House* was a documentary about five families, each with a child fighting cancer. Another, *American Blackout*, probed the violent suppression of the African American vote. *Crossing Arizona* detailed the struggles of undocumented border crossers. *God Grew Tired of Us* was about Sudanese refugee boys. *The Ground Truth* examined sad Iraq War veterans. *Iraq in Fragments* probed the effects of occupation on Iraqis. *Small Town Gay Bar* was, according to the festival's program, a "voyage to the deep South to tell a tale of the struggle for community and expression in the face of ignorance, hypocrisy and oppression." *So Much So Fast* was about Lou Gehrig's disease. *Thin* was about bulimarexia. *The Trials of Darryl Hunt* probed "the wrongful conviction of a black man for a white woman's rape and murder." Feature films at Sundance that year included three about drug addiction and five about prisoners.

Our hunger for trauma makes healing that much harder. We seduce the traumatized, who are already vulnerable, not just into telling their tales but into telling them again and again as graphically as possible. It's like asking poor old Uncle Joe to perform his swallow-the-lit-cigarette trick at every family picnic. He knows we're expecting it. He knows we will applaud.

Some cannot recover. But for those who can, recovery becomes a more amorphous goal when, as the truly traumatized are lionized, the mildly and even marginally traumatized are tempted to compete. Like all my friends, I started seeing a therapist in my twenties. In an office outfitted with colorful kilim rugs, Miró prints, and ceiling fan I recounted memories with the hopeful mien of a child pulling found items from her pocket for a grown-up to assess. I had my share of problems, but I thought them small compared to what some friends had been through and were going through. I had a place to live, I had my health, I had a nice boyfriend. Both parents were alive and well. I could not help but feel a bit like a performer, those Thursday afternoons, as if the office were an amphitheater. Therapy was my generation's version of oratory, Grand Guignol, burlesque. Unlike theater, though, I paid to perform.

Straining to make the most of my bland past, I spoke in florid metaphors, calibrating my voice. One day we came to the story of how, age ten, I spilled peanuts in Dad's backseat. That night, he roared into a parking space, scooped the nuts in one hand, jumped from the car, and flung them into the air, stamping on them as they fell, screaming at me, "Goddamn you, goddamn you." The story made me cry.

My therapist raised her pencil: "How do you feel?"

I sniffled. "He was mean."

Her eyes went wide. "Say that again."

We chorused: "He was mean."

I wept, digging my heels into the kilim rug.

She said I was abused.

She said it in the *voilà* tone you use when showing toddlers insects under rocks. She pronounced *abuse* like a clout, concussively: *uh-BYOOSS.*

It thrilled me. A pyrotechnic charge shot through me as she said so. Then she added more. She said I was a victim of "soul murder." *How on earth could this feel good?* And yet it did. I felt accepted. One of the crowd, like my friends, like the celebrities, part of a culture, part of a context, part of an era. Ushered into my own generation: the young traumatized American. At the age when Isaac Newton developed the theory that turned into calculus, the age when Florence Nightingale managed a Crimean War hospital, the age when Edvard Munch painted *The Scream*, I looked forward to Thursday afternoons when I could proclaim from that nubbly couch and hear her say "abuse."

At what point does the catharsis of narrative and the subsequent validation transform into something else? The point differs for each of us, but these days we are all too tempted to attend it and instead keep sobbing on the couch. If I sound harsh—if I seem to be saying *I'll give you something to cry about!*—it is because I have been stuck on trauma and for what? Small traumas, overplayed, because stuckness gave me an audience, because for so long feeling bad felt good.

Why would this be? Why do we no longer want to mop up the mess, let go and *go*, that sweet relief? Why do we now believe that letting go is wrong in principle? Why do we think that to forget—with or without forgiving—is wrong, is immoral somehow, a betrayal of all sufferers, back to the dawn of time? Given a choice, why do we choose to talk of torment?

Well, because pain is political.

Culturewide stuckness on trauma makes the lucky guilty. Q.E.D. It shames the strong, safe, and successful into doubting and resenting the sources of their success. As the underdog gets its day, the overdog lowers its tail between its legs and slinks away. We might experience this while reading a best-selling memoir, watching a trauma-based film, network TV or music video while munching popcorn, but it's right out of the Marxist playbook.

In that playbook, the strong and successful are bad, by virtue of being strong and successful. In that playbook—it's right there in *Das Kapital*—the strong and successful are oppressors who traumatize the weak. Look, they let this poor girl starve! They made this poor boy go to war!

In the Marxian view, life is a series of class struggles between oppressors and the oppressed. Ideally, in that view, the oppressed rise up, vanquish the oppressors, and overcome. Struggle is trauma. Oppression is trauma. The oppressed are deprived of power, undergoing sustained physical and moral injury. Trauma reveals hegemony. It proves power inequity. A population transfixed by trauma is in a revolutionary mood.

But Marxism isn't only about the rich and poor anymore. A kind of "folk Marxism," argues economist Arnold Kling, is being busily applied to every type of injustice qua trauma: "Of course," Kling writes, "for Marx, the oppressors were the owners of capital and the oppressed were the workers. But folk Marxism is not limited by this economic classification scheme. All sorts of other issues are viewed through the lens of oppressors and oppressed." Through this lens, whoever is weaker merits not merely automatic sympathy but praise: thus any impulse to shield your eyes during graphic war footage or to yawn during *Oprah* marks you as an oppressor.

It's hard to say this without sounding like a playground bully or a sneering cartoon millionaire in tux and tails, but that's exactly how the trauma peddlers want me to look. If I argue that footage of downtrodden victims is agenda-driven, you can counter that I don't care about downtrodden victims. Of course I do. But you might call me mean and who wants to be called mean? A popular bumper sticker, seen frequently around San Francisco, scolds: *Mean people suck*.

Yet politicized railings subvert the real sufferings of real people, co-opting their palpable tears.

"The vast majority of college professors," Kling writes, "are folk Marxists, even though they do not advocate for Communism. . . . Their folk Marxism is dangerous because they do not even realize the extent to which it colors their world view. . . . Every day, in big and small ways, academic speech reinforces the view that the world consists of oppressor classes and oppressed classes."

And the best way to reinforce that view is by getting stuck on exciting, emotional trauma narratives that fit the script.

The oppressed-victim skew is obvious in college courses such as "Women and Violence" at the University of Kansas and Georgetown's "Narratives of Violence." The catalog description of a University of Sussex course, "Gendering Conflict and Violence," asserts: "Statistics on violence tell us nothing about the different experiences of domestic, racist and homophobic violence. . . . Violence has socially contextual forms so that questions about power, powerlessness, victimisation and agency must be situationally located and must acknowledge the dynamic nature of systems of oppression, gender, race, class, sexualities, disabilities etc. By the end of this course, you will have an understanding of . . . the etiology of violence; an understanding of the interactive nature and complexities of violence and victimisation; a theoretical and practical understanding of the significance of social structure and gendered power for violent behaviour."

Why are we stuck? That's why.

Kelly stayed home alone in Texas while her live-in boyfriend was attending a family wedding in Europe. She felt safe in the house with her Irish setter, Pogo. Kelly had studied judo for seven years. But when a rapist climbed through a bathroom window that Kelly had forgotten to lock, Pogo never barked. Kelly did not wake as the rapist crossed the dark house and let Pogo out. The setter curled up on the porch and went to sleep.

"You never really know your pets," Kelly says now, "until disaster strikes."

The rapist crept into her bedroom. Kelly never saw him. By the time she jolted awake, she was already blindfolded and gagged. She heard his voice. She smelled his sweat.

The next day, cops dusted the house for prints. This left gray cloud shapes all over the creamy walls and doorjambs. Kelly never saw them. The rapist had told her, pressing a metallic object to her head, to wait an hour after he left before making a move. She waited what felt like sixty minutes but was actually twelve, showered— destroying evidence, the police later said—for twenty, donned a shirt and trousers belonging to her boyfriend (whose fault it was, Kelly thought, for leaving her alone), and fled the house. She drove around until dawn, then showed up at her best friend's door. They called the cops. Kelly gave them a key but would not go inside.

She would not go in even after Rick flew home two days later. He could not coax her. Neighbors were feeding Pogo, since Kelly had stopped. She hated Pogo now. Apples had rotted on the kitchen table, in a bowl.

Weeks passed. Kelly stayed with her friend. Rick cleaned the walls, begged Kelly to come home. She tried: stood on the porch, suitcase in hand. But the scrunch of the doormat beneath her feet nauseated her. She left.

She never moved back in. Renting a top-floor flat in a building with maximum security, she told herself it was transitional, but it was not. She and Rick broke up. It wasn't that she feared sex so much, but rather sex with him, because he brought the rape to mind, because she blamed it partly on his absence and because the mattress into which the rapist had forced her face that night had smelled like Rick.

She still lives in the same town but, eight years later, cannot drive past that house. She has devised circuitous routes to avoid that street. When she is a passenger in other people's cars, some- times she tells them to avoid it but sometimes she can't, and when they reach that street she hyperventilates.

"Most of me wants to forget the whole thing, just wipe it out like wiping off a chalkboard. Part of me wants to remember," Kelly says, "because forgetting might be like saying it never happened. And I wish it hadn't. But it did."

The journey onward from that horrific night has neither been nonstop, speedy, nor in a straight line. "Unfortunately," Kelly says, "that experience is mine. So it is one of all the many, many things I count as mine. And which of these many, many things that are mine do I want to think about and focus on? Not that one—because life's too short as it is."

But physically and scientifically, to what degree is it even possible to *just get over it*? How plastic are our brains? Brain science is a burgeoning but comparatively new field in which much remains unknown. Researchers have isolated the amygdala, an almond-shaped neuron cluster in each of the brain's temporal lobes, as the key area activated by emotionally intense experiences, including trauma. The amygdala processes these experiences by releasing a protein into the hippocampus, which stores memories of these events. Storage of traumatic memories serves an evolutionarily adaptive, life-preserving purpose, as remembering past fears may help us avoid future risk, danger, or death. But sometimes it proves counterproductive, when intense memories intrude upon daily life, triggered by even the slightest stimuli.

After performing experiments on laboratory animals and on people who had been directly exposed to the 9/11 attacks in Manhattan three years earlier, a team of neuroscientists from Cornell and Stanford universities posited that exposure to "acute uncontrollable stressors" can produce "extended hyperexcitability of the amygdala." In other words, the brain's trauma-processing center stays on somewhat perpetual alert. Examining their subjects' reactions to various stimuli, the team concluded that "the amygdala and closely related structures are persistently more reactive after trauma" and remain "more readily activated independently of the triggering stimulus." This hyperexcitability manifests, even years later, in "increased vigilance and fearful responses (e.g., freezing)."

Not everyone who has undergone trauma shows these effects. Scientists are still trying to work out which factors—genetic, gender, and others—render which types of people more or less able to move on from which types of trauma. Several studies have found reduced hippocampal volumes in Vietnam War combat veterans and in women who were sexually abused during childhood. Years after their traumas, these people actually had smaller functioning hippocampi than control subjects who hadn't undergone similar experiences.

The way we "handle" past traumas in present life—choosing to talk about them extensively or not, for instance—might also affect our brains, according to researchers Patricia Lester, Susan W. Wong, and Robert L. Hendren:

"It is hypothesized that the constant reliving of traumatic events is responsible for cell damage and therefore decreased volume of the hippocampus," these neurobiologists write. "It is believed that this may contribute to an individual's difficulty in processing new information, increasing the vulnerability to misinterpretation of even neutral stimuli."

Society and culture, they add, "may protect against the negative outcome from trauma by providing an acceptable way to process the traumatic event so that numbness or dissociation do not need to be used as the primary defensive mechanism." Lester, Wong, and Hendren offer the example of a twelve-year-old Navajo girl who "became psychotic after the trauma of 'accidentally' shooting her baby sister when she was repeatedly left alone to babysit for her. A cleansing ritual by the tribe's elders (which involved the family and the tribe) resulted in relief of her guilt and the subsequent disappearance of her psychotic symptoms."

This suggests that addressing individual or group trauma by ritual means might help us heal. Heck, it worked for our ancestors.

Yet in our secular culture, we rely less and less on rituals. This is partly because many of us scorn spirituality, partly because in this instant-gratification era we cannot stand to wait for anything. The whole point of rituals is that they require us to await them, build up to them, then experience the rush of them in one fell swoop. In rituals it is also implied that *for their duration*, each participant is a star. During rituals we are invited to emote, act, reenact. But when the ritual is finished, we are expected to fade quietly back into the populace, neither our suffering nor anything else about us meriting star status. In our era, we have become too stuck on ourselves to accept this fade-away. We do not want to leave the stage.

The collective urge, however, still plays a role in how we handle trauma today. This is the era of identity politics. Seeking to escape the anonymity of urban and suburban anomie, we hunger for unity, community, and solidarity. We bond with others based on shared blood, breeding, taste, faith, heritage, or history.

This groupism starts in mid-childhood. Babies and toddlers are famous for disregarding differences among themselves. Only when culture gets ahold of them, when adults fill their heads with differences, do children start to think in terms of clans and clubs and cliques: of *where do I belong*.

Identity politics *is* politics. Thus, having claimed membership in a group, one seldom speaks purely for oneself but instead speaks as if ventriloquizing all group members back to the dawn of time. And trauma is a tool. Each group has its own legitimate tragedy, its

Trail of Tears. By staking membership, you stake claim to the whole bloody kit and caboodle. This is part of what makes neotribalism so attractive. A group's crisis, even if it happened long ago and far away to strangers before you were born, bonds you to fellow members in permanent retrospect.

A solidarity in suffering.

It makes us feel more real, more a part of something in a crowded and uncaring world.

Memorizing the tribal trauma narrative is part of the initiation ritual. One learns it from elders, discusses it, feels its pain, tattoos its symbols on the skin. One watches films about it. Buys the T-shirts. These days, you can wear the trauma.

Yes, it's good to raise awareness. Yes, it's morally right to remember wrongs. To some extent we should never forget.

But to what extent?

The trouble with tribes as regards trauma is that your tribe-mates might interpret your desire to move on as a betrayal. Another popular bumper sticker warns: "No one is free as long as others are oppressed." In neotribal language, this means: *You cannot get over it until all of us do.*

Some groups' trauma narratives have inspired powerful movements. Wave upon wave of these have swept ashore in the last few decades, wreaking great change, catalyzing laws and attitudes. Others are still taking shape. Starting in 1998, Australia's annual "National Sorry Day" was established to mark recognition of the "stolen generations," Aboriginal children taken from their families and sent to government schools as dramatized in the 2002 film *Rabbit-Proof Fence*.

"Sorry Day offered the community the opportunity to be involved in activities to acknowledge the impact of the policies of forcible removal on Australia's indigenous populations," the government's online culture portal explains. Now held annually in May, Sorry Day occasions huge marches. One tradition is Sorry Books, on whose blank pages Australians are invited to inscribe their own apologies. By 2007, over half a million had signed such books: "I am very sorry that as a young adult and teacher I did not teach the truth about our aboriginal friends. I am really very sorry," wrote a signer in one Sorry Book. "Forgive my Anglo-Saxon-Celt predecessors, forgive my handed-down attitudes toward you in my blind youth. Forgive me, forgive me, for not being *with* you in your struggle. Forgive my kind," wrote an Australian named Peter. "As a West Australian farmer's daughter I am someone who has prospered from the dispossession of Aboriginal people. For this and more I am sorry," wrote another named Carmel. Zelda adds: "Saying sorry is not enough."

In 2005, the event's name was changed to National Day of Healing, at which point observations began in London as well.

My absent hip sockets are absorbed into the bigger narrative of birth defects and disability. If I say I don't think about my brace, that I don't care about it now and don't remember ever caring about it, am I being mean (and mean people suck) to all children who ever wore braces? Am I being even meaner to those needing braces but denied them?

I'm a monster.

Even when I reason that (1) my birth defect happened decades ago, (2) thanks to luck and doctors, it left no trace but an ever so slightly waddling gait because my right leg is one inch shorter than

my left, and (3) why waste time when I'm no longer clad in steel—
for my logic I feel scolded. Rebuked.

And a tad silly, because in our traumasphere my birth defect
could be a status symbol—okay, the most twisted kind. It is less
a comment on me than on the traumasphere that mentioning my
barely remembered brace can feel like a boast. It does. We have
reached a point at which laying claim to pain commands attention.
Strangers snap to it, trained to show sympathy and share. "Really?
No hip sockets? Well, I have dyslexia!"

The secret handshake. Welcome to the tribe.

Stuckness on trauma is commonly used as a criminal defense
strategy and in discussions of crime in general. The perpetrator,
we learn time after time, endured something awful in the past *and
that's why this happened*.

On February 12, 2007, eighteen-year-old Sulejman Talovic
brought a shotgun and pistol to Salt Lake City's Trolley Square
mall. Wearing a backpack stuffed with ammunition, strolling among
the shoppers, the teen went on a rampage, slaughtering five people
before dying in a gunfight with police. The Salt Lake City *Deseret
News* article about it began: "As a little boy in Bosnia-Herzegovina,
Sulejman Talovic hid in fear from the Serb military forces who
were slaughtering Muslim men and boys as war and genocide rav-
aged his country." Calling the young shooter "a child of war," the
reporter detailed the Talovic family's hunger and anguish in the
old country.

Covering brutal crimes with perpetrator profiles whose message is "Oh, but wait!" is a pat feature of the traumasphere. Trauma

as a raison d'être, as an excuse and an explanation. A never-ending end in itself.

The Man Booker Prize is one of the world's most prestigious literary awards. Its 2003 winner was D.B.C. Pierre's novel *Vernon God Little*. Its teenage narrator is on the run; his pal has slaughtered sixteen schoolmates and committed suicide. Tattooed, tellingly, across Vernon's chest is the Spanish phrase *Me ves y sufres*, "See me and suffer." Vernon repeats nihilistic catchphrases such as "I just want to fucken die." At one point, Vernon says of someone who has deceived him: "Bless his bones smashed and stuffed through the ligaments of his puking fucked eyes, bless his mouth to suck me off, take my bile so it kills him dead to a place where he stays conscious and fucken broken and cold, shivering fucken worms and slime from organs that pop and fucken waste as I laugh."

Vernon has been traumatized.

In bygone eras, the heroes of popular fiction almost universally overcame trauma rather than be consumed by it. Typical of these were Horatio Alger's hundred-plus nineteenth-century best sellers bearing such unsubtle titles as *Do and Dare, Strive and Succeed, Wait and Win*. These were tales of bootblacks and newsboys whose perseverance and strong work ethic pulled them out of poverty. But a major shift occurred after World War I, with such works as Erich Maria Remarque's *All Quiet on the Western Front* evoking a profound new hopelessness. It caught on, slowly suffusing literature in general. The 2005 Man Booker winner, John Banville's novel *The Sea*, concerns a man agonized by memories of deceased loved ones, including a childhood friend who drowned. And so it goes. The 2007 winner, Anne Enright's *The Gathering,* is fueled by paralytically harrowing memories—of a brother's suicide, a mother as unloving as a "piece of benign human meat."

The Privilege Exercise is a popular activity in schools and work-places; its script is distributed widely via the Internet. How to do the exercise? Stand with fellow participants (coworkers, classmates, club members) in a long line as a facilitator intones instructions, and obey:

"If your parents were unemployed or laid off," says the facilita-tor, "take one step back."

On the other hand:

"If your family owned its own house, take one step forward."

The exercise's thirty similar "ifs" fall into two types: those implying childhood deprivation and those implying wealth or comfort.

"If your family ever had to move because they could not afford the rent, take one step back."

"If there were more than fifty books in your house, take one step forward."

Finally the students are asked to turn and face each other, pon-dering their positions. Those whose steps forward deem them lucky and trauma-free are supposed to feel guilty and ashamed, unde-serving of their fortune. Those whose steps back deem them trau-matized are rendered the stars of the exercise, which concludes with a "critical thinking" session that amounts to apologies from the privileged group to the traumatized.

The goal of the Privilege Exercise seems to be to make the trau-matized feel not merely recognized or comforted but contemp-tuous and superior. It is yet another venue that commodifies past pain. This whips memoirists into a who-suffered-most sweepstakes, which produces ever-bleaker results.

As students, as artists, as potential lovers and friends seeking to make ourselves interesting and worthy, we sift through our backstories for ugliness. A lifetime of good decisions, of caring parents, of being lucky and not doing anything dumb has suddenly become not a source of contentment and pride but rather something to hide and to be ashamed of. Panicked as we remember endless summer lawns and gentle moms, we dredge for what might be repressed. (Therapists are often more than willing to aid in these pursuits.) We say: *Wait, wait, wait! There was this bully on our block*. And then we recount some minor unpleasantness that we had long ago tried to forget, not realizing back then that one day it would be a valuable coin.

Now an official academic discipline, "trauma theory" is the topic of college courses, conferences, and university-sponsored centers. Not to be confused with hospital trauma centers—that is, emergency rooms—university trauma centers are hubs of discussion, art, and activism.

San Diego State offers a Certificate in Cultural and Community Trauma. Boston University offers one in Traumatic Stress Studies. In 2004, the University of Washington Press published *Trauma and Cinema*, whose editors "offer the reader a plethora of images of trauma for comparison and contrast" in essays such as Andrew Slade's "*Hiroshima, Mon Amour*, Trauma, and the Sublime." Published in 2005 by the U.K.'s Sussex Academic Press, *Trauma and Ethics in the Novels of Graham Swift* "shows how the novels elaborate an ethics of alterity by means of a detailed study of one of Swift's most persistent and fascinating—yet all too often ignored—concerns: the traumatic experience of reality." Ah, yes. Ignored.

The University of Washington is home to the Dart Center for Journalism & Trauma. The Australasian Society for Traumatic

Stress Studies offers an "annual media award to recognise excellence in journalistic reporting of traumatic events in any media. The winner will take home $1,000."

Trauma: the prize.

Is a brand-new career awaiting *you* in the thrilling, rapidly expanding field of miserable experiences that made people terribly unhappy?

In his 2003 mega best seller *A Million Little Pieces*, James Frey claimed to have caused a fatal accident, spent time in jail, and been a drug addict and a wanted man in three states before using sheer willpower to break his addictions and get clean. Amid grisly depictions of bloody vomiting and sans-anesthetic root canals, Frey keeps announcing, with portentous capital letters, "I am an Alcoholic and I am a drug Addict and I am a Criminal." In 2006, the alleged memoir was exposed as having been largely fabricated. The previous year, a series of wildly popular trauma tales purportedly written by another victim—J. T. LeRoy, a young AIDS-afflicted male heroin addict who claimed to have been pimped out to truckers by his mother at age twelve—were revealed to have been authored by a middle-aged woman named Laura Albert. Before this hoax was exposed, the trauma tales had captivated numerous film stars and other celebrities, who for years publicly, enthusiastically, vaunted the shy, elusive sufferer they thought was real.

Feeding our trauma hunger, a new type of counterfeit is flooding the market. In bygone eras, hoaxsters and losers and sneaks assumed false pasts to raise their social standing. They pretended to have been brave soldiers, as seen in the 1944 film *Hail the Conquering Hero*, or Resistance fighters, as seen in the 1996 French film *A*

Self-made Hero. Today, seeking social approval, hoaxsters pretend to have been brutalized—not to have won but to have lost. In the first half of 2008, two more alleged trauma memoirs—Misha Defonseca's *Misha: A Mèmoire of the Holocaust Years* and Peggy Seltzer's alleged gang/drug memoir *Love and Consequences*—were both exposed as fakes.

Such counterfeits insult everyone who really *is* or *was* sick or addicted or interned in death camps. But our Freys and Alberts and Seltzers are like con artists anywhere, giving the public what it wants. Scanning the marketplace, aiming to make a buck, fakers feign pain.

For thousands of years, trauma and recovery were a matter of faith and ethics and pragmatism. After the Age of Enlightenment they became a matter of science.

Best known today as the first physician to diagnose multiple sclerosis, French neurologist Jean-Martin Charcot also gained notoriety in the mid-nineteenth century for using hypnosis to study what were then called hysterics. These women experienced disabling symptoms such as paralysis, blindness, fatigue, and seizures that could not be traced to any neurological source. At his clinic in Paris's Salpêtrière Hospital, Charcot theorized that certain individuals had weak nervous systems, and that these individuals were susceptible to being overwhelmed by fearsome childhood experiences, suffering mental anguish that manifested in their behaviors long after all actual traces of the incident were gone.

Thus was born the idea of trauma as we know it.

Sigmund Freud was one of many devoted students who trained under Charcot at Salpêtrière. The young Freud was further in-

trigued by experiments that his Viennese colleague, the physician
Josef Breuer, was performing on a hysterical patient named Bertha
Pappenheim, known in research papers as "Anna O." Twenty-one
years old when she began seeing Breuer in 1880, Pappenheim was
partially paralyzed and given to hallucinations, contortions, speech
difficulties, and a severe cough. At one point in her treatment, she
refused to speak anything but English, even though it was not her
native language. At another point, the highly intelligent woman
"no longer conjugated verbs," Breuer observed, "and eventually
she used only infinitives." Although other doctors had dismissed
Pappenheim as a lost cause, Breuer found that he could coax her
into trancelike states—she called them "clouds"—during which
she narrated her hallucinations and abruptly remembered traumatic incidents that had triggered her symptoms. Her paralyzed
arm, for instance, was the same arm with which she had cradled
her beloved father as he died—and she blamed herself for his death.
Pappenheim called these revelations "chimney-sweeping." Breuer
called them "catharses," from the Greek *katharsis*, meaning "to
purge" or "to cleanse." The sessions with Pappenheim gave Breuer
great faith in the power of shifting traumas from the unconscious
into the conscious mind.

Freud, too, was taken with this "talking cure." He blended it
with elements he had learned from Charcot to forge what we now
know as psychoanalysis.

"We guided the patient's attention," Freud recalled of early
talk-therapy sessions, "directly to the traumatic scene during which
the symptom had arisen, [and] tried to find therein the psychic conflict and to free the repressed affect. We thus discovered the proce-
dure which I later named *regression*." Drawing the supine patient
back "to earlier experiences," Freud explained, "forced the analysis

to occupy itself with the past." Thus Freud developed his contro-
versial theory that adult behavior is largely shaped by early childhood sexual traumas: penis envy in girls, castration anxiety in boys,
and the Oedipus complex in both, triggered by a desire for the
mother and a competitive urge to kill the father.

Today, the language of therapy is largely a language of trauma.
And the language of trauma vis-à-vis the language of therapy is the
lingua franca of the classroom, the office, the talk show, the relationship. We say: "I feel your pain."

That's largely because, at the start of the twentieth century, therapy became a fad. As with most fads, artists had a hand in launching this one. The psychoanalyst Jacques Lacan, a Parisian acolyte of
Sigmund Freud, counted among his friends the era's most influential artists: Pablo Picasso, Salvador Dalí, André Breton, and Georges
Bataille. One of the first celebrity doctors, Lacan was known to
charge patients the equivalent of $200 for sessions lasting between
two and ten minutes.

Meanwhile, a succession of major wars—merging with the burgeoning field of psychoanalysis—was bringing trauma ever further
into public consciousness and changing its image.

Treating Civil War soldiers at a Philadelphia military hospital,
an internist named Jacob Mendez da Costa noticed that many of his
patients displayed the same set of symptoms. Trembling, perspiring
profusely, the men had heart palpitations and felt exhausted. No
physical cause could be found. These symptoms were unrelated to
whatever wounds or diseases had brought them to the hospital. By
the end of the nineteenth century, this set of symptoms came to be
known as Da Costa's syndrome or "soldier's heart."

When they reappeared in the trenches of World War I, the
symptom cluster was renamed "shell shock." At first suspected of

stemming from toxins in live explosives, shell shock was soon recognized as a mental rather than physical malaise. Freud treated shell-shocked soldiers at a time when the public—and the military—still viewed such men as weak cowards. Being stuck on trauma was costly, back then. For refusing to return to the trenches , more than three hundred British soldiers were executed during World War I.

During the next world war, the symptom cluster was called "battle fatigue" or "combat fatigue." In the American military, sufferers were generally permitted a few days' rest in military hospitals before being sent back to battle. By contrast, Russian soldiers suffering combat fatigue during World War II were usually executed promptly.

All the lessons of the past several thousand years still permeated public attitudes toward shared trauma. In the mid-twentieth century, Britons told one another, "Keep a stiff upper lip" and "Mustn't grumble" and "Keep your pecker up"—*pecker* meaning, of course, nose. Americans said: "Keep your chin up" and "Never say die." The Japanese relied on *Gambatte* and *Shikata ga nai*—meaning, respectively, "Do your best" and "It can't be helped." The message in these bracing mottoes was: *Don't get stuck on your trauma. Get over it.*

The same pattern of symptoms surfaced among American troops during the Vietnam War. It was especially noticeable among veterans back home and even became a cliché: the shaky vet leaping under a table at the slightest sound, clutching at an imaginary gun.

But by then, public attitudes had changed. Traumatized vets were no longer roundly dismissed as weak cowards. Moreover, during and after a very unpopular war, they became the focus of unprecedented research, media coverage, and sympathy.

Not getting over it became the next big thing.

The 1980 edition of the *Diagnostic and Statistical Manual of Mental Disorders* included a brand-new syndrome called Post-traumatic Stress Disorder. Still associated mainly with Vietnam vets but not limited to them, PTSD was designated as appearing after exposure "to an extreme traumatic stressor involving direct personal experience of an event that involves actual or threatened death or serious injury, or other threat to one's physical integrity; or witnessing an event that involves death, injury, or a threat to the physical integrity of another person; or learning about unexpected or violent death, serious harm, or threat of death or injury experienced by a family member or other close associate." In order to be diagnosed with PTSD, a patient had to experience symptoms for at least one month.

Legitimized by the *DSM*, this fledgling pathology attracted massive attention. In 1983, Congress launched the National Vietnam Veterans' Readjustment Study. Its researchers concluded five years later that more than 30 percent of Vietnam vets suffered from PTSD. In 1989, a National Center for Post-Traumatic Stress Disorder was established under the auspices of the U.S. Department of Veterans Affairs.

"PTSD" became a household term.

Stuckness on trauma's new status as an official medical diagnosis was a portentous landmark, as well as a confluence of powerful forces—a medical industry that stood to benefit hugely from new treatments and drugs, and an antiwar movement that stood to benefit hugely from scientific proof that war was not healthy for children and other living things.

Because Western society holds science in such awe, and because the medical industry is so influential, our whole social climate can be heavily influenced by official proclamations about what is and is not an illness, who is and is not sick. When anything is designated a disease, once clinics are devoted to it and pharmaceutical firms concoct expensive drugs for it, we commit ourselves to viewing its causative issues and manifestations in a brand-new way. The media converges on new diseases, whose patient narratives offer maximum human interest. Stories on PTSD do triple duty: wowing readers with cutting-edge science, making them cry, and proffering another good reason to protest wars.

Which is not to say that PTSD isn't real. Surveying twenty years' worth of research, University of Pennsylvania psychology professor Martin Seligman saw concentration-camp survivors and POWs suffering lifelong PTSD symptoms with little or no hint of relief. Clearly, while "some of us react to our losses with resilience," Seligman observes, in other cases "we find ourselves beyond consolation"—sometimes forever. He laments that of all the most commonly discussed mental-health issues, "PTSD is the least alleviated by therapy of any sort" and that "the development of new treatments to relieve PTSD is of the highest priority."

But.

In a society where illness fuses with identity, we find ourselves tempted to claim ourselves sick. This would perplex our ancestors, who demonized schizophrenics as witches and forced Hansen's disease patients, then called lepers, to signal their presence with bells. Now as then, with trauma as with addiction, no one *wants to be ill*. Yet we cannot help but be affected by the status conferred on the sick in an era when pain is paramount and sufferers are stars. Deluged by talk shows, articles, books, songs, and films, we cannot help but wonder whether, in some ways at least, being sick is

somehow better than being healthy. We believe that being sick, and
knowing that our illness has a name, explains if not excuses those
odd things we do. And we believe that if we're sick, we will be listened to.

So now being stuck on trauma is a sickness.

When a whole society is stuck on trauma, the temptation to exploit that condition is irresistible, either on purpose or because sympathy is seductive and it sucks you in. And how easy to exploit
PTSD—which Martin Seligman dubs "the saddest disorder of
them all"—when its definitions are so subjective. According to the
Diagnostic and Statistical Manual of Mental Disorders, the disorder
can spring not only from military combat but also from violent personal assault, natural or man-made disasters, severe automobile ac-
cidents, diagnosis with a life-threatening illness, confinement as a
prisoner of war, a hostage, or a concentration-camp inmate. According to the *DSM*, the disorder can also be caused by seeing
someone killed. It can even be caused by seeing someone injured. It
can even be caused by hearing about something bad happening to
someone else. For example, according to the *DSM,* PTSD can result from hearing about an "assault, serious accident, or serious injury experienced by a family member or a close friend." To qualify
for a PTSD diagnosis, the patient must experience any, though not
all, of these symptoms: "recurrent and distressing recollections of
the event, including images, thoughts, or perceptions . . . illusions,
hallucinations, and dissociative flashback episodes, including those
that occur on awakening or when intoxicated . . . intense psychological distress at exposure to internal or external cues that symbolize
or resemble an aspect of the traumatic event . . . persistent avoidance
of stimuli associated with the trauma . . . efforts to avoid thoughts,
feelings, or conversations associated with the trauma . . . inability

to recall an important aspect of the trauma . . . feelings of detachment or estrangement from others . . . restricted range of affect (e.g., unable to have loving feelings) . . . sense of a foreshortened future (e.g., does not expect to have a career, marriage, children, or a normal life span)." Patients might also experience sleep-related difficulties and angry outbursts. They might find concentration more difficult after their traumas than before. They might also startle more easily.

Do any of these apply to you?

Sure they do.

I experienced the 1971 Sylmar earthquake (measuring 6.6 on the Richter scale), the 1973 Veracruz earthquake (6.8) while on vacation, and the 1989 Loma Prieta earthquake (7.1). I have sustained a head injury in a car accident, witnessed a boy falling from a jungle gym and breaking his arm, witnessed another driver in another accident propelled headfirst through his windshield and onto the pavement. I have heard about a classmate being raped, my mother breaking both hips, and my grandmother being mugged in Central Park. Am I ill? Are those experiences the reason I feel detached from others and fear an early death? Are my efforts to avoid talking about Teri's rape or imagining the boy's broken arm, his split humerus jutting up through the slashed skin like a blood-streaked white stake, pathological? Or am I just an average person with typical experiences?

As claims and diagnoses pile up, we lose our power to gauge pain and suffering, its extent and endurance—in others and even in ourselves. Prompted by signals everywhere we look, we check ourselves compulsively for psychic bruises and telltale signs. Hypersafeguarding our children from the specter of risk or fear and even discomfort, we get stuck not just on trauma but on the separate trauma that is the fear of trauma. Obediently, we report all glimmerings of stress.

Sometimes we ourselves can't discern whether or not we are faking it.

Aesop warned us against crying wolf.

In 1995, Billie Jean Matay sued Disneyland for the emotional distress of her grandchildren, aged four, seven, and ten, who she claimed were traumatized by witnessing employees in a backstage area half in and half out of their character costumes, holding the oversized costume heads in their hands. Court papers indicate that Matay claimed these Disney employees "devastated her grandchildren with the sudden revelation that Disney characters are not real, but make-believe." Her suit, which proved unsuccessful, followed a 1989 case in which Lonnie and Karen Boozer sued Disneyland for $1 million after their two- and five-year-old daughters spied employees carrying costume heads backstage. One of the girls reportedly required three months of therapy to recover. The case never went to court, as the Boozers settled with Disneyland for an unspecified amount.

After seeing a dead fly sealed into a bottle of water in 2001, Waddah Mustapha sued the Culligan water company. He did not swallow the fly or even drink from the bottle but claimed that his revulsion upon seeing it was a trauma that triggered a phobia of flies "that changed his personality and even killed his sex life," according to a news report. A court initially awarded him $341,777 in damages, but that ruling was overturned in 2006. In 2007, claiming that "he had trouble drinking coffee because it contained water and became anxious about getting in the shower," Mustapha resolved to bring the case to Canada's Supreme Court.

In these sue-Disneyland days, trauma is a lure, a destination. It's why you did something. It's why you did nothing.

And the traumatized are paraded past us as reminders not only that life in general is what the Bible calls a *valle lacrimarum*, a vale of tears whose cruelties—disease, death, disaster—strike us all at random, but also that we inflict trauma on each other, mainly through prejudice and institutions such as war.

The glamorization of trauma is not some random accidental glitch in Western culture. A political agenda lies behind much of it: a drive to glorify the downtrodden and vilify the powerful, the strong and the victorious. Yes, this emphasis can be traced most transparently back to Marxist philosophers, but its deepest roots go all the way back to the early days of Christianity. For while the Romans were lavishing triumphal parades on jubilant emperors, an obscure Jewish sect leader named Jesus developed a revolutionary new worldview that acted as a salve for his hounded followers: *He that is least among you shall be the first in heaven. A rich man can no more enter into heaven than could a camel pass through the eye of a needle*. Christ's message was clear—the real moral victors are you, the oppressed, the losers, the victimized, the poor. His own story embodied this philosophy: while other religions of the era worshipped warrior gods and sun gods and infinitely powerful heroes, Jesus was idolized *because* he was a victim, betrayed and crucified, unable to halt his humiliation and destruction, the ultimate beautiful loser. Christianity would take on a martial mien in later centuries, with the Crusades and Inquisition and conquest. But at its core throbbed this eternal ache: the meek, turning the other cheek.

———

Unveiled by the Duchess of Kent in 2001, the Shot at Dawn Memorial in Britain's National Memorial Arboretum commemorates the 306 British and Commonwealth soldiers who were executed for cowardice and desertion during World War I. Created by sculptor Andy de Comyn, the memorial comprises a semicircle of stakes bearing the men's names, flanking a ten-foot-tall statue of a tender teenage Tommy, blindfolded and with his hands bound behind his back, awaiting the shots of a firing squad.

Again we are crushed into our uncomfortable emotional corner. Imagining ourselves in the trenches, we feel for these lads. Would we want to fight in the Battle of the Somme? Heck, no. World War I, with its feeble premises and unthinkable casualty counts—19,240 mown down on one day at the Somme alone—was one of history's most ridiculous and pointless conflicts. Its absurdity, its losses, and its shell-shocked legions have led antiwar activists to argue, ever since, that *all* wars are pointless and ridiculous. If World War I was your sole example of a war, you could conclude that *all* wars are shams, scams, and selfish juggernauts. The artist Andy de Comyn wanted his Shot at Dawn sculpture to make "those who died all be remembered as being the same—without any stigma attached."

All those who died: in battle, in hospitals, from firing squads. But . . . they aren't the same.

Casting deserters and fighters as "being the same" conveniently erases the fact that some wars are worth fighting. Antiwar activists would like you to believe that none are, and possibly they believe it themselves.

Empathizing with deserters and forgiving them is one thing. Equating deserters with fighters is another, and it's dangerous. It equates trauma with what could be called service, duty, responsibility. If quitting—because you're afraid, you're tired, you're stuck on trauma—is morally on par with persevering, far fewer would fight. Which is fine in utopias. And this equivalency carries over into nonmilitary milieus: if quitting draws no stigma, why work, why stay in relationships, why try? Caring for deserters is one thing. To glorify deserters is to tell all those who were also afraid and tired and traumatized, *yet stayed and fought*, that they were fools.

And that their principles were foolish too.

In 2006, Britain's Ministry of Defence pardoned the executed deserters *en masse*. Pardoning deserters is one thing . . .

The shell-shocked Tommy was in agony and has my sympathy. He could not heal fast enough and was shot for that, which I find horrible.

Ten-foot-tall statues suggest hero status, right? And, shoulders thrust back, de Comyn's soldier-boy looks brave.

A local paper headlined its coverage of the memorial "Proud moment for relatives of soldiers executed for cowardice." Really? Relieved, maybe. Consoled. But *proud*? That's interesting.

This is the icon in a new antiwar West: stuck-on-trauma deserter as martyr. Deserter as no different from the man who stayed. Deserter as victim. Deserter as double victim: victim of war and victim of prejudice. Deserter as wiser than fighting man: maybe even superior.

In the age of trauma theory, we see ourselves as living not in the land of the free and the home of the brave but the land of the brutal oppressor. From lecterns, pulpits, screens, and pages we are told that we are traumatized by wars and holocausts. By racists. Fascists. Homophobes. By sexists and by sex. By childhood. Adolescence. Growing up. By small-minded small towns. By urban sprawl. By rootlessness. By staying put. By wealth, by poverty, by eating too much, not eating enough. We are told that our parents, partners, siblings, strangers, and friends traumatized us. Think they didn't? Think again.

I watched us get this way.

When I started kindergarten in 1964, my heroes were ship captains and cowboys. My favorite films were *Captain January* and *How the West Was Won*.

By the time I graduated from Berkeley in 1981, I refused on principle to read books written by men because men were sexists and rapists, because men tortured and killed women accused of being witches during what my friends and I called "the burning times"—a distant, horrifying past in which the matriarchy was dismantled by scheming, rampaging, violent males who forced their patriarchy on the human race, which started every problem since. Or so I thought.

The underdog ascends.

Like sponges, children absorb popular culture and ooze it through their pores. At five, I revered cowboys, hobbling in my hip brace pretending to ride. By nine, though, I knew how to imitate Vietnamese girls fleeing burning villages. Posing before the bathroom mirror, hair askew, I practiced looking harrowed. At night I lulled myself to sleep murmuring, "Poor thing. Poor thing."

How did I learn that?

We all did. In seventh grade, my friend Doreen appeared at school one day wearing a T-shirt with a picture of a Native American and the words TRAIL OF TEARS. Stretching it taut, gazing down, she said, "This. Is. So. Cool."

"So," I said, "what's the Trail of Tears?"

She shrugged. "Who knows?"

We saw *Love Story*. Cancer-trauma narrative. We liked Cher's "Gypsies, Tramps and Thieves." Racism-trauma narrative. Other kids wore steel POW bracelets. Tortured-by-Vietcong-trauma narrative. I wore a steel bracelet incised with the name of a *refusenik*, a Jew whom the Russians would not permit to emigrate. Anti-Semitism-trauma narrative.

All of us memorized the songs in *Jesus Christ Superstar*, the greatest trauma story ever told. My friend Suzanne saw *Billy Jack* over and over in our local theater one whole Saturday and Sunday. She screamed during the gang-rape scene each time, and sobbed aloud during the scene in which hicks harass Native Americans. When other patrons turned to stare at Suzanne, she said, "Excuse me. I'm Seminole." Well, her dad was. One-sixteenth. He said.

Around that time, an unfamiliar symbol started popping up at school. The Christian kids wore schematic eyeless fish silhouettes. Jeff in pre-algebra, who wore a fish patch on his jacket, told me what it meant. He said it was the *ichthys*, which ancient Christians scratched onto walls to show the way to secret meetings in the pagan Roman Empire, where—Jeff told me solemnly—they would have been tortured and killed if they had been caught. Its 1970s revival started in Australia.

Jump on the trauma train.

At first, our vicarious pain hurt in a harmless way, like reading murder mysteries. In our suburban never-never land, we could only imagine actual crucifixions, lynchings, Agent Orange, rednecks spouting slurs. It was fodder. But being kids, being Americans, we wanted more.

The trouble was that in atrocity after atrocity, the villains were . . . people like *us*. Up to a certain point, self-hate is purgative. Your gait has a penitent drag lest you forget. But then you can no longer bear the pounding shame and guilt—for traumas inflicted by folks resembling you but *not* you long ago and far away. The trauma-track forks. You choose one: Either, like professors of trauma studies, you choose a career composed of apology, of fetishizing underdogs, of wearing the shameful red O that means Oppressor.

Or you choose to *become* the Oppressed.

For Suzanne, it was easy. She was one-thirty-second Seminole. She said. For Doreen, it was hard until she decided her ancestors were Huguenots. And I—I had the Holocaust. Or did I? My parents were both born in New Jersey twenty years before the war.

My generation cut its teeth on borrowed traumas. We grew up barging like party crashers into whatever human-rights outrages we could find. Practice makes perfect. But we wanted to *own* trauma. So it was we, the first children of the traumasphere, who begat a new institution in it. A new medium, the oeuvre of our age: the white-middle-class Trauma Memoir. This will be our legacy, budded in a time and place of marvelous peace and prosperity. In *A Child Called "It,"* published in 1995, Dave Pelzer recounted a suburban California boyhood during which his alcoholic mother beat him, starved him, forced him to swallow ammonia, bathe in ice water, and eat feces. Selling well over a million copies, it spent two years on the national best-seller lists. Pelzer guested on *Montel Williams* and *Oprah*. The trend continues.

These tales individually are gripping, unbearably sad. As a genre they're so *us*. Exhibitionistic. Confessional yet accusatory. Graphic. Gross. (We grew up with comic books and horror films and the Crucifixion, after all.) And ahhh, the masturbatory buzz of the first-person singular. Why pretend anyone else matters, anyway?

We went shopping for traumas.

Not that the stories aren't true—well, James Frey's wasn't, but surely most others are. Beach reading by and for the bruised. A pain parade. *Broken. Parched. Dry. Smashed. Wasted. Empty.* Those are the titles of memoirs about addiction and eating disorders by William Cope Moyers, Heather King, Augusten Burroughs, Koren Zailckas, Marya Hornbacher, and Christie Pettit, respectively. We had incest memoirs: Sandy Wilson's *Daddy's Apprentice*. Erin Merryn's *Stolen Innocence*. Sylvia Fraser's *My Father's House*. Sue William Silverman's *Because I Remember Terror, Father, I Remember You*. Stuart Howarth's *Please, Daddy, No*. We had rape memoirs. Murdered- or otherwise dead-parent memoirs. Madness memoirs. Illness memoirs such as Susanna Kaysen's *The Camera My Mother Gave Me*, about her chronically hurting vagina. "My whole life," she confides to us all, "is a pain diary." In the era's paramount dead-parent memoir, *A Heartbreaking Work of Staggering Genius*, Dave Eggers—whose mother and father both died of cancer when he was young—remembers: "While reclining on the couch most of the day and night, on her back, my mom turns her head to watch television and turns it back to spit up green fluid into a plastic receptacle. . . . For many weeks she had been spitting the green fluid into a towel . . . which she would keep on her chest. But the towel on her chest, my sister Beth and I found after a short while, was not such a good place to spit the green fluid, because, as it turned out, the green fluid smelled awful, much more pungent an aroma than one might expect. (One expects some sort of odor, sure, but *this*.)"

Few of us have experienced anything nearly so horrendous. And while it might seem natural to avoid such imagery—why think about green spit-up or cancer if you don't have to?—Eggers's book became a massive best seller. To what extent do trauma narratives become best sellers based on their intrinsic literary merit—their "staggering genius"—and to what extent is it because we fear what society will think of us if we *don't* read them? We acquire status from sharing strangers' deathbed scenes and rapes, and acquire scorn by admitting we'd rather watch football instead. We've come to believe that turning away from a trauma narrative, especially one that comes packaged portentously by a major publisher or network TV, is tantamount to turning your back on all the underdogs—the sick, the sad, the poor.

And what does that make you?

As the value shift grew roots, pop and punk songs became mini trauma narratives. Jewel's "Daddy." The Scorpions' "Daddy's Girl." Madonna's "Oh Father." Christina Aguilera's "I'm OK." Fiona Apple's "Sullen Girl." Iris DeMent's "Letter to Mom," in which, when the narrator was ten, her mother's boyfriend "climbed into my bed and he left me wishing I was dead."

Motörhead sang: *Don't let Daddy kiss me.* Metallica sang: *Can you heal what Father's done?* Machine Head sang: *You molest and destroy just a five-year-old boy and you make me suffer, motherfucker.*

Like Eggers's book, Dan Barry's *Pull Me Up* describes his mother dying of lung cancer on the living room couch. Elsewhere in the memoir, Barry is assaulted by a pedophilic monk.

I've devoured trauma memoirs as if they were Milk Duds. I would have written one if I could. And yes, I tried and tried to write one, fueled by that word my therapist said which throbbed, glowing, in the air.

Abuse.

But no. When all was said and done, I knew that mine was a safe, lucky, boring life.

It wasn't so much that our generation set out to get rich flogging our trauma narratives, though some did. It was just that we were so good at it.

Terrible things happen. Realer than real. What changed is not the fact or the nature of tragedy but how we viewed it, how we wrote about it, how we clung to it for dear life and wouldn't let go. Set in San Francisco's Chinatown, the musical *Flower Drum Song*— a Broadway sensation in 1958—is about immigrants, about the trauma of arriving poor and penniless in a foreign country whose language and culture both baffle you. (In the 1961 film version, Japanese actors eat chop suey and portray offensively stereotypical Chinese, although both play and film were based on the novel by C. Y. Lee, who actually *was* a Chinese immigrant.) In one scene, an old man and his nubile daughter, fresh off the boat, turn being overwhelmed by strangeness into a hopeful song: "A hundred million miracles," they trill, "are happ'ning every day!" They go on to recount some of these miracles and affirm their gladness to be alive.

By my twenties, nothing could be less cool.

I ached to ache.

That's when I started therapy.

Right around then, in the 1980s, the West considered itself pretty sophisticated. Vietnam and Watergate had been harsh reckonings, leaving in their wake a sense of been there, done that, won't get fooled again.

Odd, then, that a book published in 1980 whose author, a suburban housewife and mother, claimed to have been raised not merely by abusive parents but Satan-worshipping ones who forced her, at age five, to watch babies being butchered and to quaff their blood . . . became a best seller.

And spawned a new genre, a *new* kind of trauma narrative in which the trauma was *so* horrific that the authors claimed to have repressed it, virtually forgotten it, for decades on end.

Michelle Smith led a seemingly ordinary life in British Columbia, Canada. But during therapy sessions with a psychiatrist named Lawrence Pazder, the young woman suddenly remembered—out of the blue, the pair would later say—shocking childhood scenes in which her mother initiated her into a Satanic cult. Smith described adult members raping her. She recounted rites involving anal penetration, excrement, and eating worms. These descriptions peppered that 1980 best seller, *Michelle Remembers*. Talk-show sensations throughout the early '80s, Smith and her psychiatrist/coauthor, Pazder, left their respective spouses to marry each other. Having died in 1963, Smith's mother couldn't be interviewed. But reporters barraged Smith's father and siblings. They said the book was bunkum.

A century earlier, Sigmund Freud had pursued the idea of "repressed memory," in which certain traumatic recollections sank deep into the unconscious and lay buried so deeply as to be beyond reach of the conscious mind, for all intents and purposes forgotten. Even if you *asked* the patient whether he had ever been molested or fallen off a horse, he would say no. Yet Freud theorized that these buried traumas wrought havoc anyway, igniting neuroses that baffled the patients.

Lawrence Pazder coined a new term: "ritual abuse."

It caught fire.

Other claims of forced childhood Satanism filled the airwaves and bookshops. Here was the renaissance of a very old variety of trauma narrative, a continuation of Eve's confession: "The serpent deceived me, and I ate" (Genesis 3:13).

It was fear of the devil, redux. The same fear had led to rampant torture and execution of accused witches during the Reformation—those dreaded "burning times." When that wave of panic subsided in the eighteenth century, it lay fallow for a while. Fear of the devil was a quaint novelty by the 1960s and '70s, providing amusement and chills in *Rosemary's Baby* and *The Exorcist*. But when *Michelle Remembers* unleashed a new Satanic panic, it was different. This time, it wasn't about moral outrage or offending God.

This time, it was all about the trauma.

Suddenly they were everywhere, the formerly Satanically abused. They spoke of vile rites, of being used after their first menses as "brood mares," impregnated by rapists repeatedly to bear an endless supply of infants for human sacrifice.

It wasn't just fundamentalist Christians who created and consumed these narratives. Throughout the '80s, the secular mainstream media framed ritual abuse as fact. Airing just before Halloween in 1988, NBC's two-hour *Devil-Worship: Exposing Satan's Underground* was promoted as an "investigative report" and a "documentary." A record-breaking viewership watched self-described "Satanism experts" and alleged victims recount what host Geraldo Rivera called "gruesome rituals" and "gruesome memories." These included the by now familiar blood-swilling, infant-butchering, and pedophilic orgies. In somber tones, Rivera told viewers that even more shocking bits had been edited out.

During a May 1989 broadcast, Oprah Winfrey sounded like a

believer as she announced: "As a child, my next guest was used also
in worshipping the devil, participated in human sacrifice rituals
and cannibalism. She says her family has been involved in rituals
for generations. She is currently in extensive therapy, suffers from
multiple personality disorder, meaning she's blocked out many of
the terrifying and painful memories of her childhood. Meet 'Rachel,' who is also in disguise to protect her identity." Turning to her
guest, Winfrey asked: "You come from generations of ritualistic
abuse?" "Yes," the young woman replied.

If "abuse" was already the era's most electric buzzword, this exotic new spin on it was irresistible. It allowed the imagination so
much play. Best of all, it was so easy to claim ritual abuse because,
when your claims involve acts performed in secrecy in houses long-
ago resold or bulldozed by people now long dead, who can prove
that you aren't telling the truth? As types of trauma narrative go,
this one is almost airtight.

At block parties and Little League games, in pubs and police-
station meeting rooms, in college classrooms and office cafeterias,
sophisticated educated Westerners were talking about the trauma
of Satanic abuse: How, they wondered, can we save more helpless
children from being betrothed to Satan, eating dung for the Dark
Lord, or being skinned for him? How, they asked as they drove
their Dodge Darts, how?

More memoirs emerged: *Satan's Underground* by Lauren Strat-
ford. *Drawn Swords: My Victory over Childhood Ritual Abuse* by
Jeanne Adams. *Blessed: Reclaiming My Life from the Horrors of Ritual Abuse* by Rosie Daymore. The topic was so au courant that it
necessitated acronyms: SRA for Satanic ritual abuse, RMT for the
repressed-memory therapy that burgeoned in those years as a new
specialty for mental-health professionals. Respectable publishers

issued RMT instructional manuals: *Treating Survivors of Satanist Abuse* from Routledge; *Satanic Ritual Abuse: Principles of Treatment* from the University of Toronto Press.

In the fad's heyday, many Satanic abuse accusations were taken to court and many people were convicted. In 1984, the office of Middlesex County, Massachusetts district attorney Scott Harshbarger charged Violet Amirault, her daughter Cheryl Amirault LeFave, and son Gerald Amirault with having done terrible things to preschoolers in their Fells Acres Day Care Center. According to the allegations, these offenses entailed robots, animal slaughter, and at least one sodomy involving a foot-long butcher knife. Analysts have subsequently decried the prosecution of this case, which was based mainly on statements from three- and four-year-olds who had been coached by adults. Gerald Amirault was sentenced to thirty to forty years in prison, Violet and Cheryl to eight to twenty years.

The ritual-abuse craze has since been roundly denounced. Many of its key figures and their claims have been discredited—too late, though, for all those convicted "Satanists" still incarcerated, thanks to a public ravenous for new trauma-narrative flavors. Gerald Amirault was freed in 2004; his sister and elderly mother served eight years each before their convictions were overturned in 1995.

Repressed memory is a gold mine.

And the message inscribed on its portal is "Never get over it."

Nor is it confined to memories involving Lucifer. In the traumasphere, the idea that traumas can be lost and found, forgotten and then miraculously remembered, is incredibly compelling.

Think your life was lucky, boring, and safe?

Think harder.

What happened that June at summer camp when all the lights went out and the counselor walked in the dark from cot to cot—?

Nothing. It was a fun summer.

It was *not*. Think again.

Several of my friends began wondering for the first time in their adult lives whether they might have been molested. At late-'80s family holiday gatherings, they began peering across tables at fathers, brothers, cousins, uncles, grandfathers, and stepfathers through new, suspicious, straining-to-remember eyes. Abruptly, to catch the males off-guard, my friends dredged up half-remembered occasions: long-ago swimming lessons, Twister games, lap-sits. *I climbed on his knee—and he squirmed!*

One friend—I'll call her Jessie—became certain that her brother and his best friend had spied on her regularly for years through a hole drilled in the bedroom wall. She said she'd repressed the memory, but in wondering why she couldn't bear to be naked in front of anyone, even her husband, a scene flashed through her head: her old bedroom, a narrow shaft of light.

"If you would just apologize," she told her brother, "I'd forgive you."

"There's nothing to apologize for and nothing to forgive," he countered angrily. "We never peeped at you. There was no hole."

Things got so fractious between them that Jessie wrote her family a letter—which she made me proofread, explaining that "the trust we had is gone" and that she still felt "invaded and betrayed." The fact that she had only recently remembered it—almost, sort of, maybe remembered it—just proved, she wrote, that it was heinous enough to repress.

She had no contact with her brother for four years. They first talked again at their father's funeral. They are cordial today, but only just.

Bamboo is a traditional motif at Japanese weddings. Often depicted on ceremonial kimonos and thinly sliced and coiled back upon itself to create elaborate bridal hairpins, bamboo is considered a good omen for couples—it represents resilience, because in nature bamboo neither changes color in fall nor dies in winter. When battered by storms or burdened by heavy snow, bamboo bends but does not break. When the snow melts and the sun shines, it springs upright again. In botanical and poetical terms, the slim but sturdy bamboo—compared, say, to the bloom-shedding cherry tree or the flamboyant but fragile, one-season-only poppy—gets over it.

We all suffer. Every trauma has its own personal arc. But it seems that science is pulling us ever closer to a time when we can simply choose to medicate bad memories away: to get over our traumas by prescription. A real-life variation on the sci-fi memory removal that turns lovers into strangers in the 2004 film *Eternal Sunshine of the Spotless Mind* is a drug called propranolol, which blocks the action of stress hormones on the part of the brain called the amygdala, where memories and emotional reactions are processed. A beta blocker originally developed as an antifungal, then later used to fight hypertension and angina, it has recently been used experimentally to treat PTSD. One woman who was diagnosed with PTSD after being carjacked at gunpoint, and then further traumatized by experiencing a street accident, was treated with propranolol and told the *Washington Post*, "I really think it helped. It helped not bring back my earlier bout with post-traumatic stress and made it easier to cope with this new incident. I look both

ways before I cross a one-way street now, but I'm not in a panic."
Advocates hope that the drug can eventually be used to help soldiers and victims of natural disasters and terrorism.

But before those futuristic scenarios come to your local drug-
store, if you are holding on to past trauma right here, right now—
well, why? What's keeping you there? Why, with a world of things
to see and do and think about, present and past, are you immobilized by that particular portion of the past? Are you its helpless
prisoner?

Martin Seligman, an expert on learned helplessness, believes
that we too often choose our own imprisonment, electing to "become victims, 'survivors' of abuse," rather than carve out other
roles and identities. One reason we do this, he ventures, is that
while past trauma hurts, it nonetheless "does not hurt as much as
failure hurts. Being a victim, blaming someone else, or even blaming the system is a powerful and increasingly widespread form of
consolation." We'd rather be hapless sufferers, laid low by outside
forces, "than 'failures' and 'losers.' . . . We are now underdogs, trying to fight our way back from misfortune. In our gentle society,
everyone roots for the underdog. No one dares speak ill of victims anymore. The usual wages of failure—contempt and pity—
are transmuted into support and compassion."

Sometimes survivors of even the most tragic traumas startle us
with their deep reserves of love and hope.

In *Keepers of Memory*, a documentary film about the 1994
Rwanda massacres, a Tutsi man sorts through bones in the ruined
church where his relatives took refuge before being slaughtered.

"We need to work," he says pragmatically, making neat piles of
the remains of those who were once his intimates, "towards life tri-
umphing over death."

Boris Cyrulnik offers the same advice. A trauma survivor himself, he hid from the Nazis as a child during World War II. The rest of his family was deported from France and died in concentration camps. Cyrulnik is now a psychologist, a world-renowned expert in the study of human resilience.

"In the West, the life of one child out of four will be rent by trauma before the age of ten," he asserts. "By the end of his or her life, one adult out of two will have experienced such a rupture and will end up broken by the trauma or will have transformed it"—into something else: a lesson, a stepping stone, art, a reason to move on.

"Confusion follows a traumatic event," Cyrulnik posits. "Our ability to think clearly is slowed down so that we can't make sense of the world, and our mental fogginess leads us to focus on a single detail that . . . [holds] us spellbound to the point where everything else is obscured."

Stuck.

Calling it a "psychic near-death experience," Cyrulnik urges the traumatized to revive themselves, to strive to ignite "a few sparks of life that we must transform into the embers of resilience."

And the sooner, the better, he believes: "We have to give meaning to the sudden disaster as soon as possible in order not to remain in this state of confusion." Those who stay stuck on their traumas too long can only "bring themselves back to life by inflicting pain on themselves. They bang their heads on the ground," figuratively or even literally, inflicting harm on themselves; then, desperate for relief, they "provoke us by displaying their mutilations to us."

Initiation rites for adolescents in many cultures entail pain and fear: that is, *induced* trauma. During the traditional manhood rite among the Sateré-Mawé people of Brazil, youths don gloves filled with a species of live ant whose sting is so potent that each is said to hurt as much as being shot with a bullet. The result can be temporary paralysis or days of uncontrollable shaking. Among the Mende people of Sierra Leone, boys' backs are slit with sharp blades in a symbolic death. The goal is to teach the young how to face trauma and move on. After such rites, as after any trauma, Cyrulnik avows, "the child has become more human, because he returns to the world of adults with a secret knowledge."

And what to do with that knowledge? What to do with past pain? Talking helps. Talking heals, Cyrulnik declares—but within reason.

"When a wounded person speaks, he affirms himself and takes up his position. As soon as he undertakes the task of a shared story, he breaks the spell of the filthy beast that had enchanted him."

But at some point, the story should end: "People who are spellbound by what threatens them remain its prisoner, spending their time repeating the same story and describing the same image."

Focusing more on actions than words, a German therapist told a reporter in war-ravaged Kosovo in 2001 that she was there to help local women start their own businesses. The women were homeless and/or had lost children and/or husbands and/or had been raped. The therapist was helping them create and process business plans. Under the auspices of a recovery group called the Kosovo Women's Initiative, several enterprises—a hairdressing project, a weaving factory, and a fitness club—were already up and running. Rather than urging them to relive their traumas, the therapist said, she was "asking these women to dream."

The past cannot be changed, of course. But Boris Cyrulnik urges us to "fill the void and become creators."

Creativity, in his view, entails not merely recitation and repetition but action and transformation. The trauma narrative is one stage in a healing process. But it's an early stage.

The song should *not* remain the same.

Hans Christian Andersen *was* the Ugly Duckling.

With his bony frame, beaky nose, and big jack-o'-lantern mouth, little Hans was chased down the streets of his Danish hometown by jeering boys who reviled his refusal to join their raucous games. He far preferred the dreamy solitude of his homemade puppet theater.

Already difficult, his young life shattered when his father died. To help his mother, eleven-year-old Hans found a factory job. As he described it many years later in his memoirs, one day at the factory he broke into song to cheer himself up. Hearing his high-pitched voice, adult male coworkers up and down the factory lines joked that surely little Hans was a girl, not a boy.

Surrounding him, they yanked down his pants.

"I screamed and wailed," he wrote in his memoirs, as the guffawing men "held me by the arms and legs. I shrieked, wild with fear, and . . . dashed out of the building and home to my mother."

Battling suicidal urges, he moved from Odense to Copenhagen at age fourteen, enrolling in theatrical courses in hopes that his creativity could earn him a living onstage. But when his lack of social graces made him "an object of derision" among his teachers and classmates, "I hid myself at home in a corner, wept, and prayed to God." Starving and penniless, he realized the stage held no future for him.

"Agonized with this thought, I stood as if crushed to the earth. Yet, precisely amid this apparently great unhappiness lay the stepping-stones of a better fortune."

Poor as he was, Andersen literally couldn't afford to stay stuck on his shattered hopes, his fears—or anything.

As the world now knows, his "stepping-stones" were stories: fanciful tales such as those he had nurtured as a lad playing with puppets. Unable to become an actor, he started writing and selling plays, poems, novels, and travelogues. At age thirty, in 1835, he issued his first volume of fairy tales.

It's hard for us to imagine now that such a book could ever be considered radical. Yet it was. Critics trashed Andersen—not for writing badly, as all agreed that he wrote well. Rather, they assailed him for "wasting" his skills on stories meant for kids.

It was an era in which children were not yet taken seriously, were still almost universally considered "best seen and not heard." Andersen challenged these conceits, insisting that children were fully human and deserved their own literature, a literature lush with memorable characters, dialogue, sound effects, and scenery.

"I've written them exactly as I would tell them to a *child*," Andersen explained at the time. To him, that was a good thing, and he proved his critics wrong. Immortal even when they were about mortality, his tales were his own traumas, transformed: He was the misunderstood, misplaced Ugly Duckling, the famished Little Match Girl, the hypersensitive princess injured by a pea. He was the Little Mermaid: a fish out of water. He was the brave boy who announced that the emperor was nude.

Once upon a time, when he was a child, men pulled down his pants in a factory and made him wild with fear.

What if that was the only story that Hans Christian Andersen ever told?

5.

PEOPLE WHO NEED PEOPLE

Stuck on Others

Set me free, why don't you, babe?

—LAMONT DOZIER, BRIAN HOLLAND,
AND EDWARD HOLLAND, JR.

L ife is like bumper cars.

It's like one continuous ride in which we greet and collide with others, constantly negotiating ins and outs. We slam, sidle, edge, sideswipe into friendship, love, alliances, affairs, associations, partnerships, klatches, and cliques. Sometimes we back out and sometimes we don't. Sometimes we stay: because we're ecstatic or at least comfortable or because it pays or it's convenient or we can't work the reverse gear on this thing.

Sometimes we're scared to leave.

In a crowded world, it's inevitable that all but the most die-hard hermits will get stuck on each other, stuck with each other, like it or not, for an infinite number of reasons in an infinite number of configurations. Disparate as these are, save a precious few, most boil down to what feels like necessity. What is peer pressure if not the perceived need to stick to protocols decreed by others, the perceived need to prove oneself? So many of life's *other* stucknesses—on habits, traumas, the present, the past, even work—can be traced back to that simple playground stress: peer pressure. We do so much of what we do because others want it, expect it, need it—or because we think they do. We filter many of our choices through others' desires, others' demands. We recoil when we disappoint or disobey. My parents said: "Whenever you must decide whether or not to do something, picture our faces suspended in the air. Are we smiling? Or are we sad?"

What we get in return is usually intangible, but it matters. I spent a lot of teenage Friday nights hanging around the local tow-truck lot because my best friend liked the drivers. My friend needed company. I loved my friend. Peer pressure slackens as we age, but does not vanish. Often it determines where we worship, how we spend our money, how we vote.

We get stuck not just on personal relationships—though later in this chapter we will look at those—but also on entire dynamics, hierarchies, and strategies. We get stuck not only on individuals and groups but ways of interfacing with the human race.

Every relationship, from the one-on-one of friendship or marriage to the increasingly complex cats' cradles of family and workplace to society, is an interplay of dependencies, of stuckness on others that sometimes makes us feel guilty and indebted and helpless and sometimes feels like paradise. Some of us are needier than others, and those needs—those dependencies—take myriad forms. In good conscience, most of us try never to "need too much." We avoid persons we deem "too needy." They exhaust us. Seeing their numbers on Caller ID, we roll our eyes and sigh. We know how one-sided those dialogues will be.

I am not independent.

Who in this world is?

My husband is almost always right.

I'm not just saying that. He didn't make me say it. We both know it. I don't feel bad about it. He just is.

He is smarter than nearly everyone. He could prove it any way you like. He has an analytical, deductive mind, is good at languages, has launched successful businesses, and strategizes taking into account future contingencies: a skill required of a chess master, which he also is.

I'm just sayin'.

It does not hurt my ego that he is smarter than I am. We do not argue over who should decide what. I do not trust my instincts. I think like a child. Stuck at the Magic 8-Ball stage, my strategies fill with holes even as I plot them. Do I *make* Tuffy make decisions— or do I *let* him? He decides and I do not, will not, because why argue for the sake of argument when whatever he says or does will in all probability be right and best? I am not joking here. It will. Time has proven this empirically true, and if I am clever at all—I am not *stupid*—then the mark of my intelligence is having found and kept someone as smart as he. Call it a gender-based power imbalance, if you like. Things go rather nicely around here.

And because they do, he is not crushed under the burden of responsibility. Decision-making is not really stressful in a pleasant house with just the two of us. Now and then an appliance breaks. He fixes it because he can. I try to help. If he asks my opinion I provide it. But the major way in which I keep things fair, in which I minimize his burden, is in requiring practically nothing. This is another intelligence of mine: the minimal desires of that politely conscientious child. I am a scavenger, a saver. Library books and a scuffed Walkman found in the street six years ago—still works— and thrift-shop clothes and Lipton tea are not just okay for me. I prefer them.

A woman named Bridgette who appeared twice on *Dr. Phil* spent $7,000 a week on clothing and accessories—most for herself, some for her dog. Her husband, a doctor, worked eighteen-hour shifts to pay her bills and the mortgage on their luxury home. I tell myself: I make/let Tuffy make all the decisions, but at least I am not like Bridgette.

I give back.

At best I am amusing, sympathetic, fun. At worst I am invisible.

It could be worse.

This is my bargain with the world. Days pass in which I neither spend a cent nor need a cent spent on me. I ask for nearly no attention. I neither demand that Tuffy buy things nor take me places nor dress a certain way. I am what you would call low-maintenance. He says he is the happiest man in the world and you will have to ask him if it's true.

I need him. He says he needs me.

Do we drill our own teeth? Deliver our own mail? We all depend. We all need help sometimes. How much help will you ask for, what kind and from whom, before you are called selfish? Irresponsible? A bum? A thief? A leech? As civilized human beings, we are asked to pull our own weight. But each variety of need, in each situation, mandates unique units of measurement and unique scales.

How much help will you ask for, what kind and from whom,

before you sacrifice your own autonomy? Whom do you love enough, whom do you trust enough, to just let yourself need them?

We are born dependent—an utter, total need that lasts for years. In this regard, Homo sapiens differ from such species as, say, desert tortoises. After depositing their eggs in burrows, females totter away, never to return. Their Ritz cracker–sized young hatch without adult supervision. Fewer than five of every hundred desert tortoise hatchlings survive babyhood. As for herring, females are far away by the time their eggs sink to the ocean floor. Humans suckle, swaddle, support in every way—knowing that, nearly always, this is temporary.

And when it is not, when able-bodied, able-brained adults do not support themselves—heads wag. Stuckness on dependence is a social issue and a political football.

At a family gathering, everyone takes turns playing with two-year-old Tessa, reading to her and filling her sippy cup. Yet at the same gathering, in the same room, the same adults scowl at Tessa's unemployed thirty-two-year-old uncle, Tyler, who still lives with his parents. Tyler and Tessa lounge side by side on the couch, both waiting for lunch. Tessa is everyone's princess. Tyler they have nicknamed the Sponge.

Who hurts?

His parents do. They love him, but supporting him is draining their savings and retirement accounts. They resent this, but because he is their son and they love him, they scold themselves for being selfish. This hurts, too. As do the looks they get from friends who nod and raise their eyebrows upon hearing that the able-bodied and reasonably intelligent Tyler still lives in his old bedroom, spending most days watching sports on TV and surfing the Web. His parents are ashamed. And so is Tyler. He savors the security he has known at home all his life, that comfortable calm he missed so much during his two years away at college. He knows what others think of him. Tyler's two younger brothers drive over on weekends with their families, talking about their homes and their jobs and their lives. He sees them mouthing "Sponge." Sometimes he considers looking for work and an apartment of his own. He's strong and capable. But at this point, the idea of moving out and living on his own is almost terrifying.

Dependence is a sneaky stuckness in America. This is a nation whose identity is based on *independence*. We celebrate Independence Day. Our founders signed a bold Declaration of Independence. In 1776, these nation builders asserted that Americans "are endowed by their Creator with certain unalienable Rights," which they defined as "Life, Liberty and the pursuit of Happiness." Americans have come to treasure independence as a legacy, as a national trait, a prize envied by others in less lucky nations.

We believe that we deserve our independence, that our forebears worked and fought and died for it. We see it as our right. We use the word "independence" interchangeably with the word "freedom."

And who doesn't want to be free?

In any society, at any time, some sector of the populace will be unable to support itself. Which sector, when and why? That varies. Infants. Seniors without family. The mentally ill. The sick. The disabled. The poor—whom even Christ said "will always be with us."

Beggars were a common sight in ancient Rome. They thronged the city gates, narrow passageways, and uphill roads where traffic jams and strenuous climbs turned travelers into easy targets. The most notorious begging spot was the Clivus Aricinus, a steep stretch of the Appian Way fifteen miles from the city itself. "On this ill-famed slope," wrote the nineteenth-century archaeologist Rodolfo Lanciani, "swarms of filthy professional beggars used to take up their station, to tax the benevolence of travellers with their impor-tunities . . . harassing them with their vociferations, until the vic-tims, to rescue themselves from such a persecution, would throw a handful of coins."

In medieval and Renaissance Europe, as Christianity implored the devout to be compassionate, churches and wealthy landowners systematically dispensed aid to the poor. Almshouses were estab-lished where large numbers of the indigent could live for free. During the seventeenth century, the town of Herefordshire alone had twenty-three such houses. Landowners periodically distrib-uted bread or other food. Guilds collected funds for members who were no longer able to work.

Even so, not all indigents were considered equal. Sharp lines were drawn between those considered the "deserving poor" and able-bodied, able-brained, yet still unemployed vagrants. These faced harsh treatment under the legal system of the day. Homelessness carried stiff penalties. According to Britain's Tudor-era Poor Law, vagrants could legally be rounded up and pinioned in the stocks for days at a time. They could legally be whipped, forced to do road re-pair or other hard labor, and sent overseas to the colonies. Recidi-vist vagrants caught more than once could be imprisoned, even hanged.

Some such people were consigned to workhouses. Unlike alms-house dwellers, who were not required to do anything in exchange for room and board, workhouse inmates were pressed into hard labor. An 1834 amendment to the Poor Law expanded the work-house system. The gloomy, horrific conditions in workhouses— where husbands and wives were typically forced to live apart—

were largely deliberate. Knowing about these dire places would have a "bogeyman" effect—scaring the masses out of becoming "too needy."

Rodolfo Lanciani's rhetoric about ancient Rome's indigents reveals the temper of his times: In his view, beggars are *filthy*. They prey on *victims*. Charles Dickens, a former child laborer himself, showed rare sympathy in such works as *Oliver Twist*, with its hungry young hero facing life on the streets, and *Little Dorrit*, whose heroine sheds "secret tears" spurred by the "anxieties and shames" of growing up in a debtors' prison.

Dickens would marvel at how much attitudes have changed since his day. Welfare systems support millions around the world, and children are generally taught to feel compassion for the needy. Canned-food drives are standard practice at schools in the United States, and student-run relief projects are increasingly popular. In the Angel Tree Project at Episcopal High School in Bellaire, Texas, teens raise funds every autumn in order to buy holiday gifts for children whose parents are in prison. EHS students also collect used clothing for disaster relief and cook breakfast for the homeless. More and more schools, clubs, and nonprofits are rallying around the needy.

And yet—

Supply free sustenance, and some people will always be accused of taking advantage. Such accusations can be harsh. Sometimes they're true.

Offered free stuff, how much should one accept? My mother scolded me when I was seven and a nice lady passed me a plate of cookies and I took not one but three. "Don't be a pig. Put two back and apologize," my mother hissed. The nice lady laughed. "No, she can have several." The word "several" instantly swelled with a magic that it has held for me ever since. I cannot hear it without tasting butter, sugar, candy stars.

But in that interchange thrummed the questions that haunt us all: How much is fair? Exactly how many is several?

On the campaign trail in 1976, Ronald Reagan regaled a Chicago crowd with the story of a woman in that city who "has eighty names, thirty addresses, twelve Social Security cards and is collecting veterans' benefits on four nonexistent deceased husbands." This "welfare queen," as the future president called her—coining a term—also "has got Medicaid, she's getting food stamps, and she is collecting welfare under each of her names." Nineteen years later in that same vein, then–Missouri senator John Ashcroft told an audience at the Heritage Foundation about a five-month-old girl who had lived with her parents and four siblings "in a squalid one-bedroom apartment in public housing. The family's principal source of income was welfare." This infant was drowned by her mother. Future U.S. Attorney General Ashcroft told the crowd: "Investigators examined the apartment. They found a scrap of paper with each child's name on it and the dollar amount that they were worth on welfare: a life reduced to the dollar amount of a welfare check."

Indigenous Australian lawyer and Aboriginal activist Noel Pearson could by no account be called an American "neocon." Yet he crusades fiercely against welfare policies in his country, calling public aid a "poison" that he claims has almost singlehandedly shattered Aboriginal culture. Citing Aboriginals' high unemployment and substance-abuse rates, as well as data revealing that Aboriginals' lives are on average seventeen years shorter than those of other Australians, Pearson contends that when transactions "are not based on reciprocity . . . the recipient gets money but gives or does nothing in return. It is money for nothing." This, he claims, sets "a poverty trap" in which "perverse incentives encourage people towards welfare and away from real employment." And this, he adds, leads to a loss of self-esteem and sense of purpose.

Many Britons were shocked when their newspapers revealed in 2006 that the nation's welfare program virtually discouraged aid seekers from marrying. While according to fixed payout rules a single person was entitled to £57.45, a couple on the dole would be entitled to £90.10 a week, total. By simply marrying each other, two individuals would say good-bye to nearly £25 a week right off the bat. They stood to lose much more, still, as singles were also entitled to higher child-support payments and larger job-seeker allowances and tax benefits. A report prepared by fiscal-policy experts Don Draper and Leonard Beighton for the family charity CARE declared that because of the skewed benefits system, couples needed to work nearly five times as many hours as single mothers to rise above the official poverty line. As a result, Draper and Beighton noted, millions of children in two-parent households were desperately poor, and record numbers of couples were divorcing or living apart purely in order to qualify for the higher single-person benefits. By making marriage itself into an obstacle, by penalizing families whose members could at least in theory share rapport and responsibilities, such a system seems designed to lock aid seekers into isolated, often lonely lives—in any case, to make them all the more dependent on outside support.

But not all welfare is public aid. Some of it is very private indeed.

Tessa's uncle Tyler, munching cereal out of the box and surfing the Web on his dad's computer, would never dream of driving down to the welfare office and applying for food stamps. But in the gimlet eyes of his brothers, he is little different from those who do.

Tyler is part of a growing demographic. Most of us know at least one person who moved back in with his or her folks after finishing high school or college, or after a layoff or divorce. It's as if a generation has lost faith in going out to seek their fortunes.

Emerging from the nest to become self-sufficient is perhaps the most important human initiation of all. It forms the crux of countless fairy tales, folktales, and sagas: *setting off to seek my fortune.* It is the ultimate stuck/unstuck challenge. Push your chair back from Mom and Dad's bounteous and fragrant table, stand up on your own two feet, shoulder that knapsack, and . . .

Scary, yes. Exciting, too. Our parents and grandparents tell us how it was for them, how at sixteen or eighteen they apprenticed, joined the military, married, went to night school, worked by day to help support their siblings, shipped out, struggled, suffered, saw the world.

Tom Lutz was inspired to write his book about the history of indolence, *Doing Nothing,* when his son moved in with him and spent days and nights—well, doing nothing.

"Having moved cross-country from his mother's house into his father's at age eighteen, young Cody's plan," Lutz writes, "was to take a year or two off before beginning college." Lutz had himself taken a few years off before starting college. But he'd spent those years "working . . . as a carpenter, line cook, factory hand, piano tuner, landscaper, gymnastics instructor, day laborer and odd-jobber, lumberjack, kitchen manager and caterer, farmhand, contractor, bartender, and musician." Thirty years later, he relished his memories of rounding up cattle. "So imagine my chagrin," Lutz writes, when day after day he woke to find Cody "lying on the couch and watching TV." As a typical day wore on, "he was watching cartoons. . . . I would come back from the library or a meeting, and he would be

there, like an Edwardian neurasthenic, dourly contemplating the
world around him from the comfort of a plush purple sofa. Had
my son become a slacker?"

Lutz questioned his own discomfort. "Why did it make me so
crazy? If he was stretched out on the sofa at the age of thirty-five,
obviously I'd have a case, but the kid was only eighteen."

So Lutz, as his son's support system, weighed these particular
needs on that particular scale and cited age as the main reckon-
ing factor. Eighteen, okay. But not thirty-five. At what cutoff age,
somewhere in between, would he say stuckness on dependence had
set in?

In 1998, a skit called "Kevin Still Lives with His Parents" aired
on *Saturday Night Live*. In it, Ben Stiller portrays a thirty-year-old
who roars into the suburban living room where his parents are quietly reading the newspaper.

"Who's been in my room?" Kevin demands. "And don't tell me
nobody, 'cause there's something I do to the door where I can tell
that somebody's opened it, and somebody's definitely been in there
and opened the door to my room!"

His mother explains that she entered the room in order to put
Kevin's clean clothes on the bed. Then she tells him that she's left a
plate of food for him in the oven. Kevin rants:

"Why did you do that? I told you to stop doing things for
me! . . . I want it to be like you barely know I'm here!"

His parents page blandly through their newspaper, discussing
an article about aphids. Kevin declares: "As soon as I get out from
under my Visa debt, I am going to move out, okay? . . . I'm sorry
I yelled. I love you both very much. I love you, Mom. I love you,
Dad. . . . I am trying *so hard*. . . . I'm gonna be living in the streets,
because I can't afford my own apartment, okay? Just because I'm

not good at saving money doesn't make me a bad person!" He begins to cry.

"Are you happy now? Look, I'm crying! Your little boy's crying like a little baby! What do you want, Dad-deeee?"

Announcing that he is going to a theater to watch *Bride of Chucky*, Kevin drives off in their car. Alone in the room again, his parents confide in each other that they can hardly wait to die.

In the 2006 film *Failure to Launch*, Matthew McConaughey plays a thirty-five-year-old who lives with his parents. They so desperately want him out of the house that they hire an attractive professional "interventionist" whose job is to lure him into independence, using the promise of sex and an engineered crisis. On a forum about this film at the popular cinema site imdb.com, one poster asks, "Who still lives with their parents?"

"I DOOOOOOOOOOOOOO," someone replies, "but im 19 and in college and its so much cheaper! . . . im pretty much stuck until someone decides they want to spend the rest of their life with me."

Another adds: "I still live at home! . . . No rent and they feed you a lot."

And another: "I'm 24 years old and I still live with my parents. I really don't like to talk about it. In my defense, I do my best to help out around here with the chores and I do my own laundry and stuff like that. . . . I have to build credit first before I can move into my own apartment and for me getting a credit card from my bank is impossible."

Another simmers: "My brother still does and he's 39 and married already. Him and his wife just recently traded my dad for the master bedroom."

Yet another: "My uncle does but he is also a complete loser."

Failure to Launch was based loosely on the 2001 French film *Tanguy,* in which a couple concoct increasingly horrifying schemes aimed at evicting their twenty-eight-year-old son, a brilliant scholar of Asian languages and philosophy who still lives with them and has panic attacks at the prospect of leaving.

Some fourteen million American adults now live with their parents. A 2003 study conducted by the Prudential financial company found that nearly seven million Britons over eighteen lived with their parents at that time. A full million of these were in early middle age. The typical reason given is that living alone is too expensive, that entry-level jobs don't pay enough to cover rent and food and fun of the kind and amount to which most young people are accustomed. But young people raised in the West in these times—raised on advertisements in an ambience of relentless materialism—demand more pleasure, faster, than perhaps any generation in history.

The Prudential researchers coined an acronym: "kippers"—for "kids in parents' pockets eroding retirement savings." Another British nickname for the same group is NEET, derived from a 2000 government document that used the term "not currently engaged in employment, education, or training." In America, they're called "twixters"—caught betwixt adolescence and adulthood.

In Japan, they're called "freeters." Coined in the late '80s, a "Japanglish" term transliterated into the Roman alphabet as *freeta* and *furiitaa*, it denotes young people who—despite a then-burgeoning bubble-economy job market—bucked the traditional school-to-salaryman route and instead stayed home. Most were supported by their parents, a small percentage performing low-paid, low-skilled, part-time work, such as at fast-food restaurants. Freeters have been glamorized in Japanese popular culture as rebels and iconoclasts. Combine this social chic with Japan's prohibitive prices, and freeterdom—with *Otoosan* and *Okaasan*, Dad and Mom, footing your bills for clothes, concerts, computer games, CDs and cigarettes—is irresistibly addictive.

In Japan, freeters are also called *parasaito shinguru*, a phonetic rendering of the English phrase "parasite singles," coined by sociologist Masahiro Yamada in a best-selling 1999 book detailing this phenomenon. Yamada drew upon Japanese Ministry of Health and Welfare statistics showing that 60 percent of single Japanese men and 80 percent of single Japanese women aged twenty to thirty-four—some ten million in all—lived with their parents at the time of his research.

While some parasite singles work and pay partial rent, a far more radical Japanese subculture known as *hikikomori*—meaning "pulling away" or "extreme withdrawal"—drop out of middle school or high school and become hermits, refusing to step outside their parents' houses and sometimes even outside their own rooms for years at a time. The media casts them variously as victims of a pressure-cooker educational system and as menacing embodiments of a once-cohesive society in collapse. Reporters have exposed and investigated *hikikomori* such as Takeshi, who spent four years watching game shows, and Yoichi, who after spending several years indoors begged his cancer-stricken father to die because "I want to claim your life-insurance money. So die."

Such extreme cases—and even mild ones such as that of Tyler and Cody lounging on their dads' couches—reveal that stuckness on dependence causes harm in all directions. It harms the supporters most directly, draining them of money and floor space and supplies, but also of self-confidence. Parents of overdependent children often blame themselves for having been too permissive or protective, for failing to prepare or motivate their offspring to be independent. The overdependent thrust their supporters into an emotional tennis match between anger and guilt, as giving feels less and less good.

Stuckness on dependence harms societies, upsetting ebbs and flows that have sustained order for centuries. And stuckness on dependence potentially harms the world. What is the tipping point? When we consume more than we contribute—physically, mentally, emotionally, spiritually, creatively, culturally—we are vacuums, black holes, quicksand.

What use are we?

But stuckness on dependence harms the stuck one, too. Sure, he or she consumes more than he or she is willing to give. But the fact that one is not rendering the world a better place can be a terrible knowledge. It erodes the soul.

Becoming independent is a herculean task in Japan, where competition is dizzyingly steep for enrollment in prestigious schools, for good grades and good jobs, for affordable housing: The average 550-square-foot Tokyo apartment was selling for the equivalent of $300,000 in 2007. In the United States, too, the young say they are daunted by competition and diminishing horizons. Born to baby boomers after abortion was legalized, Anya Kamenetz's generation is arguably the most genuinely *wanted* generation in American history. Maybe that's why, as twenty-four-year-old Kamenetz laments in her 2006 book *Generation Debt*, they've "been taught to expect the world on a plate." Yet now that "the bachelor's degree is the new high school diploma," in an era of rising tuitions and rampant outsourcing, their "lives stall out on the first uphill slope."

And there they stay, she asserts, dependent on their parents or on the imaginary lifeline that are credit cards.

Kamenetz bristles at media coverage in which the "lazy, irresponsible, possibly sociopathic 'twixter' is this decade's welfare queen." Articles about couch-bound twixters spark "prejudice against young people as a class," she complains. For her generation's woes, she mainly blames an economy that she claims rewards the old but not the young, leaving the latter poor and hopeless.

We depend not only on people but also on institutions. Information. Machines—which are themselves the work of people, countless people we will never know, each invention a legacy of countless brains and hands. We take so much for granted. We can scarcely picture ourselves in a world without freezers or pens. We take for granted not only accomplishments but ease. Compared to any other time, life now is ludicrously easy. At 6:32 a.m., you were in Paris, placing contact lenses on your eyes. At 7:10, a plane on which you sat took off for Capetown. On the plane, you used translation software to create a chart in Afrikaans. At 10:02 you took your thyroid pill and called your brother in Shanghai.

We—our bodies, our minds—actually do very little. Devices and systems and technologies, from underwater cables to synthetic fabrics, do most of the work and we depend on them. We seldom rack our brains or break a sweat. Which is nice. We are lucky, but luck makes us lazy.

But how independent are we really? How genuinely self-sufficient?

University of Texas zoologist Eric Pianka believes that we will have to find out the hard way, sooner rather than later. Human overpopulation and reckless treatment of natural resources have, the award-winning scientist believes, doomed us to suffer a devastating pandemic unlike any the world has ever known. "We bred our brains out," Pianka declared during a speech at the Texas Academy of Science, "and now we're going to pay for it." Some airborne microbe, he believes, will mutate at hyperspeed, outpacing science's effort to stop it. Scenes like the scariest from science-fiction and horror films will surround us—and then gouts of blood would blur our vision as our corpses join the billions clogging what once were dance floors and motorways.

This "great collapse," as Pianka calls it, will kill off all but a tiny fraction of humanity. The scant survivors will scrape by with pocketknives on a newly dark Earth, all previously known support systems gone.

And who will these survivors be?

"Well, it certainly won't be the weak or the meek, will it?" Pianka tells me. "I am egalitarian, but nature is red in tooth and claw."

He instructed his audience at the academy: "The first thing you should do when you go home tonight is get a real tarp. Don't get one of those crummy plastic ones; they deteriorate too fast. Start packing it with the absolute necessities you must have to stay alive. These would include things like needles and thread, a blanket, some sharp knives, pliers and wire, water containers, some string, rope, and twine. . . . Wrap them up and figure out how you can carry it on your own two shoulders because you are not going to be able to take public transport or drive your car when the time comes. And then you want to get as far away as you can from any other human beings because they will take your stuff away from you. Try to snare a rabbit, if there is still a rabbit out there to catch. And when you get that rabbit, skin it and tan its hide.

"Soon you'll be wearing it," he said.

By abdicating effort and independence, we abdicate power. Waiting to be served, we abdicate strength, ingenuity, experience. And the most crucial bit of all: knowledge. Lurching from bailout to handout, *we never learn what we can do*.

So far, specieswide near-extinction remains a theory, a horrifying fantasy. As regards scrambling for survival in the wilds, our stuckness when it comes to interacting with others will not have such apocalyptic repercussions for years to come, if ever. Dealing with relationships on an individual, day-to-day level is what concerns us most. When we're happy, when everything's gliding along fine, we don't question our friendships, partnerships, or alliances, our family dynamics or our likes and loves. But when we fight, or feel frustrated or irked or bored or yearn for something different, something more, we say: *I'm stuck*. We warn each other, too: *You're stuck*. We attribute tragedies to the victim's having been stuck with the wrong lover, friend, or crowd. An eighteen-year-old who had been accused of several robberies and suspended from an Alabama high school brought a gun to campus and shot himself to death in front of 150 fellow students in March 2008. In the comments forum of the local newspaper, an acquaintance declared, "I know Jujuan. He was a good kid. He just got stuck with the wrong crowd."

Garrett and Tom had been friends for fifteen years before Tom noticed that waves of dread washed over him whenever his phone rang and the Caller ID showed that Garrett was calling. He always answered, always met Garrett wherever Garrett suggested meeting and did whatever Garrett suggested doing—but not because Tom wanted to.

Tom's reticence had increased gradually in the two years since Garrett had stopped participating in triathlons, the hobby that had bonded the men originally. Instead, Garrett had started collecting guns—which he threatened to use on his girlfriend and her kids and on Tom, albeit always in a half-joking voice.

Tom tried, several times, to talk with him about it.

"It is my nature to be too honest, open, and therefore confrontational," Tom says, remembering how angry Garrett became whenever the topic came up. "My contribution is being brutally honest and hurtful, forgetting that people don't want to be told how mean they are."

After one too many hours spent watching Garrett wave a pistol around at a pool party, Tom went home and composed a long, eloquent e-mail explaining that his initial fondness and admiration for his old friend had turned to a mixture of affection, avoidance, and paralytic fear. He typed in Garrett's e-mail address, then hit "send."

"Better to cut your losses," Tom tells me. "The question is, why did I let myself get close to this person? The answer—one answer—is that he was so charismatic and charming *and* deceitful that I didn't see that other side, the cruel side. I do seem to attract these types; they do seem to capitalize on my sensitivity and 'goodness' "—Tom is trusting and generous—"and I fall.

"Well, live and learn. No real love lost there, at this point. It does hurt to let go of something and someone. . . . The only thing is, I could have skirted around the issue, never brought it up, and not have been confrontational.

"On the other hand, I'm glad that I am free."

I, on the other hand, am a cut-and-runner. Gone without a trace. Vanishing act. Now you see me, now you don't. This is a by-product of childishness: when personal things get tricky or sticky or slightly unpleasant, rather than talk it out, I flee. I am not proud of this, not proud to have left tattered bonds of friendship down the decades in my wake, some of them soaked in blood. I am not proud of this and always vow to change. Next time, I tell myself. Next time.

But no.

I've always been this way.

Gwen moved into the house across the street when I was ten. Her father was in shipping. They moved a lot. My mother said Gwen was mature for her years, "a little old lady in mary janes and pigtails." Bustling in the kitchen on weekends and after school, Gwen wore ruffled aprons she'd sewn herself, their pockets shaped like hearts and suns. She trilled Singing Nun songs as she baked cookies the same buttery white as her hair. She had a big, wide head-split-open smile that spread when we joked but also when she mocked me, my voice, the way I walked. Secrets I told her.

She was mean sometimes but it was easy being friends with Gwen, because she was pretty and smart and lived across the street. It was easy in the same way as fish swim into traps: once in, the fish can't turn around and swim against the current to escape. Besides, the openings are barbed.

It is easier to latch onto whoever is closest than it is to muster the effort and master the fear that would be required for the massive task of selecting, from among all of humanity, those few who are perfectly suited to oneself. It is as true for love and sex as for casual pals and BFFs.

Convenience double-crosses us, of course. Whoever is closest might turn out to be mean, or tedious, or incompatible with you in every way. But by then, you are intertwined. You have shared secrets. You are on their front porch asking them to come out and play.

You stay.

Until . . .

Gwen's family moved away after a year, to the far end of the state. We exchanged letters for while but then fell out of touch. By sheer coincidence, I saw her eight years later in a large university auditorium. We were in the same psych class.

She looked grown-up, and wore grown-up cowl-neck sweaters and culottes. I was childish, of course, and loathed myself and dressed in rags. She looked like a more dignified version of her old self and, with my lopped-off hair and orange makeup, I did not. She never would have recognized me had I not walked up and introduced myself.

We became friends again. We baked cookies as in old times and studied in cafés.

She still sang. She had spent a year in France.

She was still mean.

Now she had new things to mock me for. And no sooner would I vouchsafe Gwen a secret than she told someone: another classmate, her boyfriend, her mom.

I hear you think you saw a ghost!

I hear your carpet's full of fleas!

One night we were trimming her Christmas tree: clear plastic icicles and clip-on red velveteen bows. Two other girls were there.

"Her father," Gwen told them, smirking, pointing at me, "thinks she is still a virgin."

I picked up my backpack, turned, and left.

This is how it is with the cut-and-runners. Reach a saturation point and, without warning, flee.

I never was the kind to stay and fight.

"Hello," Gwen said to my answering machine a few times over the next few days. "Hello?"

She was neither the first nor last. I am not proud to say so, but it's true. My cut-and-running is a desperate act and only vaguely punitive. Escape elates me at first, the giggly euphoria of shock. I spend a few days relishing the tingly piety of the survivor. Afterwards—sometimes *years* afterwards—regret seeps in. I'll miss someone a bit. I'll look back at what I have lost: a discarded menagerie. I scold myself: *I should have left a note.*

Either a sorry note or a good-bye note or a note that described them to themselves: *This is how you are. This is why I left.* A character report, a kind of horoscope. I could at least have left them that. To make them change? To keep them from hurting someone else somewhere down the road? Sure. But mainly to say: *Too late.*

But what about love?

My friend Janine has a new boyfriend. That's the good news. The bad news is that even now, in these pearly early days, she feels imprisoned. Not by him. She likes *him.* But those sneaky self-sabotaging beliefs that always sprout anew with every promising new relationship are back again, with a vengeance. Each one undermines her, traps her, wraps its tendrils around her ankles, and trips her up. As Janine lists them, some look silly to her but that doesn't make them go away:

> *I'm so afraid of any sign that I'm being dumped that I can't relax.*
> *I can't trust that someone actually likes me.*
> *I'm jealous that every woman who sees him when I'm not around*
> *will take him away.*
> *I imagine that he'll jump at any chance to leave me because I'm*
> *boring and depressing.*
> *Whenever he doesn't call, I assume he's mad at me for something.*
> *If he does dump me, I'll never get over it.*

And I'll never be attracted to anyone else.

And no one else will ever be attracted to me.

And if I'm not wanted, I have no value.

I get used to being alone, then when I get together with someone
   I get used to that and I don't think I could get used to being
   alone again.

I'm not smart enough.

I'm not pretty enough.

I'm exuding something—anger, fear—of which I'm unaware.

I've just said something that ruined everything.

I am unlovable.

In this crowded world, lonely and cold and goaded biologically to reproduce, we pair off, bond, and mate. It's only natural. We scrunch our noses watching on TV how other animals do it. Hermaphroditic garden snails fire tiny virtual harpoons into one another's flesh. Bull elephant seals bite the necks of their rivals while battling over control of the local harem. Female praying mantises bite off their mates' heads while copulating—though this is rarer than once thought. Some species reportedly mate for life: the cockatoo, the whooping crane, the wolf, the swan, the Australian shingleback skink. Yet human pairings are infinitely more complex and more diverse than those of any other species on Earth because, unlike any other species, we have big enough brains to devise strategies for outfoxing biology and outthinking instinct. At the points in our life spans at which members of other species would be birthing their fourth litters—or, for that matter, would be long dead—we're still flirting and second-guessing. Along with other animals, we suffer jealousy, rivalry, trickery. But unlike other animals, we talk. And unlike other animals, we lie.

The slang we use when talking about relationships is telling: *You put a spell on me. She's got her claws in him. They tied the knot. Wanna hook up? You're mine.* It's a horror-show lexicon of capture and control. Personal development trainer Steve Nakamoto uses angling terms when writing about romance in his book *Men Are Like Fish: What Every Woman Needs to Know About Catching a Man.* Females, Nakamoto urges, should prepare various types of "bait" ("Recapture your lost innocence"), attach these to a "hook" ("Know exactly what you want"), and finally swoop in with a "net" ("Get him emotionally attached").

We're so capable of complicating our lives that the topic of stuckness vis-à-vis relationships alone already fills enough books to stock a library. So out of the countless varieties of this type of stuckness, let's look at the big three:

You're stuck in a relationship and you know it.

You're stuck in a relationship and you don't know it.

You're not stuck in a relationship, but you think you are.

The first category is poignant at best, usually painful, and sometimes lethal. It can go on for months, years, lifetimes. Whole libraries' worth of books have already been written on this topic, too. It could be the theme of marathon film festivals, round-the-clock TV talk shows. Help lines and safe houses beckon. The resounding chorus is: *Get up, get out. Retrace your trail of crumbs. Change your locks. Call a lawyer if you have to. Go.*

Category #1 encompasses the consciously bored, furious, frustrated, frightened, and/or abused who, despite the clangor of warning bells, remain unwilling or unable, too lazy or too afraid or too self-unaware, to free themselves. Hardly a week goes by in which we don't encounter this category at its most extreme, in the form of news stories about people who murdered the lovers and ex-lovers who tried to leave them.

And we can barely imagine life in the type of society where even *attempting* to come unstuck from relationships is, for women at least, punishable by death. Legally. Officially. Religiously. Newspapers report on only a fraction of the so-called honor killings in which women perceived as having "dishonored" their families by having premarital or extramarital sex or trying to escape arranged marriages are murdered by their own brothers, cousins, uncles, and even fathers. As reported in Germany's *Der Spiegel*, twenty-three-year-old Hatin Surucu "divorced the Turkish cousin she was forced to marry at age sixteen . . . and began dating German men." On a cold evening in February 2005 while waiting at a bus stop, the single mother was shot dead—with three bullets to the face. Her youngest brother confessed to the crime.

Then again, some of us are stuck and don't know it. Or we sort of do but won't admit it. The prospect of breaking up and reentering the world of the unattached is fearsome enough to keep many of us half-asleep in dead-end relationships idling on and on in cul-de-sacs as our friends and families nag us about So-and-so. Not that So-and-so will kill us, but they say he or she is holding us back, dragging us down. Our friends and families say this out of love. Our reflex is to drown them out, to defend So-and-so, to chant *We're happy and you're jealous and you wouldn't understand*. We've pretty much all been on both ends of the argument. Some of us have even been So-and-so.

Jerri, a Connecticut lawyer, remembers all those middle-school mornings that began in the predawn dark with an icy whoosh as her mother flung back Jerri's sheet and blankets, shrilling *Get up, Jerri-bean!*

"I would stagger down the hall to the bathroom knowing I only had, like, two minutes to get ready," Jerri recalls. "My mom would be standing by the front door holding her car keys, going 'Come on, come on.' I'd tell her I had to pee and she'd say, 'Can't you just hold it in and do it later?' She was *that* desperate to leave. I'd run out in mismatched socks, shirt inside out, not having brushed my teeth."

Jerri and her mother bundled into the car in the dark, the rest of the neighborhood fast asleep.

"Then we were off—to find Maurice."

Jerri's dad had moved out when Jerri was a baby. Raising Jerri alone, her mother had dated a few guys. Just as Jerri was finishing sixth grade, her mother met Maurice. For the first few weeks of their romance, Maurice came over for dinner nearly every evening— and slept over. Jerri hated those nights, the sounds that shuddered through the walls.

But soon his interest waned. Maurice was very popular with women, it turned out. They loved his jive talk and his faux kung-fu kicks.

But although he stopped visiting and even phoning Jerri's mother, "she wouldn't let go. She stalked him," Jerri says, "and that's what we were doing every morning. Mom found out the names and addresses of his other girlfriends and every morning we drove in the dark from house to house, all over town, looking for his car parked out in front of one. That would reveal who he'd spent the night with. Mom would park right behind his car and cry and write in her journal and say all this really graphic sexual stuff that I didn't understand—that I didn't *want* to understand. I'd be

half-asleep and she'd be going on and on about orgasms. After staying behind Maurice's car a while she would take me to the pancake
house, where she talked and wrote in her journal some more, then
she dropped me off at school."

This went on for over two years. "Finally he married one of
those other ladies and moved out of town.

"I learned much too much, much too young. I was stuck in her
car," Jerri says, "stuck on her schedule and stuck in the sick little
echo chamber of her sexual obsession. Heck, yes, I was jealous of
Maurice. I know I should say my poor mom couldn't help it, but
she could. She was clear-thinking enough to get dressed every day,
to drive a car, go shopping, have a job. So shouldn't she also have
been clear-thinking enough to notice that she was talking to a child
about testicles at 5:30 a.m.?"

Truth hurts. So we avoid it, whether that urgent little voice is
coming from a friend or relative or inside our own heads.

But because those first two categories—stuck and you know it,
and stuck and you don't—could fill whole volumes, and *have* filled
them, let's look at another aspect of this issue. A lot of us aren't
stuck in our relationships but think we are. A vast number of us
have perfectly decent, healthy, ostensibly happy relationships. Yet
we are led to believe that these relationships—largely by virtue of
being long term—are dull, oppressive, repressive, and unimagi-
native.

That they hinder our growth.

Right this minute, untold masses believe—or, as directed by
powerful forces throughout popular culture, the media and academia, are starting to fear—that they're stuck in their relationships.
That they're not having enough fun. Enough sex. Enough adventure. Enough of what a friend of mine called "soul connection" but

could not define more clearly than that and, for its putative lack, left her adoring husband. Believing they're stuck, so many couples fidget. Fret. They think they're missing out. These restless, would-be-happy people eye their perfectly good partners and think, anguished: Out of two-billion-plus options, I chose *you?*

Quiz these masses. Make them take polygraphs. Multitudes among us are actually happy ever after.

But—

Powerful forces want us to believe we're not.

When my friend Megan first started a relationship with a married man, I was furious. I asked her how she could do such an awful thing to an innocent woman—his wife—and I predicted that Megan would end up sad, angry, and lonely.

"You don't understand," she said, flicking the long hair she had already dyed caramel for him. "His wife refuses to have sex."

"That's the oldest story in the book," I wailed, then mimicked a man's voice. "*My mean bitch of a wife won't have sex with me*. Boo freakin' hoo."

"In Taylor's case," she said, "it's true."

Taylor told Megan he would never leave his wife. He wanted both of them, wanted the double incomes and the house and the security of marriage as well as Megan once a week, an hour each time. Leaving his house to drive to Megan's, Taylor always told his wife that he was heading to the gym. He carried a gym bag as "proof." Megan would be there twenty miles away in her apartment, waiting in the pretty underwear she'd bought that week, her lavender eyes ringed with the kohl he liked, a tray of carefully arranged cut fruit and pastries on the coffee table. He might stay to eat these afterward but he might not, might instead zip his trousers while scrubbing his face at Megan's sink, already thinking of the freeway.

She would call me afterwards, often in tears.

"I said I loved him and he didn't say it back. I called him my soul mate and he just sat there."

"He's taken," I'd say.

"But you don't understand," she said. "Without him I have nothing."

"Without him," I fumed, "you have the chance to meet someone who isn't an asshole."

"You don't understand," she said. "You have a *husband*."

Well, yeah.

She drew out the word "husband" so long that I thought it might snap like chewing gum. Was it an insult or a compliment? I "have" him, sure, as she put it, though that verb makes him sound like a captive, an allergy, or a kitchen appliance. She meant that Tuffy and I have been together too long to remember the new-fella urgency she felt. The thrills.

I had been with Tuffy for all of the twenty-plus years that I had known Megan. During those years, men had been interested in Megan. Some had professed their love and proposed marriage, but she rebuffed them all. They were not her type, she said: They were too skinny, too dull, their hair too sparse, their academic pedigrees too small. They were too available. She was stuck on a type: slick, suave, smart, smooth-talking, *taken*. She was also stuck on competition, on being the other woman. Thus she was stuck on two-timers, liars, and cheats: the ones who get away. She reeled them in. And then, time after time, they got away.

And although Megan fumed imagining Taylor in his suburban

home, pouring wine for his in-laws while wearing a Santa hat, although she envied the ubiquitous thereness of married life, she rejected all offers from single men. Deep down, she thought steady relationships were dull.

That she would feel this way is no surprise. Throughout Western culture these days, a lot of effort and a *lot* of money is spent on convincing us that we are faithful to our partners not by choice but out of boredom and convenience, faithful because of rote mainstream conformity, faithful because we fear being single again or fear our true desires. Powerful forces want to break us up, for reasons this chapter will probe. They want people like Megan to think infidelity is cool and harmless or at least inevitable. Ironically, two of the most prominent among these forces are intractable ideological enemies: capitalism and its opposite. Yet both of these target couplehood in principle with equal ardency. The undermining of stable relationships is a crucial step toward the ultimate goal of each. For each, it is a means to an end but the horrifyingly funny fact is that these are two simultaneous, disparate ends. It is a cosmic convergence of mindbending scope and perversity, in which our poor little hearts are tools in the massive hands of two archenemies, armed politically and economically and philosophically.

And who could withstand that?

Powerful forces out there would look at me and Tuffy and intone: *You're stuck.*

I am? Fine. I wish you were, too.

The first horseman of this homewrecking apocalypse is capitalism. Companies with goods and services to sell hate happy couples.

The main objective of all marketing is to make the consumer feel inadequate. Unsatisfied. Unsettled. Incomplete. The goal is to fill consumers with such yearning for what they lack that they sit up and shout: *"I'm missing out!"*

Marketers want to keep you wanting what you do not have. If you already have a partner, ipso facto marketers want you to want something else: another partner, a different partner, many. For entirely venal reasons, using twenty million catchy tunes and airbrushed flesh, marketers tell us we are bored with what we have. Crushingly bored, and that a new improved alternative awaits, if only—

They chant: *You deserve the best!*

And: *Don't settle for less!*

And even if those slogans are assigned to antiperspirants and chocolate bars, they mesmerize us. Eyeing our partners, we subconsciously murmur those refrains.

Am I settling for less?

Are you the best?

Fortunes are at stake. Companies with goods and services to sell get richer off us when we are single and searching and dissatisfied than when we are paired up, in love, serene. The restless, craving customer is the good customer. The lonely, bored, insecure customer is the good customer. The predatory, promiscuous customer invested in being perpetually attractive is the perfect customer.

Lovebugs, on the other hand, forget to shop.

A happy couple is an advertiser's nightmare. Happy couples occupy cocoons à deux: comfy, self-sufficient, sealed. To paraphrase an old joke: You can always tell a happy couple . . . but you can't tell happy couples much.

They aren't listening.

No longer dressing up, no longer going out: frayed sweats, mussed hair, beer, DVDs. Happy couples "let themselves go." And are the envy of the world. We have the life we want already, says the happy couple. We're smarter than you. Love songs say:

Money can't buy me love.

You're everything I need.

I don't need anything but you.

I've got my man. Who could ask for anything more?

Sure, certain industries rely on couples and families—travel, automobiles, real estate. But these are outnumbered by industries that bank on singlehood and sex with near-strangers, on self-display and desperation.

And if getting us into that state means convincing us that our partners are dull-witted, obese old drones, they will. With zero compunction. *They must.*

And in the far corner . . .

You say you want a revolution?

Happy couples will not make Molotov cocktails.

Happy couples love the status quo. They want stability. They have stability. They generally do not want to turn the world topsy-turvy. They like the world. They do not want new rules. Nor do they wish to be swept up and swept apart in some wild war, even a social war. They want just to be left alone. In pairs.

Yet throughout the West thrums a revolutionary movement, struggling to overthrow the status quo, capsize society. Envisioning a world they say will be more peaceful, fair, and fun, its advocates aim to shatter institutions and traditions that they blame for all our current ills. Religion, politics, distribution of wealth—*revolt*. Its advocates are anarchists and socialists, primitivists and naïfs and agents provocateurs. Some are subtle, speaking in ever more chic buzzwords. (Struggle. Hegemony.) Others are overt. They do not pretend otherwise. At least at universities, the revolution calls itself by name. Walk through your local college. Peruse its bulletin boards. Audit a class session or two. You will emerge chanting and perhaps thinking:

The West invented prejudice.

The worst offender is America.

Privileged? Apologize!

It's all about power and class.

Rise up and fight.

Comb faculty Web pages and after a while it will become numbingly repetitive as liberal-arts professors from literature to languages to anthropology to history and beyond cite Marx and Mao and social class among their specialties. Some were famous in the '60s for their radicalism. Log on and play spot the revolutionary.

Happy couples are automatic obstacles to revolutions, because revolutions can be kindled only amid massive societal unrest. Happy couples produce nuclear families, and Karl Marx and Friedrich Engels made no bones about their dislike of these, proclaiming in *The Communist Manifesto:* "Abolition of the family! . . . On what foundation is the present family, the bourgeois family, based? On capital, on private gain. In its completely developed form, this family exists only among the bourgeoisie." In other words, it's the enemy. Elsewhere, as in his 1884 treatise *The Origin of the Family, Private Property and the State*, Engels wrote approvingly and extensively of polygamous and other types of "open" family. The *Manifesto* continues: "The bourgeois family will vanish as a matter of course . . . with the vanishing of capital"— i.e., with the revolution. It goes on to rail against "bourgeois claptrap about the family and education, about the hallowed correlation of parents and child." This Marx and Engels deem "disgusting."

"The Communists," they declare, "have no need to introduce free love; it has existed almost from time immemorial." Charging that bourgeois men "take the greatest pleasure in seducing each other's wives," the *Manifesto* deduces: "Bourgeois marriage is, in reality, a system of wives in common and thus, at the most, what the Communists might possibly be reproached with is that they desire to introduce, in substitution for a hypocritically concealed, an openly legalized system of free love."

Marx and Engels could have made a fortune in advertising. Take two pure, innocent, incredibly exciting words and make a phrase:

Free.

Love.

Who could resist? What's not to love about freedom and love?

Nothing, as long as we realize that in this context "free" and "love" mean "nonmonogamous" and "sex." As long as we realize that they are often co-opted to promote a political agenda, wielded for the purpose of making couples feel stuck. Monogamous and faithful, you are not "free," according to this lexicon. Perforce, you are a slave. Blurring the definition of love devalues its noble, spiritual side, the treasured love for which one waits and aches and is— think of heroic rescues and valiant self-sacrifice—willing to die. This blurring of its meaning is also deliberate. Love in its noble sense is difficult to find: the wait and the uncertainty while waiting are anathema in an instant-gratification world. Dreaming of future happiness with someone yet unmet, exploring hearts and minds, are not for the lazy. Like truth, love can hurt. On the other hand, sex is a comparative cinch. You say you want a revolution? Which requires the abolition of the family?

Convince a populace that love does not exist.

In her book *Against Love: A Polemic*, Northwestern University media studies professor Laura Kipnis portrays cheating spouses as freedom fighters escaping what Kipnis calls "domestic gulags." Echoing Marx and Engels, Kipnis asserts that we pretty much all want to cheat on our partners and should just admit it, because cheating is a breath of fresh air, a righteous rebellion against the "emotional stagnation and deadened desires" endemic to long-term partnerships.

"What can't you do because you're in a couple?" Kipnis asks, then answers herself: You can't have privacy. You can't have secrets. You can't scatter crumbs, and you can't have sex with just anyone. You can't have fun, basically, declares Kipnis. She views affairs as salubrious and monogamy as not just unnecessary but ludicrous, likening it to "voluntarily amputating a healthy limb."

Professor that she is, Kipnis duly compares marriage to factory labor: "Marx's question remains our own to this day," Kipnis quips. "Just how long should we have to work before we get to quit and goof around, and still get a living wage?"

We hear it everywhere: love is a myth. *Cosmopolitan* magazine ran a feature in its October 2007 issue titled "The 'I Love You' Horrors," in which women gave ostensibly true accounts of those horrible, mockable moments when men pledged their love. "All I could do was laugh," one account reads. "The next day we both pretended it hadn't happened." Another recalled: "I didn't know what to do, so I gave him a pat on the back."

Love: that old mood killer and deal breaker, its pronouncement a laughable gaffe, better ignored, like breaking wind.

But sex is real.

Sex sex sex sex.

Did someone mention sex?

You don't have to be a eunuch or a nun to notice how relentlessly not just sex but a very specific sexual aesthetic is promoted in Western culture. It's an exhibitionistic, in-your-face, pro-promiscuity aesthetic, it's high pressure and it's everywhere, from *Sex and the City* to suburban pole-dancing classes to "pimp" as a mainstream and multipurpose verb. And it has the baseball-bat-to-cranium subtlety of any propaganda. Happy couples cannot help but second-guess their own contentment in the throbbing, greased-flesh glare of music videos, in mainstream journalism that is ever more explicit.

"He had his finger up my ass," columnist Christine Borden muses in "Sex on Tuesday," a weekly column in U.C. Berkeley's *Daily Californian* newspaper. Borden is recounting an encounter with a man she did not know well. "Wait, yes, that was indeed his finger. And that was definitely my ass." Of this maneuver, she sniggers: "It's so juvenile and so four years ago. I can't believe guys outside of high school still think it's cool. . . . Pussy play is assumed if you're going into my pants, but the ass is something extra."

Say the reader has never been similarly penetrated, not four years ago or now. He or she cannot help but think: *What am I missing?*

Am I stuck?

"Free" is perhaps the world's most potent word. Twine it with "love" and promiscuity is cast as liberating. This suits both agendas perfectly. Capitalists sell goods and services that they claim liberate the customer from toil and from waiting and uncertainty. Power tools liberate the user from exertion. Fast food frees the hungry from having to buy and tote and cook ingredients or wait to eat. Medicines free the sick from symptoms. Soap and antiperspirant and mouthwash free the average person from fear of embarrassment. An abundance of flavors, brands, and colors frees the customer to choose. Thus, in the capitalist view, promiscuity frees consumers from the same-old, same-old drudgery of "hi dear" couplehood into an infinitely more exciting realm where everyone is hot hot hot and having *so much fun* and if you buy this, you can, too.

But liberation was also a big favorite with Marx and his fellow revolutionaries. "Communism is the doctrine of the conditions of the liberation of the proletariat," Engels explained in *Principles of Communism*. "The people liberate themselves," proclaimed Che Guevara (shortly before he began his work of facilitating hundreds of executions at Cuba's La Cabaña prison). Liberation is a valiant principle. Until its proponents attempt to "liberate" us from our relationships—in principle.

This idea got a big boost from Erica Jong's 1973 novel *Fear of Flying*. Its narrator, a young married woman named Isadora Wing, decides to act on her fantasies about a man who isn't her husband. She emerges from the brief affair with a radical new image of herself as sexually autonomous and free. The book was a massive best seller, an instant classic, and is now a standard in women's studies courses. In it, Jong coins a feminist catchphrase, the "zipless fuck," which she describes as "absolutely pure. It is free of ulterior motives. There is no power game. The man is not 'taking' and the woman is not 'giving.' No one is attempting to cuckold a husband or humiliate a wife. No one is trying to prove anything or get anything out of anyone. The zipless fuck is the purest thing there is."

Untold numbers of married women took this book to mean: *Sister, you're stuck.*

For many, the novel was a permission slip.

Wendy Shalit's first book, *A Return to Modesty*, published in 1999, when she was in her early twenties, advocated premarital abstinence. It aroused fierce, hooting derision among elite critics. Eight years later, as a married young mother, Shalit was shocked to see sexually themed merchandise aimed at children, even at babies. A quick Internet shopping trip illustrates this issue. Crimson-lipped Bratz Babyz dolls. Lace-trimmed thongs in little girls' sizes, printed with cartoon characters. Tiny T-shirts emblazoned with the word LUST. Bibs proclaiming I'M TOO SEXY FOR MY DIAPER. A site called Tshirthell.com sells tiny shirts that read PLAYGROUND PIMP, on which "pimp" takes the form of building blocks.

In her book *Girls Gone Mild*, Shalit laments a loss of innocence. In their exaggerated cynicism and exhibitionism, young girls are oppressed in a sinister yet unacknowledged way, she argues. In the years since her own adolescence in the '80s, "being publicly sexual has become the only acceptable way for girls to demonstrate maturity." For reinforcing this ethos, Shalit blames not only the fashion and entertainment industries but also parents, teachers, doctors, therapists, and journalists who are sexual-revolution veterans, having come of age in the '60s and '70s. Such crusaders, Shalit claims, "view virginity as a boil to lance."

Another border blurs—between liberation and exploitation.

But that's the *plan*. The more promiscuous a populace, the more it mocks and mistrusts couplehood. And thus the more it pleases both horsemen of the apocalypse. The promiscuous spend more money in their endless quest to look good and go places seeking other people who go places and look good. Meanwhile, the promiscuous do not form nuclear families.

From both sides, we're fucked.

Not in a good way.

A movement is afoot to elevate the slut.

She is cast as a brave embattled soldier in books such as—well, *Slut*, Leora Tanenbaum's 2000 cri de coeur against "slut bashing." In the first decade of this century, a new nonfiction subgenre has arisen in which educated middle-class young women quit their ordinary day jobs to become sex workers—for fun, for cash, to prove a point—then write about it. Brook Busey-Hunt, who writes under the name Diablo Cody, was a college graduate working in an ad agency when she started stripping and lap dancing in sleazy Minneapolis clubs for what she calls "a huge adrenaline rush." Pussy Ranch, the website she created to detail her new adventures, was immensely popular, leading to a book deal. In the book, a 2005 memoir called *Candy Girl*, she remembers: "I desperately wanted to be a stripper." After her first shift in a local sex club, "I felt like a common whore," she enthuses. "It was the best day of my life." *Candy Girl* is typically stocked in bookshops' feminist studies sections.

Candy Girl launched an illustrious career. Busey-Hunt is now an Academy Award–winning Hollywood screenwriter. She is also now married, but the arc of her career manifests the ethos that powerful forces want to promote and reward.

Among the guest stars who performed during *American Idol*'s sixth season in 2007 was the Senegal-born rapper Akon. Although he sang only "clean" songs on *Idol*, Akon was at the time well known for his hit single "I Wanna Fuck You," about hooking up with a stranger seen in a club "cuz pussy is pussy." (A censored version of the song, titled "I Wanna Love You," was also released.) By presenting Akon twice on the immensely popular family show *Idol*, the ostensibly conservative Fox network introduced tens of millions of viewers to—and endorsed—an artist who in turn endorses casual sex with strangers. By mainstreaming Akon, *Idol* and Fox consciously or not mainstreamed his message, paralleling it with those of the show's main sponsors, Ford and Coke.

The scholars are in on it. "The Virtues of Promiscuity" is the headline of an article that ran in the *San Francisco Chronicle* in 2002. Under the headline is a teaser: "The latest anthropological research shows that female infidelity is good for the family, the community, and even the gene pool." Well, why didn't ya say so?

" 'Slutty' behavior is good for the species," proclaims the article, in which Pennsylvania State University anthropologist Stephen Beckerman scorns what he calls "the male-female bargain," also known as garden-variety monogamy. Instead, he hails South American tribal groups such as the Bari, Tapirapé, and Ache, whose women have sex with multiple lovers when they wish to become mothers. Not knowing that pregnancy results from a single sperm cell, these tribes believe that pregnancy results from an accumulation of sperm from numerous donors and that the child inherits qualities from all these men. Thus, these cultures view children as having multiple fathers, all of whom offer support. In the "small egalitarian horticultural" societies Beckerman cites, women are "shielded from the effects of male sexual jealousy" and help to raise one another's kids.

But what do the Bari, Tapirapé, or Ache societies have to do with us? Most of us belong to established societies that are neither small, egalitarian, nor horticultural. Modern Western women tend not to raise one another's children, nor—given our sophisticated knowledge of how babies are conceived—will numerous men eagerly support the same woman and child. Beckerman seems to be arguing that if we consciously changed our sexual morals and mores, we could acquire the social benefits these tribes possess; we, too, could have communal parents and sexual freedom and be jealousy-free. But do we want the rest of the package? Life expectancy in the cultures he cites is remarkably low. Promiscuity in the Bari, Tapirapé, and Ache tribes is aimed at producing as many babies as possible, given that so few survive into ripe adulthood. Illness, tribal combat, and violent confrontations with outsiders take huge tolls, especially on reproductive-age men.

In order to get this good-for-us sluttiness, do we want also to adopt primitive living conditions and scientific ignorance?

Spicy pipe dreams aside, the couple-centered West is unlikely to transform itself into a polyamorous playland any time soon in emulation of obscure South American villages. Cherry-picking aspects of other cultures and decontextualizing them is of little use when it comes to assessing our own motives and relationship issues. You could just as easily point to the practices of certain African tribes and announce, "Clitoridectomies are good for marriage."

Relationship issues are too personal and too pressing to tackle via a crash course in anthropology. Bored by her nattering? Irked by his burps? Your solutions are not in *National Geographic*.

Or at the zoo. Yet another set of experts and social engineers would have us emulate not obscure human societies but other animal species. They select and praise certain sexual traits among these species—again, with the same goal in mind: Make the monogamous feel stuck.

Around the turn of the latest millennium, journalists and scientists and social scientists took a sudden interest in bonobos, an endangered species of pygmy chimpanzee numbering just a few thousand and native to a space between two rivers in the Democratic Republic of Congo. They are distinctive for having more sex than other apes, and more kinds of sex, including same-sex sex. Unlike any other species of nonhuman apes, bonobos have been seen performing face-to-face sex and oral sex. Researchers have also described bonobos using sex as a form of greeting and apology, as a means of resolving disputes, and as a favor traded for food. Articles and programs about bonobos promptly started popping up everywhere. "Sex-crazed bonobos may be more like humans than thought" was the headline of a typical story that ran on the Discovery Channel's website, complete with photographs of mating pairs. One online forum discussing bonobos called them "Hot Sex Monkeys!!!"

"If men would only give up their silly desire for world dominance," Maureen Dowd wrote in the *New York Times* in 2002, "the world would be a much finer place. Look at the Taliban. Look at the Vatican. Now, look at the bonobo."

These rainforest creatures, she tells us, "have an extraordinarily happy existence.

"And why? Because in bonobo society, the females are dominant. Just light dominance, so that it is more like a co-dominance, or equality between the sexes." Male bonobos, Dowd tells us, are "happy to give up a little dominance" knowing that female bonobos, "after a busy day of dominating their jungle, [are] primed for sex, not for the withholding of it."

One might as well shout in the reader's ear: *Are you less sexy than a bonobo?*

Awash in this cacophonous chorus, we question our commitments. Are they really commitments—or cowardice? We question our sense of stability, of loyalty. Are we building a life together or marching in place, in lockstep, following an obsolescent status quo? Just by coupling up, are we throwbacks—Mr. and Mrs. Myth? As Laura Kipnis would have it, our vows and pledges are mere vestiges of a sexist, classist, fearful, funless antiquity. And fidelity is just a relic.

Chanting "Love does not exist" along with our professors and TV shows and MP3s, how could we not grow disillusioned? How could we not focus on our partners' flaws and feel unfree? And see ourselves not as *sticking with* him or her, but stuck?

We are genetically coded to stick together, at least to some extent. It is a primal code, an endlessly repeating poem: produce young who will survive long enough to produce young. Unlike fish or insect parents, mammalian parents stay with their young until the latter can live independently, safeguarding them and rearing them and teaching them survival skills. Among Homo sapiens, with our drawn-out maturing process and long life span, this can occupy nearly two decades. The presence of two parents provides offspring with double sustenance and double vigilance, which makes those offspring likelier to survive—and bond, and reproduce. So from prehistory forward, a pattern has evolved that predominates in most cultures: human males and females meet, mate, reproduce, and stay together.

This makes sense as an evolutionary strategy only if you're female. If you're male, you're wired for promiscuity, a vital arithmetic in which men's bodies sing: sow more seeds, see more sprout.

And as a result we see the back-and-forth tension between men's and women's genetic needs—and, further, between conflicting needs and wants within each of us—that have produced human culture.

"Because children take so long to raise, men inherited two needs," says Joe Quirk, whose book *Sperm Are from Men, Eggs Are from Women* details what he calls "the science of relationships." Feeling stuck after a few years of partnership with someone makes plain biological sense, he says.

"Men need to impregnate a fertile body. And they need a good mother to raise the result. These are separable needs." The male, Quirk says, reasons subconsciously: "Just because I invest my love and labor in one woman to make sure our offspring survive doesn't mean I don't have spare sperm. Can't hurt to toss a couple extra out there and see if they take. Some of my ancestors succeeded at the fathering strategy. Some succeeded at the fornicating strategy. They've all passed on their desires to me."

It's the same for women, more or less: "Because children take so long to raise, women inherited two needs. They need a good nest to raise the healthy baby. They need good genes to raise the healthy baby. The best nest might come from your husband. The best genes might come from somebody else's husband. It's hard to get both in the same guy."

If we inherit a falling-in-love gene, "we also inherit the desire to sneak hot genes on the side," Quirk tells me. "We come into this world tormented.

"Humans tend to consult our feelings. Well, where do our feelings come from? Emotions are instincts. Lust is an instinct. Marriage is an instinct. Desires that dominate in our psyches are those that are best at getting genes into the next generation. Our desires are designed to get us to the next life stage."

And life is hard. For most people, it's harder spent alone.

But the what-ifs seep into us like an IV drip—from *Desperate Housewives* and *Footballers' Wives*, from Akon and Diablo Cody and not just one but three totally unrelated pop songs titled "No Such Thing as Love."

Living amid limitless opportunity induces what psychologists call "choice overload," an automatic sense of regret and disappointment— the anxiety of being offered many choices and picking the wrong one. Studies have shown that, given more than a handful of options, *no matter what we choose, we will later wish we had chosen something else*.

Just by living in the modern West, you wander through a constantly changing, unlimited array of romantic and sexual options. This creates anxiety: a bigger, more volatile and potentially lifelong version of eating Boston cream pie in a restaurant and wishing desperately that you had ordered lemon meringue instead.

In prehistoric times, when humans lived in caves and traveled in small bands, the number of potential mates for young people was extremely limited. Perhaps only one or two individuals in the clan were even in the right age group. Later, as humans settled into villages, the pool expanded. At that point, each matable young male (or his parents, in societies where parents chose partners for their children) had dozens of nubile females to choose from. With the rise of cities, international travel, public schooling, and universities, our choices expanded exponentially. It has become much easier to find partners but, paradoxically, it has also become much easier to regret our choices, because *for the first time in history we are able to see all the options that we didn't pick*.

Thousands upon thousands of attractive people parade through our lives—of whom in previous eras we would have been blissfully unaware. With the rise of mass media and globalized culture the situation has intensified even further, because not only are we aware of all those other people in our vicinity whom we didn't get, but our psyches become saturated with images of the most appealing people in the entire world: geniuses and superhotties plucked from Ukraine and Brazil and the Massachusetts Institute of Technology and beyond, photographed and filmed and quoted and interviewed, their faces and bodies and words plastered over every imaginable media outlet, forever taunting: *This is what you missed out on*. Since, in this oppressive patriarchy of ours, in heterosexual pairings males still do most of the choosing, women comprising the lower 99 percentiles of attractiveness—which is to say, almost all of us—now find ourselves competing for men's attentions with the top 1 percent. And none of us are ever allowed to forget, while observing our partners, the looming proximity of others more beautiful, intelligent, accomplished, sexy, fun, and young.

Both horsemen know about the paradox. And win.

For the most part, our ancestors paired up less by love and choice than force and protocol. For much of history, in most of the world, marriages have been arranged. Priests, augurs, and parents pushed together hapless, helpless brides and grooms who'd never met before, to forge family alliances, for good business, to settle debts. A nervous pair of strangers' conjoined zygotes, under a faraway sky so many years ago, spawned whoever spawned whoever spawned whoever spawned whoever spawned whoever spawned whoever spawned whoever spawned you.

Did such people sometimes fall in love with the strangers they wedded? Sure, the lucky ones. Were they stuck?

They probably didn't think so. To our ancestors, whom they were with and the fact that they would stay with their partners until death was simply how things were, for better or worse.

They knew of no alternative. Like the wild regret spawned by choice overload, feeling stuck in relationships is itself a luxury of our times. We feel stuck in relationships *because we can*.

But that doesn't always mean we *are*. Sometimes yes. Sometimes no, although our impatience and outside influences always tell us yes, yes, yes, move on.

"By the time you read this, Florence Levy Caesar and I will have been married for sixty years," comedian Sid Caesar wrote in his memoir *Caesar's Hours*. "By the time you finish this book, you will realize that the reason I am alive today to tell my story is because of Florence." When the pair wed in 1943, "I was making $66 a month. I didn't have the money to buy her anything," so he made up little songs and poems for Florence in lieu of material gifts. In those days, he says, "I was fixing toilets in Brooklyn." Within a few years, he'd been discovered and was making over $3,000 a week for his unique brand of sketch comedy. As his career soared and he landed film roles and a popular TV series, he struggled with barbiturate abuse and alcoholism. Florence never left him. Was she stuck? Were they?

"She has stood by me through the tests of time and great adversity. She provided emotional support for me and our family, saved my life countless times, and always loved me. She is the most beautiful version of the Rock of Gibraltar I will ever see."

Separate yourself from your professors and from literary lap dancers and pimp-my-everything and other primates. Separate yourself from horsemen playing tug-of-war with your body and soul. Sidestep the music and the fairy tales and revolutionary chants. And think:

Am I happy with So-and-so? Is he or she happy with me?

How do I define happiness, and how do we?

Where will this lead, and if it leads to where we are right now, here, this far and no farther, forever and ever, is that agony or is it ecstasy?

Because I am not someone in a novel or depicted in a magazine. I am not a hunter-gatherer or a chimpanzee.

Think: This is me without you. This is me with you.

We will never stop wondering, in this limitless, shimmering pool: What if? That is a question we can never answer. But you, *and only you*, know: What is.

We like to tell ourselves that anything is possible. This is a lovely, dangerous enchantment. Sometimes believing the possibilities are endless drives us mad.

"I can do better. I can do better," sings Avril Lavigne.

Maybe she can.

Or go mad trying.

6.

TAKE THIS JOB AND . . .

Stuck on Work

We've hauled some barges in our day.
—AMERICAN FOLK SONG

Janine studied acting at the Lee Strasberg Institute. She worked as a continuity person and assistant director on several Hollywood blockbusters. She directed a full-length indie feature film. Now she's an office manager at a TV studio. She answers phones, transfers calls, greets visitors. Some would call this quite a comedown, a lower rung on the career ladder than her skills and experience would seem to merit. Janine feels that her job is leading nowhere and doesn't pay enough, but when she sits down to write a list of pros and cons about it, the list begins to look something like this:

> *I'm comfortable in the security of having been here for years and it*
>   *won't stop, unlike film production jobs that end when each*
>   *project wraps up.*
> *I love the people here.*
> *It's easy, so I have no stress or pressure.*
> *The hours let me have a life.*

I love the perks of working on the lot, such as being able to watch
   first-run films for free.
I love having the 401k and retirement and health insurance.
The office is near my apartment, my mom's nursing home, my
   doctor's and dentist's offices, and my favorite hair salon.
I can work out in our building's gym and walk at lunch.
I can stay late and write my own screenplay in my cubicle.
I'm afraid that if I quit and took a more demanding job, I'd never
   finish my screenplay and thus never get back to doing anything
   really meaningful.
I feel safe here.

So she stays, the pros somehow outnumbering the cons. Not entirely stuck, but . . .

From the telemarketer to the civil engineer to the clerk to the surgeon, every job on Earth (except those done by slaves, who unfortunately do still exist) is the result of a highly personalized equation, an arithmetic of wants plus needs plus hopes plus dreams subtracted from realities. Variables include location, desperation, hours, benefits, coworkers, conditions, difficulty, security, and autonomy. The calculations happen consciously or not, under duress or not.

Jenna and Sarah were college roommates. Jenna is a prestigious big-city celebrity attorney. Sarah trains horses in a rural valley. Work-related stress gives Jenna insomnia. She loathes many of her clients. She wants more kids, but barely has enough time now to spend with her only child. She feels terribly guilty about this. And she feels stuck.

So does Sarah. She loves horses. She loves working outdoors. But she worries constantly that she'll be injured and then unable to work. And she isn't earning any benefits.

Add. Multiply. Subtract.

Try what I call the Deathbed Test. Imagine yourself on your deathbed. (Go on, it's just a fantasy.) From that vantage point, look back at what you did for a living.

Was it worth it?

You've got three options:

Keep your job and seethe.

Keep it and stop seething.

Switch.

Keeping it and seething is simplest. Chances are, you're already doing this. It affords you the frisson of venting—without having to risk anything or move a muscle. The ready-made "lazy and afraid" career-management strategy is staying and seething.

Staying *without* seething requires effort: the inner workout of exercising optimism and patience, of finding silver linings when your impulse is to shout "Take this job and shove it!"

Switching is the most strenuous workout of all. It's not just mentally and physically hard but also terrifying, as it means learning new skills and routines and agreeing to take orders from and get along with a new set of strangers.

Yet switching is also easy in at least one sense. If one keeps switching at the first sign of dissatisfaction, one need never learn resilience, patience, or endurance. One is never forced to find inner peace. Instead, one just escapes—perhaps to face the same problems again in the next workplace. In which case one is not stuck in a job, per se, but stuck on starting over—stuck more on discontent, on the idea of being stuck at work, than actually stuck at work.

New York University business professor Amy Wrzesniewski interviewed janitors at an urban hospital about their work. Even though they all did virtually the same tasks under the same conditions, they did not all regard it in the same way. While some scorned the job, others prized it, viewing themselves as participants in a powerful caregiving network.

"The same type of position can have a wide range of meanings" to those holding that position, Wrzesniewski concluded. "Depending on whether they see their work as a job, a career, or a calling," she added, different workers "have different ways of shaping their work and their relationship with their environment."

The happy janitors don't consider themselves stuck. The unhappy janitors do.

I'm not saying: *Be a janitor and be happy as hell about it*. I'm just saying that stuckness at work is one of the most subjective, eye-of-the-beholder stucknesses.

Someone who seems stuck in what you think is a mind-deadening, humiliating, or unrewarding job might surprise you by finding it worthwhile—or even loving it. Your definition of "reward" and theirs might differ, but *their* definition, since they're the ones doing the job, is the only one that matters. The hospital janitors are one example. My mother is another. She has volunteered at a UNICEF folk-art shop for nearly forty years. Through thick and thin, rain or shine, Tuesdays through Saturdays from noon to five she is there. Neither she nor her fellow employees have earned a cent. Relatives always tut-tutted that as a certified teacher and former department-store executive, Mom could—and should—have a "real" job. But money mattered little to her. She and my dad were frugal, and his income as an engineer covered household expenses. For her, the "payoff" has been selling handicrafts to the people of our hometown for a worthwhile cause.

By 2005, Annie Volinski had been waitressing at the same New Jersey diner for fifty years. She had no plans to retire. "Not everybody loves their job," Volinski's sister told a reporter, "but she does." Saying that she'd "never really had a bad customer," Volinski explained that the job gave her "a reason to get out of bed in the morning."

It's all about context. Moroccan leather tanners earn the equivalent of less than five American dollars per day, which comprises twelve hours spent hip-deep in water fetid with flesh, lime, and the pigeon dung that is used as a softening agent. The reek nauseates passersby.

Yet the Moroccan leather tanners filmed in 2007 for the TV program *Dirty Jobs* presented themselves as proud experts creating a useful and sensually pleasing product. The camera panned over them stroking soft, supple finished leather that had entered the tannery days earlier as stiff, gory hide.

On the flip side, someone who appears successful and dynamic might surprise you by feeling stuck. As a marketing executive for a major food conglomerate, Monique earns more than all her friends. She supervises a large staff, develops new product lines, and travels extensively. Yet despite her power in the boardroom, Monique would rather be in a *classroom*. Her dad was a high school history teacher whose students sent him thank-you letters long after graduating. When Monique told her college career counselors how much she admired him and wanted to emulate him, they talked her out of it.

"They actually scoffed. They said I was too smart for teaching and I should raise my expectations, that a person with my brains belonged in the business world."

She remembers the enthusiasm—"a sense of mission," she says—with which they shepherded her into an MBA program. "They just told me my youthful aspirations were silly, and I believed them and now I'm so used to the perks that it feels too late to change. But I'll always regret it, deep down."

The early Roman hero Cincinnatus didn't listen to naysayers. Originally a humble farmer, he was elevated to the then-official post of dictator to help fend off an invasion. After his military exploits were successful, many Roman citizens expected Cincinnatus—even begged him—to stay on and become dictator for life. But Cincinnatus famously gave up absolute power and went back to his farm. In his heart, he knew he'd rather be a poor farmer than an emperor.

Most of us linger somewhere in between: frustrated, frantic, bored, feeling unrewarded, unrecognized, unchallenged, under-utilized, and underpaid. And in this crowded world, we might very well be correct. We are pinned into position by strictures internal and external, both within and beyond our control. Career counselors can say what they want, but anyone who has so much as flirted with the job market knows that life isn't fair.

We have to make deals with it.

When Craig was hired to manage the largest in a new chain of sporting-goods stores, he was told that it was because of his strong background in design and media production. Company higher-ups envisioned exciting in-store displays and local cable-TV spots, which Craig was told he could create. But those plans were shelved when the company changed owners six months after he was hired. With twins on the way, Craig didn't want to risk quitting. Eight years later, he still manages the store. He helms a capable and energetic staff and has been rewarded with generous bonuses. Some days it feels like an impossible grind.

On weekends, he makes videos for local bands for free (or for concert tickets). His job didn't turn out to be the venue for his art that he thought it would be, but his job supports his art.

We are more inclined to feel stuck at work than in almost any other aspect of our lives. That's because work—pretty much by definition—sucks. For what is a job, for all but the lucky few, but long stints spent doing what we would not normally choose to spend long stints doing, in a place where we would not normally choose to spend long stints, with people we barely know and do not necessarily like. Work is, after all, *work*.

"What work I have done I have done because it has been play," a nearly seventy-year-old Mark Twain told a *New York Times* reporter in 1905. "If it had been work I shouldn't have done it. . . . The work that is really a man's own work is play and not work at all. Cursed is the man who has found some other man's work and cannot lose it."

Because we spend most of the waking hours of our adult lives working, our jobs become fused with our identities. When we ask strangers, "What do you do?" we aren't asking what they do on vacation or in bed. We're asking what they do for a living. The answers to "What do you do?" almost always start with "I work at" or "I work for" or "I work in" or, even more tellingly, "I am"—a teacher, waiter, mortgage broker, zookeeper.

On one episode of the TV crime documentary show *The First 48*, Detroit cop John Morell declares: "Being a homicide detective is not something you do. It's something you *are*." The United States is a nation built on work, built almost within memory by men and women bearing hammers, needles, oars and beams, fenceposts and microscopes and drills. A significant percentage of American folk songs are work songs: from heartbreaking spirituals to sea chanteys to cowboy melodies to tunes about mills, mines, riverboats, trains. Sung at school, on road trips, around campfires, those songs cast workers as heroes, proud and bold: *Come all you rounders who want to hear the story of a brave engineer* . . .

And in those songs, work inspires dignity, pride, and adventure.

In an ostensibly classless society, work is seen as the ticket to success—if not for oneself, then for one's offspring. Upward mobility beckons in the land whose popular board games are called Careers and Monopoly.

That's a massive lot of pressure to put on a job. No wonder we squirm and feel stuck.

What did you sacrifice in order to join the adult workforce? Free time. Free choice. Your youth.

We expect a great deal from our careers because they must compensate for all we have relinquished. We glance around the workplace and a tiny voice, below any frequency our conscious minds can catch, whispers: "I gave up the sandbox for *this?*"

Work brings money and power, sure. But adult burdens and responsibilities are so oppressive as to arguably outweigh the benefits. You gave up your childhood to start working because that's what civilized people do. You gave it up because the alternatives—being dependent on others or the government, being indigent and/or breaking the law—seemed too dangerous, shameful, and/or unlivable. You gave it all up and that, you thought, was that.

But on some level it wasn't, and you still mourn what you've lost.

Because I am so childish, I am more conscious of and more resistant than most to the idea of donning grown-up clothes to perform grown-up tasks with grown-ups in a grown-up setting to earn a grown-up salary. Even now, I just can't seem to accept it. When we were ten, I overheard my friend Rhonda pointing out her father to our teacher: "He's that nice man," Rhonda said, "in a suit." He was. My dad, too, was a nice man in a suit, driving to his office at dawn and returning at dusk. My mother, too, contended in the baffling realm of customers and cash registers. I shuddered at

the thought of someday joining them, those legions rendered faceless by their daily commutes and their universal martyrish pall,
their complaints about back stock, the boss, and Bob in Account-
ing. Picturing my future, I didn't want to be a hobo living under a
bridge. Then, as now, I believed that able-bodied adults should
support themselves and pull their own weight. Calculating my
strengths and weaknesses, I knew, even at ten, that one of my skills
was saving money. I would have to save as much as possible—
starting right then—because when I grew up, I wouldn't want to
work much, thus I wouldn't earn much. This would be okay as
long as I knew how to save.

And that's pretty much what happened. But more on that later.

Like brushing our teeth, sending e-mail, or any other routine,
jobs—even difficult and complex jobs—get easier with practice.
We get through most of our workdays on autopilot—not just the
work itself but also the transit, interactions, and interpersonal protocols. As with other routines, we are seduced into doing it again
and again because we are used to it. We gripe about feeling unchallenged, but challenge often hurts.

Fantasies of changing jobs are escape fantasies. We picture
drawling *Take this job and shove it, I ain't workin' here no more* as our
coworkers break into applause. We picture walking out that door
feeling so free.

Job dissatisfaction is a national sport.

A 2007 report issued by the Conference Board, a business-
research nonprofit, indicates that less than half of Americans are
satisfied with their jobs. That figure has plummeted in the twenty
years since another Conference Board survey found that, in 1987,

over half—61 percent—of Americans were *satisfied* with their jobs. How, as a society, have we become so inclined to feel stuck at work? How did "Take This Job and Shove It" become our new national anthem? Why is it that, the instant you begin to wonder whether you might be stuck at work, a chorus rises up to shout *You most certainly are!*

We're stuck in a perpetual state of job dissatisfaction partly because work sucks but also largely because we're stuck in a perpetual state of dissatisfaction about *everything*, because that is the state in which advertisers strive to keep us, and advertisements suffuse nearly every aspect of modern life. The more restless and dissatisfied we are, the more money we'll spend searching for happiness. The persistent goal of those with things to sell, no matter the concept or commodity, is to make us want something different, something new, and/or something more: be it a partner, a career, or possessions that only higher salaries can buy. In their eyes, the ideal consumer is the bored, fidgety consumer who responds to these plaints: *See how happy all those other people are? Don't you want what they have?*

It's like a hypnotic suggestion. Like a hex.

We're stuck in a perpetual state of job dissatisfaction, too, because we have largely lost our powers of self-appraisal. If we can't see our skills *and* limitations, how can we know what we want to do or should be doing? Yet in this stimulus-overloaded society, powerful forces want to get their hands on our self-image and self-esteem, and we are shown fun-house mirrors and fairy-tale mirrors and told that this is us.

We're stuck in a perpetual state of job dissatisfaction, too, because we're stuck in a perpetual state of financial anxiety—or actually stuck in perpetual debt. In this materialistic society, money burns holes in our pockets. Trying to escape debt, we're forever scrambling to earn more than we spend. This is the most important add/subtract/divide in our lives, yet we stare at those numbers and scratch our heads as if we missed that lesson in second grade. As soon as our wages increase, so does our discretionary spending. On that fiscal treadmill, no job can ever pay "enough." Thus, what we actually do all day matters less than how much we earn.

Interviewing her fellow twentysomethings for her book *Generation Debt*, Anya Kamenetz noted a pervasive sense of "real disappointment" among "millions of young people trapped in low-wage jobs" because "the nature of youth jobs has changed in the past generation, tilting decisively toward the grinding, the impersonal, and the dead end."

Really? At what point in history were youth jobs systematically stimulating, personal, and promising?

One bitter young interviewee, mired in student-loan and credit-card debt, derided her retail job and called college—where she'd been led to believe that a degree was her ticket to meaningful work—a "scam."

"Following your heart," Kamenetz concludes, "can lead to low income, unemployment, and a lifetime of debt."

Well, sure—especially if our hearts race off on wild, smiley-face stampedes unmoored to reality. And/or if we expect too much too soon. In fields such as plumbing and drafting and tool-and-die-making, only after a three-to-four-year apprenticeship with a master is one eligible to take a test that, if passed, allows one to obtain a journeyman's license. Further years of experience await before one can certify as a master.

We've lost our patience along with our attention spans. But most important, we've lost our ability, even our desire, to save. Much of the debt that young Americans accumulate, and which panics them as they enter the working world, occurs via abundant credit-card use in college or even before. A study by the nonprofit research group Demos reveals that credit-card debt among Americans age eighteen to twenty-four rose a whopping 104 percent between 1992 and 2001; in 2001, the average eighteen-to-twenty-four-year-old carried nearly $3,000 in debt and spent some 30 percent of his or her total income on debt payments—double the 1992 average.

What a huge gamble: spending money you don't actually have, based on how much you want to have or imagine that you will someday have. And spending it on what? American eighteen- to twenty-four-year-olds pay for at least half their purchases with credit cards and debit cards. While some of that spending goes toward tuition, housing, and other essentials, much has been shown to be for luxuries that young people—or any people—in previous generations and other cultures would never dream of buying. That sense of entitlement leads directly to job dissatisfaction. Young people don't just *dream* of rich futures, they're staking their whole well-being on such futures.

So young, so far in hock, they're stuck before they start.

Nearly any entry-level wages will seem small to someone with a four-figure debt. Playing perpetual catch-up, you're guaranteed to feel restless and resentful. Whatever even dimly silvery lining a job might have is overwhelmed by incontrovertible numbers.

This isn't the job's fault. It's the debt's fault. Which is, more or less, the debtor's fault.

And most Americans are debtors.

And thus we wish our working lives away.

––––––––

The trouble with jobs is that by the time you have one, you've already invested so much in it—time, training, energy, perhaps years in school or a cross-country move. And think of all the other opportunities you turned down to choose this one! Quitting would make you look unwise and ungrateful. You'd be chucking your investment.

Coming unstuck always has its downsides.

Terry, an event planner in Pennsylvania, says she's getting better at recognizing those moments when it's absolutely right to let go—and then letting go.

"So many things that I got into," Terry says, "seemed to be things I desperately wanted and for a while seemed to give me a new identity: the chrysalis emerging. And yet in each one there came a point of cumulative disenchantment." For years, she was an editor at a major New York publishing house. But then "I got sick of the continuous bitchy backstabbing and the way marketing superseded any belief in a good story and fine writing." She saw the same pattern in a nonwork situation, during a four-year stint in martial arts: "I got tired of the near-slavish devotion to whatever the master of the dojo proclaimed. I was getting my ass kicked in fight class and finally realized that it was upsetting me profoundly to get beat up. I wasn't strengthening my character; I was just hurt and scared all the time.

"In each of these cases," Terry says, "I left the situation feeling guilty and inadequate, as if I were quitting because I couldn't hack it. There is some truth in that, most blatantly in the karate situation. The black belts were wiping the floor with me. In publishing, I was a senior editor, quite good at what I was doing—developing new series with authors—but I wasn't good at, and had no interest in, the office politics which were necessary to survive. So I quit."

These changes "forced me to reevaluate what was really part of me," Terry says. "It sent me deeper into my own core creativity. It pushed me into a new phase of my life, and there is something in that which seems inevitable and right."

While quitting feels like liberation or escape to some, for others it is just the opposite—serial quitting itself as a form of being stuck. It is the manifestation of giving up, yet never accepting giving up—careerwise, perpetually neither here nor there.

Had you asked my friend Megan "What do you do?" last year, or in the past twenty years, she would have told you, "I'm a free-lance copy editor." Pressed further, she would have said that she specialized in copyediting art books. Strangers always said, "That sounds so cool!" But Megan always shrugged when asked about her work. She shrugged hard, hair sliding over her face like a screen she could hide behind.

She was indeed a freelance copy editor. Publishing firms sent manuscripts to her home and she corrected their grammar, spelling, style, and punctuation for $16 an hour, no benefits, no guarantee that she would ever get another.

Had you asked Megan "What do you do?" a longer time ago—say, more than twenty years—she would have said something entirely different. She would have smiled and said she was a writer.

Writing was all she had ever wanted to do. Writing was what her teachers told her she was born to do. She won creative-writing prizes in middle school, high school, college. Upon graduation, she told her parents she was writing a novel and they promised to pay her rent while she wrote.

And wrote.

And wrote.

She quit the novel eighty pages in. It was about pilots and she lost interest. She started another one, about a punk band.

She wrote.

And wrote. (Her parents paid her rent.)

And quit.

Every few months, Megan would become swept up in a new topic of interest. Bullfighting. Mount Rushmore. Minks. Abruptly dropping her last topic and her writings on it, she plunged into researching the new one, collecting its artifacts, redecorating her apartment. Stockpiling cold cuts and Snickers bars, she started writing in a frenzy, new novel after new novel begun, half-done, trashed.

One fall, Megan finished a mystery. It took place in her Alabama hometown and its heroine, like Megan, was mixed race. Unlike Megan, its heroine was confident and mathematically inclined.

Megan acquired an agent.

The agent was pumped. She said it was a great season for mixed-race heroines. But the rejection slips came thick and fast. They all said, basically: Beautiful writing, not ethnic enough.

The agent told Megan to write another draft, this time with Caribbean grandparents.

Megan complied. She really tried. But the Caribbean grandparents were wooden, their speech inauthentic, said the new rejection slips.

She quit.

And that was it.

At first she said she wouldn't write. And then she said she couldn't write. By then she said she wanted to, but no words came. Her folks no longer paid her rent. She loved to shop. She got a series of library jobs but always quit. By that time, whenever she spoke of writing, it was always with a this-is-history tremor, the way you might discuss scrimshaw or cooperage. She started free-lance copyediting. Its very mention made her flinch. Not that any-thing is ostensibly wrong with copyediting. It is a highly skilled if often underappreciated profession that requires a vast depth of knowledge in a vast breadth of subjects, applied meticulously un-der intense deadline pressure. Copyediting is not objectively bad or shameful, but to Megan it was, because it wasn't writing—and she had hung all her hopes on writing.

We prefer the other kind of story, the kind in which a freelance copy editor becomes a best-selling novelist.

We revel in rags-to-riches sagas. They glow at the core of Amer-ican mythology. They are to us what fairy tales and parables and even prayers were to our ancestors: blueprints of possibility. We scan these tales of invention and reinvention in the same way that bygone peoples scanned night skies and stared in wonder at the chrysalis.

Here's a true story: As a teenager, Larry Brilliant thought he would be a philosopher. That was the young Midwesterner's major at college—but when his father was diagnosed with cancer, Bril-liant switched his academic focus from minds to bodies. He studied medicine, earned an M.D. degree, and had just begun his career when, in 1970, Brilliant was himself diagnosed with cancer. After successful treatment, the young physician spent ten years in India, helping to eradicate smallpox from that country as he traveled from village to village with an inoculation team. Back in the United States, Brilliant took an interest in the burgeoning high-tech field; in 1985, he cofounded The WELL, a seminal online community. Brilliant is also an inventor and a professor of international medi-cine. He launched the nonprofit Seva Foundation, aimed at ending blindness worldwide. In 1998, he became CEO of a major broadband firm. In 2006, he was appointed to an executive directorship at Google.

Retelling such parables, we wonder: Could that be me? *Should* it be me? Am I doing the right work right now?

Then the dissatisfaction sets in, digging away at us like burrs in our shoes. And it's so hard to draw the lines between motivation and inspiration and frustration. Do the burrs spur us to yank them out and march on—or do they leave us lame and aching by the side of the road?

By age twelve, Charles Dickens was helping to support his family. He worked ten-hour shifts in a foul-smelling bootblacking factory. At fifteen, Dickens became a law clerk, and although this was ostensibly a big step up, he felt stuck there. He loathed the endless circuitous detail—as illustrated in his novel *Bleak House*, about a court battle that drags on and on for years. In his twenties, Dickens gave up law and became a journalist. At the time, this was considered a career downshift. Journalism was less prestigious than law. Yet Dickens came into his own here, writing true-life sketches and serials that paved the way for his classic books.

Should I stay or should I go?

Tragically, slavery in the modern world is alive and well. Present-day abolitionist groups estimate that right now, tens of millions of men, women, and children are enslaved: literally owned by other human beings.

Only slaves are literally, technically stuck in their jobs.

And when we complain about *our* jobs, we forget this.

The very idea of changing jobs—or even choosing them in the

first place—is a modern Western luxury. We take for granted our ambitions. We cherish lofty ideals in which we're self-actualized. The average American college graduate changes careers three times in his or her lifetime.

Work was not always thus. In much of the world, it's still not.

Had you asked a medieval carpenter whether he was "following his heart" or "doing meaningful work," he would have scratched his head and eyed you as if you were mad. Had you asked a Chinese steelworker in 1968 if she longed to "take this job and shove it," you and she might both have been arrested.

For most of history, workers did not select their jobs but inherited them. Most careers were determined before birth: you did whatever work your parents had done, often in the same place, later training your offspring to do it, too. A Saxon farmwife grinding grain between stone slabs all day could not realistically plan to become a boatswain or nurse, just as her husband who grew and harvested that grain could not walk through the door one night and announce that he was going to become a cobbler. The shepherd counting ewes on a hillside would not send out résumés. The night watchman was set for life, stuck, even if he was afraid of the dark.

Before the Industrial Revolution, most people lived all their lives in the same villages where they had been born. Each village had its blacksmith, baker, tailor, and such—usually the sons of the previous blacksmith, baker, and tailor. In such a fixed environment, suddenly switching careers would mean intruding upon a neighbor's established vocational territory and threatening to steal his clientele. In most towns and villages, this would have been seen as socially repugnant. Such interlopers would be shunned on principle.

Being stuck at work, the way we see it, is a modern conceit. It's a privilege, just the thought.

Exceptions in history stand out because they are exceptions. Despite imperial China's rigid class structure, poor peasants could attain high civil-service posts if they passed the *keju*, the imperial examination. A standardized test on literature, Confucian philosophy, military strategy, and other topics, from 605 to around 1905, the *keju* was open to all men—then even, in its last years, to women as well. Many rags-to-riches sagas were recorded, although even the smartest, most ambitious rural youth would have been daunted by the prodigious studies required for taking the test and the difficulties of reaching the testing place. In his ninth-century poem "After Passing the Examination," Po Chu-I remembers how hard he studied: "For ten years I never left my books."

With the advent of Chinese communism, of course, one's work and workplace were decided by the government, not the worker. This has begun to change only recently.

In the West, after centuries of career immobility, the Industrial Revolution forever altered the nature of employment. From the late eighteenth century onward, factory towns and metropolises drew massive numbers of workers who, leaving their villages, sought their fortunes doing new types of work. As we know from the writings of Dickens and others, for all its hopes and dreams this mobile workforce also faced new depths of misery and poverty. But a new idea was born:

Choose what you do.

Empires and frontiers are all about job mobility—for colonists and pioneers and to some extent, for better or worse, for the colonized, too. When everything's in flux, opportunities are everywhere and identities morph overnight. Frontiers demand self-reinvention.

Kit Carson was only nine when his father died in 1818. The

sixth of ten children, Carson dropped out of school to help his mother run the family's Missouri farm. But at fourteen he made his first career switch, apprenticing himself to a saddlemaker. Bored, he switched again two years later, becoming a fur trapper. At the time, this was one of the most lucrative trades in America, a brutal and bloody but burgeoning business. From 1829 to 1840, Carson trapped along major waterways, learning several Native American languages in the process. This multilingualism and his familiarity with the Western wilderness came in handy when Carson switched careers yet again, becoming a guide for the famous explorer John C. Frémont during explorations of Oregon and California. Later still, Carson became a mail courier, soldier, and rancher. He delivered goods to President James K. Polk. By the time Carson died at age fifty-eight, he had held at least seven different adventurous careers.

Novels featuring Carson—such as *Kit Carson, the Happy Wanderer* and *Kit Carson, King of Scouts*, written *about* him, but not *by* him—started appearing during his lifetime and continued to be penned and published long after his death. The new film industry capitalized on him as well with such productions as *Overland with Kit Carson*. Mid-century kids relished Carson's exploits in comics and on TV.

As interpreted by the American masses, Carson's motto might have been: *Better dead than stuck*. A legend in his own time, he was the embodiment of the enterprising, bootstrapping, rags-to-riches, rugged American, the classic American of his era. And that era was the era around which America continues to dream itself.

In 1893, historian Frederick Jackson Turner began circulating his "frontier thesis." Its premise was that westward expansion, more than any other aspect of American history, had forged a national identity unlike any other in the world, and that this identity was inextricable from attitudes about work. American culture, Turner avowed, was ambitious, restless, optimistic, and opportunistic. It got this way because, advancing across a seemingly limitless landscape that they felt was theirs to possess and shape, Americans bubbled with creative "nervous energy" that fed a "dominant individualism" that in turn kept them forever on the move, fueled by "that buoyancy and exuberance which comes with freedom—these are traits of the frontier."

In Turner's day, most immigrants had led utterly different lives and held completely different occupations before reaching American shores. They would reinvent themselves continually as the frontier expanded and demanded, as they headed westward to where, Turner wrote, "the wilderness ever opened the gate of escape to the poor, the discontented and oppressed."

Twentieth-century frontier theorist Ray Allen Billington developed these ideas further. Former careers and former identities, Billington wrote, were swiftly "outmoded in a land where prestige depended on skill with the axe or rifle rather than on hereditary glories." High-class ancestors couldn't help you in a Montana blizzard—but ingenuity could. For the bold ones, the ones willing to learn, new jobs and careers sprang up incessantly in a wilderness "where so many material tasks awaited doing," Billington wrote. And even when those jobs were grueling, they offered at least a soupçon of dignity because the workers doing such jobs felt part of something big and fluid and new:

"The pioneer, accustomed to repeated moves as he drifted westward, viewed the world through rose-colored glasses as he dreamed of a better future, experimented constantly as he adapted artifacts and customs to his peculiar environment, scorned culture as a deterrent to the practical tasks that bulked so large in his life, and squandered seemingly inexhaustible natural resources with abandon."

Frederick Jackson Turner believed that wholesale personal transformations created a "cultural democracy" in which Americans like to consider themselves their own bosses, always free to stay or go, forever free to say *Take this job and shove it*.

Even as the plains were paved over and the frontier has become ever more metaphorical, it still beckons. "Since the days when the fleet of Columbus sailed into the waters of the New World," Turner wrote, "America has been another name for opportunity." Most new immigrants and those millions still yearning to immigrate would no doubt agree with Turner, although his words—because they portray the frontier spirit as a good thing and because he downplayed the bloody downside of Manifest Destiny—are near-anathema in American classrooms today.

One reason we so often feel stuck at work is this core cultural credo that says if we're *not* reinventing ourselves at every turn, we're betraying the American dream. This credo tells us that doing the same thing all your life is pitiable, that missing or deferring an opportunity to change renders you a loser. It haunts and taunts us *even if we're satisfied with our current lives, and even if we like what we're doing right now*. Our society expects us to change, change, change, so we end up feeling guilty and driven if we don't. So if we don't feel stuck, we don't actually feel American.

The dot-com boom was another frontier. During its peak, a weird energy crackled in the air, giddy go-for-it jitters as office after office was revamped with foosball tables and zebra stripes; and the cafés, restaurants, and bars in dot-com districts overflowed with flashing-eyed neopioneers fresh out of school, a sleek new kind of geek. With all the stories about billion-dollar investments springing from sketches drawn on cocktail napkins, suddenly it seemed that no one ever need feel stuck at work again. Exuberant self-indulgences shimmered in store-window displays because a new workforce was earning enough to buy musical toilets and desktop sorbet makers. In those days, hearing about but never quite getting invited to lavish office parties where everyone got fencing lessons and to which sushi chefs would be flown in from Japan, I used to think: *This is the gold rush*. But the difference between it and the gold rush of the 1850s was that this one wasn't real. Even at its height, a cloud of puzzlement swirled overhead: this is all so exciting, but where is the money coming from? It's not as if anyone was plucking fist-sized nuggets from a riverbed, *real* gold like at Sutter's Mill, with intrinsic value. Rather, the profits at most dot-com companies were illusory, or plainly nonexistent. Within just a few years, the entire dot-com culture collapsed, and what had been seen as a brave new frontier turned out to be a false one, a *fools'-gold rush*, a hallucination. Yet for a while there, the Wild West spirit was alive again, albeit with databases instead of pans and saddlebags. It revealed that we still dream those dreams.

In communist China before the recent wave of reforms, the most lucrative jobs were called *tie fan wan* or "iron rice bowls"—as in a food-providing vessel that can never be broken. The main iron rice bowls in the Mao years were civil service and military posts, handed to party elites and their relatives. By contrast, the proletariat worked and even lived wherever the state assigned them. No questions asked: they went, and stayed, where they were sent—not quite slaves, but certainly stuck.

When Deng Xiaoping came to power after Mao died in 1976, he eradicated many iron rice bowls as part of his reform-oriented "Beijing Spring." A new wave of privatization spurred open competition, which in turn spurred an Industrial Revolution–type exodus from China's countryside to its cities. This unprecedented mobile workforce is now estimated at 100 million. The Chinese are less stuck in their jobs, but now face a new crisis: the meritocracy. Assigned employment was numbing and unfair, but at least it was certain. Now the Chinese must fight millions of others for jobs that they actually want, and now that they can entertain the idea of change, they can get stuck in whole new ways.

In the United States. our collective assumption is that college means access to "good" jobs, to riches and happiness. But ironically, we often mistake an unlimited array of potential jobs for an unlimited array of potential jobs *that we are qualified to do.*

It is only when comparing myself to others that I feel stuck.

As a child, I dreaded joining the adult workforce but dreamed of someday writing articles for the magazines I liked to read, *Tiger Beat* and *Sunset* and *Fate.* I imagined their reporters meeting socialites and pop stars and seers.

I wrote for the school papers and yearbooks in middle school and high school, but in those years never actually met any professional writers. I knew nothing of how their careers came about, knew nothing of internships or networking or protégés. I vaguely imagined, even throughout college, that good writers simply got discovered—like Lana Turner or Jesus Christ.

After earning an English degree, I sent query letters to magazines, offering to write articles on topics that interested me. Garden statuary. Dude ranches. Seances. Koi carp. The big magazines never responded but from the medium-sized and small ones I got assignments and, after my stories ran, modest checks.

At the same time, my ex-classmates were finding permanent positions at important publications—*Time*, *The New Yorker*, the *Washington Post*. One was writing for *Playboy*. They were flying all over the world on expense accounts, meeting rappers and dictators.

I thought it wasn't fair.

But it actually was. It was perfectly fair.

My ex-classmates did things I wouldn't/couldn't/didn't do. They deployed skills I lacked. They took risks I wouldn't/couldn't/didn't take.

They dressed like adults. I did not.

They had bravado, social skills, an air of normalcy. I did not.

They moved to snowy metropolises. I did not. I wouldn't/couldn't/didn't (and don't) even drive. So I freelanced for obscure magazines: spent mostly free days interviewing cemetery managers, yard-gnome artists, koi breeders, and ghost hunters for magazines whose names you do not know. If you had asked me then if I was stuck, I would have said no—then yes, remembering my ex-classmates. Yet was I? Those yard gnomes and graveyards and bright sherbet-colored fish sparked the idea for my first book, co-authored with Tuffy, whom I loved.

How things worked out has mirrored my strengths and weaknesses. I always knew what I was good at and capable of and willing to do. And I knew just as clearly what I was bad at and incapable of and unwilling to do. I knew which of these might change and which would surely not. I am bad at having mainstream ideas that can be sold for lots of money. But I am good at making a few dollars go far. I am bad at relinquishing freedom. But I am good at not wasting it.

What makes *American Idol* so popular is that it forces its participants to recognize their own strengths and weaknesses. As a singing competition judged by music-industry insiders on national television, it promises blunt honesty. And we have as a society become so used to the opposite—so used to the relentless bolstering of self-esteem amid tut-tuttings that we must never judge our fellow human beings—that we are, as a society, muzzled and gagged. And deep down we resent this. At some level, we realize that accurate judgment is crucial. It reveals our strengths and weaknesses, and until we see these clearly we will forever flail and wander, lost. Self-awareness, forced upon us *American Idol*-style, is a magnificent if unwelcome gift.

In intellectual circles, I am often teased for watching *Idol* and find myself cornered, defending it. The teasers imagine that what they dislike about the show is its lowbrow populism. But what really troubles them, whether they realize this or not, is that *Idol* puts people in their places. Its judges judge fairly, if flamboyantly. And we the viewers are so relieved at this that we embrace a brand-driven network show as if we were pilgrims. We've been starved of reality checks for far too long. The mass enthusiasm for *Idol* has less to do with music than with gratitude. This show can teach us how to feel less stuck in life and at work.

During the Seattle auditions for the show's 2007 season, contestant Kenneth Briggs confidently told the judges before singing that he would win. Moments later, after Briggs had botched an 'N Sync number, judge Simon Cowell declared: "Your dancing is terrible, the singing was horrendous, and you look like one of those creatures that live in the jungle with those massive eyes." Another Seattle hopeful, Jennifer Chapton, was chewing gum as her audition began and removed it only after judge Paula Abdul pointed out that gum can interfere with singing. After telling the judges that in voice and technique she resembled superstar Mariah Carey, Chapton sang poorly. When the judges rejected her, she began singing again—only to be rejected again. "It was a terrible audition," said Cowell, a successful music producer. He advised Chapton to give up singing and "get a job down in the port." It was brusque, but like all reality checks it was ultimately kind.

"Your opinion don't mean nothin'," Chapton retorted. "You don't know nothin' about music."

These are easy targets. But until we summon the courage to appraise ourselves truthfully, we run the risk of being as far off the mark as they are. Ambition is grand. But we will believe ourselves stuck forever unless *we know who we really are and what we can actually do.*

The striking thing about those *American Idol* rejectees is the total disconnect between their talent and their perceptions of their talent. Bad singers by any standard, they believe they're great singers— so great that they're willing to risk being judged on national TV by industry professionals. They seem unaware that their performances will be aired not as art but as comedy. Sitting at home, watching, we wonder: Can they not hear themselves? Who encouraged these people to sing, much less said they had a shot at stardom?

Because somehow, somewhere, each of these bad singers was told things that sent them on a totally fruitless career path, chasing dreams almost certain to be dashed. Even among gifted singers—

and dancers, writers, athletes, artists—few earn a living at it, much less become stars.

And yet—

Disconnect is our other national malaise. It makes millions stuck.

I call it Mirror, Mirror Syndrome.

In the fairy tale "Snow White," the vain queen gazes expectantly into her looking glass and intones: "Mirror, mirror on the wall, who's the fairest of them all?" Obediently, the mirror tells the queen that it is she. For years and years it says so, until one day the mirror replies that the queen's seven-year-old stepdaughter Snow White is fairer. The queen flies into a homicidal rage.

We are that queen. Our mirrors are our parents and teachers, who think they are helping us by saying: You are a star.

And anything's possible.

Psychology professor Jean Twenge calls this a new mantra, a catchall compliment, encouragement, and a cri de coeur that, as the child of baby boomers, she grew up hearing herself. "Can little girls grow up to be mathematicians who are also supermodels who are also astronauts?" Twenge asks in her book *Generation Me*, mimicking the wishful thinking. "Of course! Anything's possible!"

Barraged with praise, the young are blinded, hypnotized, and paralyzed. Twenge describes a recent college graduate who, soon after being hired for an entry-level position at a large firm, "told a startled manager that he expected to be a vice president at the company within three years. When the manager told him this was not realistic (most vice presidents were in their sixties), the young man got angry with him and said, 'You should encourage me and help me fulfill my expectations.'"

What mirror on what wall gave him that idea?

Observing her own San Diego State University students, Twenge laments their lofty aspirations, which hover far above both job-market realities and their own gifts.

Those aspirations mainly entail getting rich.

In a 2007 Pew Research Center survey, 81 percent of eighteen-to twenty-five-year-olds declared that their "top goal" is "to get rich"; 51 percent asserted that their top goal is "to be famous." Some respondents marked *both* "rich" and "famous" as their top priority.

That's a recipe for feeling stuck in virtually any job, anytime. Those who seriously, not just in fairy-tale fantasies but seriously, believe that they are meant to be rich and famous will feel devastated if they become not stars or even executives but, say, stage-hands or sound engineers at theaters or stadiums, much less limo drivers or Teamsters installing the seats.

Social engineers have experimented on generations of children with the odd notion that a self-fulfilling prophecy counts as a valid societal miracle cure: Tell all kids they're great, all smart, all stars, albeit in assorted ways! Believing that anything is possible, they'll study hard, improve their grades, grow up fulfilled and rich, and prove us right!

That is, the way to make all kids successful is simply to tell them they'll all become successful, that *anything is possible* meaning *you deserve the best*.

Pipe dreams.

Nature sorts itself into hierarchies, no matter how hard we try to impose controls or stack the decks or wish. Ask wolves, gorillas, seals, and CEOs: somebody always comes out on top. We might all have an equal shot, but only some will win.

Some are just better shots.

"No one loves basketball more than Marty Nemko. But Marty Nemko is never going to play in the NBA because Marty Nemko is a slow white boy," says Marty Nemko, a California career counselor and the coauthor of *Cool Careers for Dummies*. Even as a child, he always knew the difference between his skills and his wishes, between his fantasies and his actual future. Such self-knowledge "is liberating," Nemko says. "Accept reality. Accept yourself."

Nemko prides himself on being able to tell the difference between those who really want to change and those who don't but say they do. Many people, he complains, hire career counselors merely for show: not to do what the counselors advise but to look motivated, busy, to earn kudos for seeking advice.

"They just want to tell their Junior League friends that they want to get out of their rut and do something else," Nemko says. "I won't take that type as a client."

With those who sincerely want to switch, he assesses aptitude and attitude and advises them accordingly.

"A car needs an engine and a transmission," Nemko says. "Your intelligence is your engine and your gumption is your transmission. You need both. If the engine isn't good and/or the transmission isn't good, you can tune that car up all day and it isn't going to run.

"It's fun to have a pity party. It's fun to talk about yourself in fifty-minute therapy sessions—but that's not enough to get you unstuck. Human beings do not change readily."

And he refuses to lie to people about their aptitudes. Mouthing anything-is-possible platitudes to those with limited skills or intelligence "would be bullshit," he avows. "It would be perpetrating fraud. And I would incur great personal guilt, knowing that when they find out they can't change, they're going to feel like hell."

"These days even busboys . . . seek specialness," writes Hal Niedz-viecki in his book *Hello, I'm Special*. "The star system has infiltrated the minds and expectations of new generations. With Nike be-stowing $1 million on a thirteen-year-old soccer player, Mountain Dew signing up a thirteen-year-old snowboarder . . . few students today anticipate their lives as middle-class drudges." That house-and-car status to which millions in previous generations aspired seems puny and dull to many young people now. What were once considered the hallmarks of success are now just considered the ba-sics, what everyone gets as a matter of course. *Merely* having a com-fortable place to live, a nice car, plenty of food, and all the latest pleasure-giving and time-saving gadgets would seem, to a large percentage of the coming generations, like being stuck. In order to rise above the morass, they want *more*.

Thus, Niedzviecki concludes, we are pressured into job dissat-isfaction and other modes of restlessness by "the notion that we must always be shaping and telling our special tale of ascendancy." That's hard, in an expensive and competitive world where even satisfying non-star jobs don't grow on trees.

In other times and places, limitations on what one could become in life were mainly social, political, and cultural: gender, class, vil-lage, heritage. Such limitations are external, obvious, largely in-transigent. In the modern free world, our limitations are mainly internal. Aptitudes, attitudes. Skill sets, mind-sets.

But the idea of limits has itself come to be suspect. Because the American frontier once seemed so limitless, the very idea of limits now inflames us with fury, suspicion, and resentment. In the 2007 film *Gracie*, an athletic teenage girl yearns to be a soccer star. But the film is set in 1978, when big-time professional organized tournament team sports for females still lay decades in the future. When males ridicule her dreams and skills, Gracie is about to quit. But then her mother reminisces about her own youthful dream of becoming a surgeon. Of course that dream, dreamed in even more sexist times, was deferred.

"If you want to limit yourself," Gracie's mother tells her, "that's fine." She gives the word *limit* a mocking, sinister spin. "But don't let other people do it for you."

Is it really so shocking to point out that some of us are suited to be janitors by aptitude, by attitude? When I was hired to work at a national park the summer after my sophomore year of college, dishwashing was all I could be trusted to do, given my inexperience. Were I to seek a national-park job again today, I might find myself right back in the dishroom, as I *still* have never worked a cash machine or wrangled horses (though I have more or less learned to clean a house). I have two college degrees, but still lack most of the skills that matter when it comes to national-park jobs: food-service skills, equine skills, climbing skills, office skills, retail skills, rescue skills. Were I to seek a journalism job today, despite years of experience in the field, my options would be limited by my antisocial nature and refusal to drive, among other things. In the broad employment spectrum, some jobs hold high status and some hold low status, and some workers doing low-status jobs are in fact doing jobs to which they are perfectly suited. If they believe, nevertheless, that they should be higher up the ladder, they'll feel stuck. The most crucial, yet most politically incorrect question of our era might well be:

Do you have what it takes?

Well, do you, punk? Do you have what it takes to be an astronaut, a financier, a superstar? Or does it just feel good to say so?

Delusion and denial are quicksand.

———

Often we get stuck at work through no fault of our own: it is others who keep us stuck. Maybe they tell us it's for our own good. Usually it's for theirs.

"When you listen to Jimi Hendrix's records," muses rock 'n' roll historian Richie Unterberger, "you don't think of a guy who's getting stuck."

Certainly not! The persona that surrounded Hendrix in his brief lifetime and surrounds him even now, so long after his death at age twenty-seven in 1970, was all about innovation. He was the one who picked guitar strings with his teeth, the one who performed an electrified "Star-Spangled Banner" at Woodstock.

And yet, Unterberger says, Hendrix was "under continuous pressure" not to change. For Hendrix, performance was work. And as a result of this pressure—from fans and managers—Hendrix, like many superstars who get boxed into personas and styles, was just as stuck at work as the accountant down the block who wants to be a forest ranger.

"The stuff Hendrix did in his first years—not just the music but the flamboyant stage presence—was so successful," Unterberger says, that professional advisers, colleagues, and friends "pressured him to keep doing the same thing over and over again. Is there a name for not being able to say no? That was his problem." Hendrix always performed his own classics at concerts "because he was afraid not to, because he felt that his fans couldn't accept stuff from him that might be new and unfamiliar, that they wouldn't be able to accept any new statement that he might make. This contributed a lot to the confusion of the last year or two of his life," when he couldn't seem to complete any new projects. "And even though he was getting so bored with 'Foxy Lady,' " Unterberger says, "he did not have the will to *not* play it."

For a lionized superstar, the prospect of losing some portion of the adulation to which one has become accustomed—along with the "instant perks" accompanying this adulation, as Unterberger puts it—is often daunting enough to quell any limb-climbing experiments.

"Hendrix couldn't see his way to having short-term pain for long-term gain," Unterberger adds. Early in his career, Hendrix could never have foreseen that the very vibrancy that had launched him would soon burden him.

"He kept dragging this obelisk," which was his own brilliant past, Unterberger says,

Like everyone else in that era, Hendrix knew very well how many fans and critics Bob Dylan alienated and (at least for a while) lost by playing electric guitar on his 1965 LP *Bringing It All Back Home*. Today we can hardly imagine such a move sparking controversy, but at the time it was a major change, an innovation that constituted rejecting the folk-music roots that had made Dylan famous. Critics and fans felt betrayed. At a 1966 concert in London's Royal Albert Hall, cries of "Judas!" greeted Dylan from the audience.

For actors, the phrase "defining role" is telling and ironic. Sometimes a defining role becomes a damning role, miring the performer at a certain point in his or her creative development, at a certain moment in popular culture.

George Reeves played *Superman* on TV in the early '50s. After two seasons, at age forty, he wanted to move on. Forming his own production company and arranging to star in a new adventure series whose pilot screenplay he had written himself, he was offered a substantial pay raise to keep playing Superman. He accepted it—but reluctantly, said many close to him. The American public so identified Reeves with this one role that he could barely get any others. Fans spotting him on the street addressed him as "Superman." He did a guest spot on *I Love Lucy*, in a 1956 episode titled "Lucy Meets Superman," which finds Lucille Ball's character deliberately putting herself into perilous situations so as to lure Superman to her son's birthday party. A colleague would later report that around that time, Reeves would often say, "Here I am, wasting my life." Three years later, he committed suicide.

A. A. Milne is best known as the author of *Winnie-the-Pooh*. This is as true today as it was for the last thirty years of his life—to Milne's eternal consternation. In fact, he was a versatile writer: a journalist, novelist, memoirist, poet, and playwright before publishing that classic children's book in 1926. He would likely have made many more bold career shifts subsequently if only his fans had let him. But they didn't, expecting him instead to tarry in toyland forever. For Milne, who died feeling stalled and embittered, *Winnie-the-Pooh* was an airless, teddy-bear-shaped box.

Of Roger Moore, who played James Bond in seven films between 1973 and 1985, the blogger who calls himself "Marcus Aurelius" observes adroitly: "I am sure Mr. Moore has been in other works but I know of only an appearance on *The Muppet Show* and in that appearance most of the skits were of an 007 nature."

Leonard Nimoy is the prime example of the typecast actor. A self-parody for decades, stuck in his role as Mr. Spock on *Star Trek*, he has long since stopped trying to escape from his box.

During the 2006 Super Bowl broadcast, Nimoy appeared in a TV commercial for the painkiller Aleve. In the ad, he is shown—as himself, not Spock—walking down a hallway talking on a cell phone, telling someone that his hand hurts too much to flash the classic V shaped "Live long and prosper" hand signal that was his *Star Trek* trademark. The person to whom he is speaking suggests that Nimoy try Aleve. He does, then walks onstage and flashes the sign successfully—to an audience of Trekkies.

Even noncelebrities get "typecast" at work. When Robyn, a New Jersey boutique owner, got her first job in retail, management asked her whether she was skilled at working cash registers or wrapping presents.

"I said, 'Neither,' knowing that gift wrappers and checkout clerks had to stay out front for their whole shifts—and I wanted to be in the aisles helping customers and restocking and reorganizing the merchandise. The fact is, I was great at gift wrapping. And I'd been operating cash registers for seven years. I was good at it—but I was *also* good at helping customers, restocking and reorganizing, and I *preferred* those. I'm multitalented, but if I told management the whole truth, then I might get stuck using just one or two of my talents—the ones I was less interested in using. That would have been stultifying."

The trouble is, excelling at a certain skill or job-related task can end up hamstringing you, ironically as that sounds. In every profession, a hierarchy puts the lowest-skilled and lowest-earning workers at the bottom, the highest-paid managers and owners at the top—and, in the middle, a core of workers moderately to highly skilled at one or more activities that keeps the company humming, be it teaching or sales or computer programming or tree trimming. A worker who is part of this middle core might think—for it certainly seems logical—that doing his or her job *really, really well* is a sure ticket to a promotion. Yet often the opposite proves true. The best teacher or salesperson or programmer or trimmer in the company becomes too valuable *as* a teacher, salesperson, programmer, or trimmer to lose. Others in the middle core who exhibit talent at other (perhaps extraneous-seeming) skills more suitable for management positions will be promoted ahead of the best teacher or trimmer, who remains moored by his or her own excellence. This is what Robyn was afraid would happen to her if she revealed herself as "too good" at gift-wrapping and checkout clerking. Superstar though he was, this is also what happened to Jimi Hendrix. Being "too good" at guitar-burning, crowd-pleasing stage antics stalled his creative progress.

So in any job, we must be a bit cagey about which skills we cultivate and demonstrate. Who stands to gain from our excellence at this skill or that?

Our fellow living things exert almost constant effort throughout their waking hours. For food, for shelter, for escape, and to procreate, they run, hunt, fight, prey, slay, swim, fly, dig, build, undergo mitosis, navigate, and photosynthesize. They root. They rut.

If they could talk, our fellow living things would not define these activities as work but rather as *life*. They have no choice. Their actions are instinctual, evolutionary mandates toward survival of the species. Penguins swim icy seas because they must. Daisies strain toward the sun and shed seeds because, if daisies are to continue to exist in the world, this is what they do and what they are.

If they could talk, our fellow living things might define work not as what they do to survive in the wild but as what they are forced to do, unnaturally, when removed from their natural habitats. For lions in a zoo, "work" might mean pacing in a pen. For pet dogs, "work" might mean having to sit still.

Jeffrey Moussaieff Masson thinks so. In the late '90s, the psycho-analyst turned animal-rights activist adopted four dogs. He wrote about them in his book about canine emotions, *Dogs Never Lie About Love*. But Masson owns no dogs now. Nor, he tells me, will he ever again: "I still love dogs. I think they're amazing. But I don't believe we can give them the ideal life. Living with us, they're not living the life they were meant to live, which among other things would mean our spending the whole day with them."

For human beings as well, work means being removed from our natural habitats and denying our impulses and instincts. Sitting or standing in one place all day, calculating figures or operating machines or performing some other repetitive task as part of an elaborate undertaking to make some stranger or corporation rich: how different are we from pet dogs, zoo lions, or lab rats?

Among all the living things, only humans really have the power of choice. Only we can hesitate and abdicate and choose our actions to the extent that we do and still survive. We have evolved and civi-lized ourselves beyond having to fret that our species will disap-pear. We do not *need* to labor—or do anything at all—in the sense that a spider *needs* to spin.

So why do we?

Like other living things, we work for food, sex, shelter, and es-cape. We just don't do it so directly. Most of us neither slaughter nor harvest the prey and produce we eat. Most of us do not build our own homes, do not seize potential mates by the throat and mount them in public. Instead, we work for our own personal sur-vival in sophisticated, abstract, symbolic ways. These actions are remote from the primal instincts they serve. We scrub gymnasium floors, analyze data, or perform nasoplasties in order to eat. Yet for centuries, this surreal situation, this abstraction, has been second nature. Our human ideas of work are strange, but we take them for granted: that we must work in the first place. And how much. For what.

We may or may not be stuck in our jobs. But most of us are stuck on believing *that we have to work*. A lot. For as much money as we can.

Even a "good" standard job is bribery. For pay, you've made those sacrifices, traded your youth, autonomy, time, body, and to some extent your mind. Like circus seals coaxed with sardines to clap, all but a very few human workers are coaxed to perform prescribed tasks in prescribed ways for prescribed rewards. We burn away our days.

Think a new or different job will make you happier? Think a new office, new boss, new title, or new type of work will uplift or fulfill you? Harvard psychology professor Daniel Gilbert begs to differ. A pioneer in the new field of "happiness science," Gilbert seeks neurological and sociological sources for bliss. His book *Stumbling on Happiness* asserts that we're pretty much wrong about what we want and what we think we deserve.

Wrong, too, Gilbert theorizes, are our predictions about what in work and life in general would and should make us happy—or, for that matter, sad.

We humans are inept "affective forecasters," Gilbert concludes: For all our wishing and hoping and even planning, no matter how intently we try to picture the emotional effects of various options, we tend to mispredict. And even after making huge shifts or reaching milestones, he argues, we tend to slide back to our baseline emotional states: to whatever place on the happy-sad spectrum we're accustomed to occupying. Once a glass-half-empty type, the theory goes, always a glass-half-empty type. In other words, don't get your hopes up.

Yet Gilbert endorses ambition, as long as it's realistic and not pie-in-the-sky.

"When our ambition is bounded, it leads us to work joyfully. When our ambition is unbounded, it leads us to lie, cheat, steal, hurt others, and to sacrifice things we value . . . our longings and our worries are both overblown, because we have within us the capacity to manufacture the very commodity we are constantly chasing."

A few months ago, my friend Jed applied for yet another job that he didn't get. He'd been unemployed for a year. So although he was already quite familiar with rejection, this latest one filled him with an especially sickening dread. Jed was thirty-two and engaged to be married. A graphic designer, he adorned T-shirts and designed event flyers for friends as a hobby, for free. He had spent the year sending his résumé to every company within a hundred miles of his apartment that advertised for full-time work even remotely related to graphic design—or to graphics or design. He had long since stopped caring whether he believed in what those companies were doing or selling. He just wanted a job.

And yet—luck wasn't with him. Most of the time he couldn't even get an interview.

Desperate and depressed, Jed volunteered to teach an art class at a local after-school program. His rapport with the students caught the attention of administrators, who offered Jed a long-term part-time teaching job, for pay. To round out his income, Jed summoned his initiative, went through his Rolodex, and began seeking further freelance projects, designing shirts and flyers not just for friends for free but for friends of friends for fees, then for friends of friends of friends. Finally, word spread far that Jed was operating a small design business out of his apartment.

Working late one night while listening to music, Jed had an epiphany: he realized that he had spent a year stuck not in a job but stuck *searching for a job*. It had been a grueling, dispiriting stuckness, and in the process he had put the rest of his life on hold—even postponing his wedding, ashamed to imagine his fiancée's relatives murmuring to one another: *he's still unemployed*. Sitting before his computer, working on a freelance flyer in the wee hours, his favorite music blaring through his headphones, Jed sat imagining how his life would have looked if he *had* gotten one of those jobs for which he'd applied so desperately.

He pictured how a typical workday would look, pictured himself climbing grumpily out of bed at six. (He hates rising before nine.) Then he pictured himself dressing in a suit and tie, even slacks and a polo shirt. To Jed, anything more formal than shorts and a tank top—though in all honesty he prefers working in pajamas—feels like a straitjacket. He pictured himself toiling in a silent cubicle, forbidden a CD player, even an iPod.

But music inspires his creativity, improves his art.

Had he gotten one of those jobs, he would have had to sacrifice some of his values and some crucial aspects of himself.

And why?

These days, Jed says: "That last rejection was a blessing in disguise."

———

Many of us would opt out of working altogether if we could opt out without either fear or shame—say, if we won the lottery.

A few among us, a lucky consortium, feel a calling to a job that perfectly matches our desires. A sense of mission.

But what is the likelihood that some job will surface for you someday that answers all your prayers? Fulfills your dreams? It happens, sometimes by design but sometimes by surprise. My friend Miguel was an auto mechanic right out of high school. At twenty-one, he was already married with two kids, and glad to find a job in an automobile factory. The benefits were especially welcome as two more kids arrived. At age forty, Miguel felt stuck at the factory, doing the same tasks daily amid the sparks and clashing steel, in the isolation chamber of a thick protective mask. Then two tragedies befell him. His father-in-law was diagnosed with cancer and came to live his last days at Miguel's house. Then Miguel's brother, dying of AIDS, also came to live with him. Miguel worked at the factory throughout this tragic time: with four kids in school, he couldn't even think of quitting. But he devoted every spare minute to his sick loved ones. After the second funeral, Miguel reflected on his last conversations with the sick men. They had thanked him. They had said he was making their final days easier.

They said he had a gift.

Having been an auto mechanic, a union organizer, and a dad since he was very young, he had never thought much about his other talents. Prompted now, he talked it over with his wife. She was quick to point out Miguel's patience, his eagerness to listen, and his tolerance for what others would call awkward silence—honed, perhaps, over all those years spent in the isolation of his factory mask. She reminded him that most people are repulsed and/or afraid of the ill. Yet he was not.

He started volunteering at a local hospice.

He enrolled in a program to earn a certificate in hospice work.

He quit the factory and changed jobs as soon as his youngest child turned eighteen.

Had you asked Miguel ten years ago whether he would ever enjoy a career with the dying, he would have rolled his eyes in disbelief.

And yet.

His new career is not perfect. He earns less at the hospice—it's a nonprofit—than at the factory, where he enjoyed seniority and union privileges. He cannot help his kids as much as he would like to with their college fees. And certain old friends avoid him now— "as if," Miguel says, "I was contagious."

Lost friends. Lost privileges. Lost wages. Lost benefits. And yet.

This is Miguel's equation.

EPILOGUE

No time to wallow in the mire.

—Jim Morrison, "Light My Fire"

The journey of a thousand miles
starts with a single step.

—Lao-tzu

Well, Megan didn't make it out. She didn't make it out of that relationship with the married guy. She didn't make it out of the job she didn't like. She didn't make it out of debt. She moved around a lot: four apartments last year alone, all within two square miles. This constant packing up and relocating was a blunt, too-literal metaphor for what she really wanted, what she said she wanted—other, harder kinds of moving on.

Within days of unpacking, she would start scanning the classifieds for another place—a larger one, said Megan, or a smaller cheaper one, or one without noisy kids upstairs or one with a better view. It was a frenetic game of musical chairs. She occupied some of the flats so briefly—two weeks, a month—that I never even saw them. She lost thousands of dollars' worth of deposits because, departing abruptly, she broke every lease.

Peering at the map in his Corvette, Taylor drove from the sub-
urbs to Megan's successive new flats on those allotted Thursday
mornings. He would stay with her an hour or half an hour, eat her
pastries and fruit or not, then go.

One fall day in a panic, Megan moved to Oregon.

The rents were cheaper there. She told me she was terrified of
how much she loved Taylor, how much she hated his wife. "I've always dreamed of living in the woods!" She surfed Internet dating
sites, met local guys—a lawyer and a Druid and an ex-Jesuit monk.
I begged her, "Don't compare them all to Taylor." Megan said, "I
won't." She loved the bitter smell of pinesap in the air. She was
happy and sad.

She rented a cute, cheap apartment. Got a dog. She said she
e-mailed Taylor only now and then. She made a date with a divorced
nuclear engineer.

One late November day she called me, crying. She confessed
that she had lied to me, that in fact she had been texting Taylor
constantly. "And last night," Megan sobbed, "he wrote back calling
me a burden."

"Have you any idea," she said, "how that feels?"

I said, "He is hundreds of miles away from you. Also he is a
cheating, lying, sleazy bastard and good riddance. What about that
engineer?"

She had cancelled their date.

She sniffled. I pictured pine needles and deer outside her window as she blew her tiny nose. She said, "I must stop loving Taylor,
right?"

"Right," I said.

She said she was going to walk her dog and see an art show.

Then, sometime in the next day or two, she died. A lot of pills were missing from the bottles in her bathroom and the coroner would later say it was an overdose. Was it deliberate? She left no note. Remembering the smart set of her small square jaw, the wry twist to her lips when she was right, the arrow-sharp precision of her writing, I think: Heck, of course it was. This is what I mean when I say that coming unstuck does not always have fairy-tale endings. When I started writing this book, she was still alive. She told me to write it for folks like her. Before I finished, she showed me what she thought of my help, all my brilliant advice. All her life, nearly every one of her choices made her more stuck, yet she kept choosing, eyes wide open, then eyes closed. She had attempted suicide twice before, over Taylor. After the first time she said: "If it had worked, I would be free."

Now two boxes of her belongings lean, still sealed, against my wall. They were gathered and FedExed by another friend, one of the men who had professed his love for her. The boxes are not much smaller than Megan was, thus I cannot help but picture her leaping out of one: *Surprise!* Alternately, I picture the boxes as coffins. This is horrible. I should just open them. But then . . .

I am stuck.

No news there.

I am stuck in lots of ways right to this very minute. Still childish. Still wearing tattered trousers from a closet shelf stacked high with neatly folded tattered trousers. Still observing other ladies who look more finished than I do somehow. More polished. Preened. And thinking: *I should*—

But I'm not.

And the ten thousandth day of my not-changing comes and goes.

I fear too much. I am afraid of terrorists and death and looking like a fool. And I'm so very lazy. But—

Compared to how I used to be . . .

We are all works in progress, each of us in various stages of stuckness.

The twelfth card in the tarot deck is called the Hanged Man. Despite its frightening name, the card depicts not an executed criminal or a suicide but a wide-eyed young fellow dangling by one ankle from a T-shaped Tau cross or a tree. His free leg crosses jauntily over the bound one. Set against a bright blue sky, the figure looks blissfully calm. He's hanging, and it's unclear how or when or even if he will escape. But he's alive. His face is placid, patient, ringed in sunlike yellow rays. He does not seem doomed. He's just stuck.

As interpreted by tarot readers for hundreds of years, the Hanged Man is not a harbinger of disaster. He's a ray of hope.

Typically, his appearance in a tarot spread is said to vouchsafe a range of messages, such as: Surrender. Wait. Relax. Release. Accept. Take stock. Contemplate. Sacrifice. Renounce. Have patience. Adopt a new point of view.

In his classic 1911 *Pictorial Key to the Tarot*, Arthur Waite— co-creator of one of the world's most popular decks—notes that the Hanged Man is suspended not from a grim gallows but from "living wood, with leaves thereon." Moreover, the man's "face expresses deep entrancement, not suffering"—and thus, Waite writes, "suggests life in suspension, but life and not death." To

Waite, the card promises "intimations concerning a great awakening."

What better metaphor and messages for we, the stuck? Suspended in time and/or in space, we watch the world pass by.

The Hanged Man seems to say: *Your time will come.*

You're either moving or you're not.

Sufficiency and lack, like progress and inertia, are all in the eye of the beholder.

Are you stuck or taking stock?

Are you stuck or are you where you should be?

The only one who can answer is you.

What is the flame that melts your ice? The solvent that dissolves your glue? The bulldozer that clears your wreckage? The bolt cutter that severs your chains?

Your choices, one and all.

"We who lived in concentration camps," wrote the Viennese psychologist and Auschwitz survivor Viktor Frankl, "can remember the men who walked through the huts comforting others, giving away their last piece of bread. They may have been few in number, but they offer sufficient proof that everything can be taken from a man but one thing: the last of the human freedoms—to choose one's attitude in any given set of circumstances, to choose one's own way."

Even while we are stuck, we can be savants. Skills are hidden deep within our stucknesses. The trick is finding them.

After publishing his first novel to critical acclaim, Michael Chabon began another. It was about an architect. It was going to be titled *Fountain City.*

"I thought it was going to be this little, slender book, maybe two hundred and twenty-five pages," Chabon later recalled. But no matter how hard he worked on it, he couldn't seem to whip it into shape:

"Five and a half years later, I found myself with an eight-hundred-plus page monster."

He didn't like it. Neither did his agent. He was stuck.

To the novel's initially simple plot, Chabon kept adding new threads—about baseball, French cooking, ecoterrorism. "A lot of other things had all worked themselves into this thing," he marveled in retrospect. "Maybe one problem was that I never sat down and asked myself what this book was about. You might think that was sort of an obvious question that a writer would want to ask himself, but I think it eluded me."

After the manuscript topped a thousand pages with no end in sight, he said, "I was about to start the ninth draft of this novel. I was so sick and tired of it. I didn't know how I was going to fix it or even what was really wrong with it."

Stuck. *Stuck*.

So he quit.

And he promptly started writing another novel, *Wonder Boys*—about an author struggling with a two-thousand-page manuscript for a book he can't seem to whip into shape. Chabon wrote this novel quickly, drawing on intense personal memories such as "the deep mortification and embarrassment of working on the same project for that long a period of time. By the fifth Thanksgiving that rolls around, you're sitting with your family, and they ask about the book almost with dread." He'd hit his stride. For his next novel, Chabon won a Pulitzer Prize.

In the depths of his own stuckness, he became an expert on stuckness. That was a gift.

We choose to pour the whiskey down the sink. Or go to work again. Or keep a promise. Or let go. Or tell someone you love him.

Or just hold your ground.

"I used to sell paintings," says my friend Shane. "For years, I would go door to door, office to office, literally with paintings in hand. Sometimes I would have worked an entire day and made zero sales, and felt so deflated . . . it was hellish. I started cursing God, existence, everything.

"One day I made zero sales, had no money, and needed to sell a painting. I went through an entire office building, office to office, receptionist to receptionist, asking to show the paintings, showing them anyway, doing whatever I could, to no avail."

It was the last of several buildings he had tried that day.

"I was so exhausted, depleted, and depressed that I just sat on the floor in the lobby near the elevator, feeling sorry for myself."

He thought of going home, but stayed.

"At that moment, someone walked up to me and said, 'You were just in our office; you had some nice paintings. Can I see them again?' I unrolled the canvases and spread them out in the middle of the lobby, and she started pointing to this one and that one, and then another person saw the commotion and joined in—then another, then another. I ended up selling half a dozen paintings in ten minutes to three or four people and I made my daily quota.

"I was stuck—and became unstuck," Shane marvels, "simply by just being there."

———

For Leigh, a judge in Alabama, getting unstuck translates into a fight for control.

"We get stuck in intolerable situations often precisely because we resist them. Our efforts to control the Awful Thing end up controlling us," Leigh muses, "but we feel that we can't let go of these efforts because we believe the thing that threatens us will then destroy us. Only in a crisis, or upon a realization that our control measures are themselves fatally self-destructive, do we let go. And then we find that the Awful Thing that threatened us was just a threat to be faced, a change that could be survived.

"Some of us who have forced ourselves to the brink, and survived, eventually learn to recognize this wish to control when it arises, and we practice letting go instead. Calling the Awful Thing by its name, and asking for help from outside the self, have proven amazingly effective for me. It's a process of overcoming a problem by surrendering to it, and then outliving it."

For the long haul, the true molt and transubstantiation, it's about tracing that stuckness back to how it started. Seeing that and—oh. Making another choice. How many breathless moments spent straddling bridges' guardrails come down to this dialogue:

I'll never change.

I can't.

I can.

Can't.

Can.

NOTES

CHAPTER 1. ONCE UPON A TIME: STUCK IN THE PAST

page 7 "In Tennessee Williams's play": Tennessee Williams, *The Glass Menagerie* (London: Methuen, 2000).

page 11 "We try to get used to this idea": Omar Khayyam, *The Rubaiyat*, trans. E. Fitzgerald (Mineola, NY: Dover, 1991).

page 17 "Now a prolific writer of true-crime books, Carol Anne Davis says": Carol Anne Davis, personal interview with the author.

page 23 "Islamic fundamentalism . . . idea of returning to a pristine imaginary past": Emran Qureshi, "The Man Who Knew Too Much," *The Globe and Mail*, August 30, 2003.

page 25 "For the most part, we were shy, gentle creatures": Dorothy Allred Solomon, *Predators, Prey and Other Kinfolk* (New York: W.W. Norton, 2003).

page 26 "My classmates' moms": Ayaan Hirsi Ali, *Infidel* (New York: Free Press, 2007).

page 28 "Charlotte Brontë described the latter": Charlotte Brontë, *Shirley* (New York: Penguin, 2006).

page 34 "A popular country-rock singer": Dan Halpern, "Lone Star," *The New Yorker*, August 22, 2005.

page 37 "Those early articles in *Chronicles*": Chilton Williamson, Jr., "What Is Paleo-conservatism? Man, Know Thyself!" *Chronicles*, January 2001.

page 38 "Most people who were liberals in 1968": Arnold Kling, "Stuck on 1968," *TCS Daily*, January 27, 2006.

page 43 "When she's striding in a tight-bodiced": Christine Lampe, personal interview with the author.

CHAPTER 2. SEMIAUTOMATIC: STUCK IN THE PRESENT

page 55 "A thinly disguised Snyder": Jack Kerouac, *The Dharma Bums* (New York: Penguin, 1976).

page 59 "The result, according to philosopher": "Philosophy and the Habits of Critical Thinking," conversation between John Searle and Harry Kreisler at the University of California, Berkeley, September 22, 1999, http://globetrotter.berkeley.edu/people/Searle/searle-con0.html.

page 59 "I am a compulsive spender": Greg Bruns, personal interview with the author.

page 64 "Along with its other merits": Boris Cyrulnik, *The Whispering of Ghosts* (New York: Other Press, 2005).

page 68 "That our truncated attention spans": *Diagnostic and Statistical Manual of Mental Disorders,* 4th ed. (Washington, DC: American Psychiatric Association, 2000).

page 70 "Even children remain remarkably inert": Peter Fimrite, "Children Detach from Natural World as They Explore the Virtual One," *San Francisco Chronicle*, October 22, 2007.

page 72 "Maria von Trapp": Maria von Trapp, *Yesterday, Today and Forever* (Green Forest, AR: New Leaf Press, 1998).

page 72 "There is nothing other than this present moment": Charlotte Joko Beck, *Nothing Special* (San Francisco: HarperSanFrancisco, 1994).

page 73 "During the voyage": Homer, *The Odyssey*, trans. Samuel Butler (Roslyn, NY: W.J. Black, 1944).

page 75 "Instant gratification was already": Ralph Waldo Emerson, "Success," from *Society and Solitude* (Boston: Houghton Mifflin, 1892).

page 77 "By working hard, one could emulate God Himself": John Calvin, *The Necessity of Reforming the Church* (Dallas: Protestant Heritage Press, 1995).

page 78 "By the dawn of the twentieth century": Max Weber, *The Protestant Ethic and the Spirit of Capitalism* (New York: Routledge, 2001).

page 79 "Setting the tone for its gushing exuberance": Anthony Ashley-Cooper, First Earl of Shaftesbury, *Characteristics of Men, Manners, Opinions, Times* (Cambridge: Cambridge University Press, 1999).

page 80 "From the Disneyfication": Michael Shermer, "The Ignoble Savage," *Skeptic*, August 2003.

page 80 "In his book *Constant Battles*": Steven LeBlanc and Katherine E. Register, *Constant Battles* (New York: St. Martin's Press, 2003).

page 82   "In 1979, historian": Christopher Lasch, *The Culture of Narcissism* (New York: W.W. Norton, 1978).

page 84   "In the 1980s, test scores": "Toward a State of Esteem," California State Senate archives, http://www.sen.ca.gov/ftp/SEN/SENATOR/_ARCHIVE_2004/VASCONCELLOS/05ESTEEM/ESTEEM.TXT. Also, Anne Taylor Fleming, "Will the Real Self-Esteem Stand Up?" *New York Times*, November 9, 1988.

page 85   "We create a 'socially constructed reality' ": John Shindler, "Creating a Psychology of Success in the Classroom: Enhancing Academic Achievement by Systematically Promoting Student Self-Esteem," California State University at Los Angeles website, http://www.calstatela.edu/faculty/jshindl/cm/Self-Esteem% 20Article%2011.htm.

page 87   "There are no long-term studies": John P. Hewitt, *The Myth of Self-Esteem* (New York: St. Martin's Press, 1998).

page 88   "In her book about the children of baby boomers": Jean M. Twenge, *Generation Me* (New York: Free Press, 2007).

page 88   "In experiments performed": Jill Elish, "Teen Career Plans Out of Sync with Reality, FSU Study Says," Florida State University website, http://www.fsu.com/pages/ 2006/08/28/TeenCareerPlans.html.

page 90   "I am twenty-four years old": Anya Kamenetz, *Generation Debt* (New York: Riverhead, 2006).

page 91   "According to a Harris Poll": "College Students Tote $122 Billion in Spending Power Back to Campus This Year," Harris Interactive press release, August 18, 2004.

page 92   "Spending too much": Paul J. Lim, "Drowning in Debt?" *U.S. News & World Report*, July 31, 2005; also Brian Unger, "Americans Spend Billions on Halloween," National Public Radio, October 30, 2006.

page 93   "Rather than wait or accept fate": Diane Fanning, personal interview with the author.

CHAPTER 3. OOPS! I DID IT AGAIN: STUCK ON HABITS

page 95   "One night when he was twenty-one": Ron Saxen, *The Good Eater* (Oakland, CA: New Harbinger, 2007).

page 95   "Kate Holden was a smart little girl": Kate Holden, *In My Skin* (New York: Arcade, 2006).

page 102   "In July 2007, Michael and Iana Straw": "Nev. Couple Blame Internet for Neglect," *San Francisco Chronicle*, July 16, 2007.

page 105   "Your redneck pals": "Binge Eating Disorder," from a National Institutes of Health/National Institute of Diabetes and Digestive and Kidney Diseases website, http://win.niddk.nih.gov/publications/binge.htm.

page 106 "But how much funnier is Homer's made-up monster": *Diagnostic and Statistical Manual of Mental Disorders,* 4th ed. (Washington, DC: American Psychiatric Association, 2000).

page 106 "Is alcoholism a disease?" "Is Alcoholism a Disease?" American Academy of Family Physicians website, http://familydoctor.org/online/famdocen/home/common/addictions/alcohol/130.html.

page 107 "Like any other addiction": Gillian Flynn and Liane Bonin, "Internet shopping made easy," *Entertainment Weekly*, June 18, 2007.

page 107 "Addiction is a brain disease": Alan I. Leshner, interviewed by Bill Moyers as part of the 1998 PBS series "Close to Home."

page 110 "And the disease theory": AA Services, *Alcoholics Anonymous: Big Book,* 4th ed. (New York: Alcoholics Anonymous World Services, 2002).

page 112 "In a 1784 pamphlet": Robert H. Coombs, *Addiction Counseling Review* (Mahwah, NJ: Lawrence Erlbaum Associates, 2005).

page 112 "Drunkenness is a physical": Catherine Booth, *Strong Drink Versus Christianity* (London: S.W. Partridge & Co., 1879).

page 114 "The conventional wisdom": Andy Denhart, "Is Being Hooked a Choice?" Salon.com, January 10, 2000.

page 116 "Stanton Peele is another skeptic": Stanton Peele, *Diseasing of America* (San Francisco: Jossey-Bass, 1999).

page 118 "In England, Hansen's disease": Edmund Martens, *De Antiquis Ecclesiae Ritibus* (Venice: Venetiis, 1783).

page 123 "Occupants of our brave new narcissistic electronic world": Lee Siegel, *Against the Machine* (New York: Spiegel & Grau, 2008).

page 124 "Popularized in its current form": Friedrich Nietzsche, *The Will to Power* (New York: Vintage Books, 1968).

page 125 "Texas A&M": James Scheurich, "Glossary of Postmodern Terminology," Faculty website, http://www.edb.utexas.edu/faculty/scheurich/proj6/pags/glos.htm.

page 131 "To aid in the diagnosis of Pathologic Gambling Disorder": Leena M. Sumitra and Shannon C. Miller, "Pathologic Gambling Disorder," *Postgraduate Medicine*, July 2005.

page 132 "It was a brainchild": "Can't Quit Gates' Xbox? Clinic Has 12-Step Program," *Forbes*, June 8, 2006; and Smith & Jones Wild Horses Center website, http://www.smithandjones.nl/eng/index.html.

page 134 "Since then, according to NIDA": Nora Volkow, "Message from the Director," National Institutes of Health/National Institute on Drug Abuse website, http://www.nida.nih.gov/about/welcome/messagemeth405.html.

page 134 "Matthew Knippenberg was charged": Court document, Case No. 15C01-0511-FC-72, March 30, 2007, http://www.in.gov/judiciary/opinions/pdf/03300703mpb.pdf.

page 135   "At a 2001 trial in Chicago, Elizabeth Roach": Lucinda Hahn, "Buyer's Remorse," *Chicago Magazine,* April 2002.

page 135   "Fox News legal analyst": Lis Wiehl, "Addiction: The New 'Twinkie Defense,'" Fox News website, http://www.foxnews.com/story/0,2933,210321,00.html.

page 136   "On the other hand, most of our ancestors would not have lost their jobs": Morten Andersen, "Animal Bordellos Draw Norwegians," *Aftenposten,* September 14, 2006.

page 136   "Yet in Massachusetts in 1642": William Bradford, *Of Plymouth Plantation* (New York: Knopf, 1952); and James A. Cox, "Bilboes, Brands, and Branks: Colonial Crimes and Punishments," *Colonial Williamsburg Journal*, Spring 2003.

page 139   "As one among countless examples, Philip Morris paid": Ray Conlogue, "Why Can't Hollywood Kick the Habit?" *Toronto Globe and Mail,* February 13, 2001; and William Triplett, "Smoking in Movies to Affect Rating," *Cinema Fusion*, May 10, 2007.

page 141   "Young rap and hip-hop fans": Pacificic Institute for Research and Evaluation website, http://www.pire.org/more.asp?cms=294.

page 143   "Attracted by logos": Susan Gregory Thomas, *Buy, Buy Baby* (New York: Houghton Mifflin, 2007).

page 144   "Such ads have been banned in Sweden": Brandon Mitchener, "Sweden Pushes Its Ban on Children's Ads," *Wall Street Journal*, May 29, 2001.

page 144   "To coincide with the release of *Shrek 2*": "General Mills and DreamWorks Bring the Magic of Shrek to the Supermarket," *Business Wire*, May 27, 2004.

page 144   "More themed products": Commercial-Free Childhood website, http://www.commercialfreechildhood.org.

page 145   "Child-development expert": Susan Linn, *Consuming Kids* (New York: The New Press, 2004).

page 147   "Companies spend $30 billion": Michael Crowley, "Junk Deal," *Men's Health*, July 20, 2002; and Mark Androvich, "Analyst Predicts Game Advertising to Exceed $2 Billion by 2012," *Games Industry*, June 28, 2007.

page 148   "In one experiment, Columbia's Sheena Iyengar": Sheena S. Iyengar and Mark R. Lepper, "When Choice Is Demotivating," *Journal of Personal and Social Psychology*, December 2000.

page 149   "Choice overload expands beyond consumer products": Barry Schwartz, "You Have Choices I Never Had," Slate.msn.com, April 29, 2004; and Barry Schwartz, "Can There Ever Be Too Many Flowers Blooming?" in *Engaging Art: The Next Great Transformation of America's Cultural Life*, ed. Bill Ivey and Stephen Tepper (New York: Routledge, 2007).

page 151   "A seminal teachers' handbook": Jack Canfield and Harold C. Wells, *100 Ways to Enhance Self-Concept in the Classroom* (Englewood Cliffs, NJ: Prentice-Hall, 1976).

page 154   "On a website maintained by Alateen": The Forum, Al-Anon Family Group Headquarters, Inc., website, http://www.alateen.on.ca/share/esh6.html.

page 155   "One night in 2003, superstar fashion designer Calvin Klein": Cathy Horyn, "Calvin Klein Is Seeking Treatment for Substance Abuse," *New York Times*, April 5, 2003.

CHAPTER 4. THE HORROR, THE HORROR: STUCK ON TRAUMA

page 163   "Before the advent of psychotherapy": Rachel Yehuda, "Changes in the Concept of PTSD and Trauma," *Psychiatric Times*, April 1, 2003.

page 168   "Published ten years later": Marya Hornbacher, *Madness: A Bipolar Life* (New York: Houghton Mifflin, 2008).

page 171   "Martin Seligman finds this troubling": Martin E. P. Seligman, *What You Can Change . . . and What You Can't* (New York: Vintage Books, 2007).

page 172   "An inside look at bullying": *The Oprah Winfrey Show*, aired January 26, 2004, http://www.oprah.com/tows/pastshows/200401/tows_past_20040126.jhtml.

page 173   "Trauma was a virtual theme": "Sundance Unveils Competition Lineups for '06 Fest; 84 World Premieres to Screen at Upcoming Event," *Indiewire*, November 28, 2005.

page 177   "But Marxism isn't only about the rich and poor": Arnold Kling, "Folk Beliefs Have Consequences," *TCS Daily*, January 23, 2006.

page 180   "But physically and scientifically": "Exposure to Trauma Can Affect Brain Function in Healthy People Several Years After Event; May Increase Susceptibility to Mental Health Problems in the Future," American Psychological Association press release, May 6, 2007.

page 181   "The way we 'handle' past traumas": Patricia Lester, Susan W. Wong, and Robert L. Hendren, "The Neurobiological Effects of Trauma," *Adolescent Psychiatry* 27, 2003.

page 183   "Sorry Day offered": Australian Institute of Aboriginal and Torres Strait Islander Studies website, http://www1.aiatsis.gov.au/exhibitions/sorrybooks/personal/sorrybooks_personal_p1.htm.

page 185   "On February 12, 2007 . . . Sulejman Talovic": Ben Winslow and Nedim Hasic, "A Child of Violence: Talovic Survived Genocide," *Deseret Morning News*, February 15, 2007.

page 186   "Its 2003 winner": D.C.B. Pierre, *Vernon God Little* (Edinburgh: Canongate, 2003).

page 190   "Sigmund Freud was one of many": Sigmund Freud, *The Standard Edition of the Complete Psychological Works of Sigmund Freud* (London: Hogarth Press, 1955).

page 196 "When a whole society": *Diagnostic and Statistical Manual of the American Psychiatric Association,* 4th ed. (Arlington, VA: American Psychiatric Association, 2000).

page 198 "In 1995, Billie Jean Matay": "Matay v. Disneyland." Court TV Library, http://www.courttv.com/archive/casefiles/verdicts/matay.html.

page 198 "After seeing a dead fly": "High Court to Hear Fly Phobia Case," CBC News Canada website: http://www.cbc.ca/canada/story/2007/06/22/fly-water.html, June 22, 2007.

page 200 "Unveiled by the Duchess of Kent": "Proud Moment for Relatives of Soldiers Executed for Cowardice," *The Northern Echo,* November 13, 2006.

page 205 "In the era's paramount dead-parent memoir": Dave Eggers, *A Heartbreaking Work of Staggering Genius* (New York: Vintage Books, 2001).

page 208 "Michelle Smith led a seemingly": Michelle Smith, *Michelle Remembers* (New York: Pocket Books, 1989).

page 209 "During a May 1989 broadcast, Oprah Winfrey": Transcript of program: http://usajewish.blogspot.com/2007/02/vicki-and-devil.html; video: http://www.you tube.com/watch?v=R8RHl1KdM0w.

page 211 "In the fad's heyday, many Satanic abuse accusations": "Gerald Amirault's Freedom," *Wall Street Journal,* April 30, 2004.

page 213 "A real-life variation on the sci-fi memory": Rob Stein, "Is Every Memory Worth Keeping?" *Washington Post,* October 19, 2004.

page 215 "Boris Cyrulnik offers the same advice": Boris Cyrulnik, *The Whispering of Ghosts* (New York: Other Press, 2005).

page 216 "Focusing more on actions than words": Harriet Rubin, "Terrorism, Trauma and the Search for Redemption," *Fast Company,* October 2001.

page 217 "Hans Christian Andersen *was* the Ugly Duckling": Hans Christian Andersen, *The True Story of My Life*, trans. Mary Howitt (London: Longman, 1847).

CHAPTER 5. PEOPLE WHO NEED PEOPLE: STUCK ON OTHERS

page 224 "Beggars were a common sight in ancient Rome": Rodolfo Lanciani, *Ancient Rome in the Light of Recent Discoveries* (Boston: Houghton Mifflin, 1898).

page 227 "On the campaign trail in 1976": " 'Welfare Queen' Becomes Issue in Reagan Campaign," *New York Times,* February 15, 1976.

page 227 "Nineteen years later . . . senator John Ashcroft told": Tom Lutz, *Doing Nothing* (New York: Farrar, Straus and Giroux, 2006).

page 227 "Indigenous Australian lawyer": Noel Pearson, "Working Towards Peace and Prosperity," *The Australian,* October 26, 2005.

page 228 "Many Britons were shocked": Marie Woolf, "The Perfect Recipe for a Prosperous Marriage: Split Up," *The Independent,* November 26, 2006.

page 228   "A report prepared by fiscal-policy experts": Steve Doughty, "Single Mother Gets £100 More in Tax Credits a Week Than Working Couple," *Daily Mail*, November 26, 2006.

page 232   "The Prudential researchers coined an acronym": "The Kippers Who Won't Leave Home," BBC News, November 17, 2003.

page 232   "In Japan, they're called 'freeters' ": Susan J. Pharr, "For Japan, a 'Lost Decade' and After," *Harvard Magazine*, November 2001.

page 233   "While some parasite singles work": Maggie Jones, "Shutting Themselves In," *New York Times*, January 15, 2006; and Phil Rees, "Hikikomori Violence," BBC News, October 18, 2002.

page 234   "Born to baby boomers after abortion was legalized": Anya Kamenetz, *Generation Debt* (New York: Riverhead, 2006).

page 235   "University of Texas zoologist Eric Pianka": Eric Pianka, personal interview with the author. Also, lecture at the Texas Academy of Science in Beaumont, Texas, March 3, 2006.

page 243   "The slang we use when talking about relationships": Steve Nakamoto, *Men Are Like Fish: What Every Woman Needs to Know About Catching a Man* (Freeware: Java Books, 2002).

page 244   "Newspapers report on only a fraction": Hillary Mayell, "Thousands of Women Killed for Family 'Honor,' " *National Geographic News,* February 12, 2002.

page 244   "As reported in Germany's": Jody K. Biehl, "The Death of a Muslim Woman," *Spiegel Online*, March 2, 2005.

page 252   "Happy couples produce nuclear families": Karl Marx and Friedrich Engels, *The Communist Manifesto* (New York: International Publishers, 1976).

page 254   "In her book": Laura Kipnis, *Against Love: A Polemic* (New York: Vintage Books, 2004).

page 254   "We hear it everywhere: love is a myth": "The 'I Love You' Horrors," *Cosmopolitan*, October 2007.

page 255   "He had his finger up my ass": Christine Borden, "Sex on Tuesday," *The Daily Californian*, January 23, 2007.

page 256   "But liberation was also a big favorite": Friedrich Engels, *Principles of Communism* (New York: Monthly Review, 1952).

page 256   "This idea got a big boost": Erica Jong, *Fear of Flying* (New York: Signet, 1973).

page 257   "In her book *Girls Gone Mild*, Shalit": Wendy Shalit, *Girls Gone Mild* (New York: Random House, 2007); and Margaret Talbot, "Little Hotties," *The New Yorker*, December 4, 2006.

page 258   "Brook Busey-Hunt": Megan Scott, "Unlikely Pole Dancer Tells Strippers' Story," *Orange County Register*, March 10, 2006; and Diablo Cody, *Candy Girl* (New York: Gotham, 2006).